Palgrave Studies in Communication for Social Change

Series Editors: **Pradip Ninan Thomas**, The University of Queensland, Australia and **Elske van de Fliert**, The University of Queensland, Australia

Advisory Board: **Silvio Waisbord**, George Washington University, USA, **Karin G. Wilkins**, University of Texas at Austin, USA, **Thomas Tufte**, Roskilde University, Denmark, **Zaharom Nain**, University of Nottingham, Malaysia Campus, **Rico Lie**, Wageningen University, The Netherlands, **Claudia Mitchell**, McGill University, Canada, **Jo Tacchi**, RMIT University, Australia, **Nicholas Carah**, The University of Queensland, Australia, **Zala Volcic**, Pomona College, Claremont, USA

Communication for Social Change (CSC) is a defined field of academic enquiry that is explicitly transdisciplinary and that has been shaped by a variety of theoretical inputs from a variety of traditions, from sociology and development to social movement studies. The leveraging of communication, information and the media in social change is the basis for a global industry that is supported by governments, development aid agencies, foundations, and international and local NGOs. It is also the basis for multiple interventions at grassroots levels, with participatory communication processes and community media making a difference through raising awareness, mobilising communities, strengthening empowerment and contributing to local change.

This series on Communication for Social Change intentionally provides the space for critical writings in CSC theory, practice, policy, strategy and methods. It fills a gap in the field by exploring new thinking, institutional critiques and innovative methods. It offers the opportunity for scholars and practitioners to engage with CSC as both an industry and a local practice, shaped by political economy as much as by local cultural needs. The series explicitly intends to highlight, critique and explore the gaps between ideological promise, institutional performance and realities of practice.

Titles include:

Tina Askanius and Liv Stubbe Østergaard (*editors*)
RECLAIMING THE PUBLIC SPHERE
Communication, Power and Social Change

Levi Obijiofor
NEW TECHNOLOGIES IN DEVELOPING SOCIETIES
From Theory to Practice

Pradip Thomas and Elske van de Fliert
INTERROGATING THE THEORY AND PRACTICE OF COMMUNICATION AND SOCIAL CHANGE
The Basis for a Renewal

Sonja Vivienne
DIGITAL IDENTITY AND EVERYDAY ACTIVISM
Sharing Private Stories with Networked Publics

Palgrave Studies in Communication for Social Change
Series Standing Order ISBN 978–1–137–36166–0 (hardback)
(*outside North America only*)

You can receive future titles in this series as they are published by placing a standing order. Please contact your bookseller or, in case of difficulty, write to us at the address below with your name and address, the title of the series and the ISBN quoted above.

Customer Services Department, Macmillan Distribution Ltd, Houndmills, Basingstoke, Hampshire RG21 6XS, England

Digital Identity and Everyday Activism

Sharing Private Stories with Networked Publics

Sonja Vivienne
Flinders University of South Australia, Australia

© Sonja Vivienne 2016
Foreword © John Hartley 2016

All rights reserved. No reproduction, copy or transmission of this publication may be made without written permission.

No portion of this publication may be reproduced, copied or transmitted save with written permission or in accordance with the provisions of the Copyright, Designs and Patents Act 1988, or under the terms of any licence permitting limited copying issued by the Copyright Licensing Agency, Saffron House, 6–10 Kirby Street, London EC1N 8TS.

Any person who does any unauthorized act in relation to this publication may be liable to criminal prosecution and civil claims for damages.

The author has asserted her right to be identified as the author of this work in accordance with the Copyright, Designs and Patents Act 1988.

First published 2016 by
PALGRAVE MACMILLAN

Palgrave Macmillan in the UK is an imprint of Macmillan Publishers Limited, registered in England, company number 785998, of Houndmills, Basingstoke, Hampshire RG21 6XS.

Palgrave Macmillan in the US is a division of St Martin's Press LLC, 175 Fifth Avenue, New York, NY 10010.

Palgrave Macmillan is the global academic imprint of the above companies and has companies and representatives throughout the world.

Palgrave® and Macmillan® are registered trademarks in the United States, the United Kingdom, Europe and other countries.

ISBN 978–1–137–50073–1

This book is printed on paper suitable for recycling and made from fully managed and sustained forest sources. Logging, pulping and manufacturing processes are expected to conform to the environmental regulations of the country of origin.

A catalogue record for this book is available from the British Library.

Library of Congress Cataloging-in-Publication Data
Vivienne, Sonja, 1970–
   Digital identity and everyday activism : sharing private stories with networked publics / Sonja Vivienne.
     pages cm
   Includes bibliographical references.
   ISBN 978–1–137–50073–1 (hardback)
   1. Online identities. 2. Digital storytelling. 3. Online social networks. 4. Social change. I. Title.
   HM851.V624 2015
   302.30285—dc23   2015021818

*This book is dedicated to my mum
Who never got to read it, or see my floppy hat
But nevertheless weighed, in her hands,
The significance of a
'Final' Draft
Before moving on to greater mysteries...*

Contents

List of Figures x
Foreword by John Hartley xi
Preface and Acknowledgements xiv

1 Introduction 1
  What is a digital story? 3
  Everyday activism and social change 4
  Participatory culture and the digital divide 10
  Social convergence: Publicness and privacy 12
  Queer community voice and intimate citizenship 14
  Roadmap 15

2 The 'Social' in Storytelling 18
  Personal storytelling for social change 18
  The emergence of digital storytelling 24
    Cultural significance, critical problems 27
  Potentials of online storytelling 35
    Digital storytelling in online spaces 39
  Intimate Citizenship 3.0 42

3 Identity: Nominalisation, Authenticity and Incoherence 44
  Understanding identity in theory and practice 45
    Nature versus nurture: Theoretical frameworks for identity 45
    Claiming identity in practice: The problem of visibility 49
    Nominalising queer 53
    Disrupting categories 60
  Crafting 'authenticity' 63
    Performance and self-representation 63
    Narrative coherence 65
    Partial opacity and inadequate communication 71
    Transgression, complexity and fluidity 76

4 Case Studies in Voice — 86
Mediating voice in theory and practice — 87
Facilitating voice: Working with groups — 91
   What's Your Story? — 91
   Positive Stories — 97
   Rainbow Family Tree — 101
Orchestrating voice: Speaking across difference — 108
   The gift of the voice: Rhetorical devices and tonal qualities — 109
   Social movements, framing processes — 118
   Emotive language and social norms — 127

5 The Private in Networked Publics — 132
Publics and audiences — 133
Imagined publics and social convergence — 135
Networked identity work — 136
   Building bridges: Tributes, affirmations and provocations — 139
Publicness and privacy — 143
   Digitally mediated identities — 147
   Curated exhibitions of selfhood — 150
Otherness and outness: A typology — 152
   Textual approaches to production — 153
   Modes of content sharing — 166
Agency and ownership — 171

6 Provocations: Digital Storytelling ≠ Social Change — 174
Micro — 175
   'Authenticity', coherence and congruence — 176
   Nominalisation, framing devices and bracketing — 180
   Negotiating meaning — 182
Meso — 185
   Grassroots sustainability — 185
   Online curation — 186
   Institutional facilitation — 187
   Collective engagement and mindful listening — 189
Macro — 193
   Appeal of genre — 193
   Marketing — 194
   Speaking across difference — 196
   Measuring social significance — 197

7 What Lessons to Bear Forth?	**201**
Retracing the journey... and takeaway insights	201
New horizons	205
Intimate Citizenship 3.0	209
Notes	211
Bibliography	213
Index	223

Figures

1.1	Intimate Citizenship 3.0 – The sharing of private stories with networked publics as everyday activism	9
3.1	Brown Baby	51
3.2	Stealth Crip	52
3.3	Blue for Boys? Pink for Girls?	58
3.4	Brian as Brenda	69
3.5	I am Sarah	78
3.6	Sisterhood	81
4.1	Greg's Sermon	99
4.2	Rainbow Family Tree home page	103
4.3	Rainbow Family Tree community engagement	107
4.4	Where did we come from?	115
4.5	Rowan's Family Tree	116
4.6	La La Land	121
4.7	Gay Rights Rally – Adelaide 2011 screen shot	123
5.1	Back to Happiness	140
5.2	O.M.G. ... Is she really?	142
5.3	That's so Gay!	157

Foreword

'It's OK, we're both quite strong'. This is the punch line of a story Sonja Vivienne tells at the beginning of this book, returning to it at the very end, where she uses it to draw out some of the hopes she holds for the approach to 'Intimate Citizenship 3.0' that preoccupies her throughout the intervening pages.

Perhaps this line called out to me, as it were, because it seems apt for Sonja herself. It refers to the extra burden of heavy lifting – conceptual, political and, in this case, literal – that must be borne by those who lead lives outside of mainstream expectations. Not for them the easy confidence of 'self-expression', because it's not always clear in advance what such a self might be, what is risked in expressing it and how it should be expressed, which depends very much on who's asking. Here, the careless assumptions that scaffold everyday encounters – in the hardware store, for example – can present themselves as quite a different kind of scaffold, not one that props you up.

As a researcher, Sonja is interested in social advocacy as well as self-expression. As an advocate, she wants to advance the cause of queer communities (for which she has an inclusive definition). As she outlines in her own preface, 'self-expression' in such circumstances is just as fraught with pitfalls for the facilitator who wants to 'give people a voice' as it is for those who want to say something true about themselves.

To combine these educational and civic ambitions is hard enough, especially in a professional and institutional context, but then there is the added problem of personal risk. Expressing one's self in this context can be frightening, even dangerous. When Sonja set out as a researcher, among those she wanted to hear and to understand her story were her own family.

She had to be strong enough for two to manage all that – strong *professionally*, as a queer storyteller and social change agent, and strong *personally*, for self, family, children, peers, colleagues and even for those who block the way with awkwardness, problems and hostility.

This book triumphantly brings those strengths into alignment, thereby integrating self-representation with community or civic advocacy, in open acknowledgement of what might be at stake in the attempt, for all parties.

The result? What follows is a cool-headed and expert appraisal of how digital identity can be established, and how civic activism can be used to pursue social change, even when identity is uncertain or risk-laden and when activism makes entirely reasonable professional demands that don't take personal costs into account. The book also charts a personal journey, which shows that self-expression for social change is challenging for everyone involved: for the storyteller, the facilitating *animateur* and the dispassionate academic observer (who may be all the same person). It's hard work conceptually, organisationally and in practice, as well.

'We're both quite strong', being plural, also made me think about my own relationship with the work Sonja has been doing. Although I don't know that it ever came up in our day-to-day meetings, I shared her interest in how a queer family might understand and communicate with and about itself, not least from the children's point of view, since that situation characterised my own childhood.

After my father died, my mother had only one further long-term relationship. It was with a woman. We children were never led to think that we had 'two mums', but they lived together for about eleven years. This was in the late 1950s and early 1960s. Women couples were not as rare as you might expect. But the lesbian scene, if there was one, did not include children. In our case it took the banal form of mutual house visits by various couples 'in old-style hats and coats' (as Philip Larkin might have put it), for cards, drinks... and a good row.

The sexual nature of the grown-ups' relationships was not mentioned, of course. It was hiding in plain sight, oddly secret but at the same time routine. In my teens, a 'helpful' neighbour took it upon herself to explain it all to me, in a manner that rather too eagerly anticipated a shocked and scandalised response. But my sisters and I had already worked it out.

In any case, much more important to us was an unstable home and uncertain selfhood. Our peculiar family life did not equip us with the communicative strategies needed to share our anxieties, to understand our selves (whatever they were) or to seek and support like-circumstanced others (if there were any).

When it came to mums (there were no dads), we were of the Larkin generation. There was only one thing to do:

'Get out as early as you can'. ('This be the verse', 1971)

The 'get out' for my sisters was London and marriage; for me it was education and an academic career. Profession trumped person.

'Self-expression' had to be smuggled back in, or remain unspoken. Civic action remained *impersonal*. All of us had to wait until we were much older to bring private self and public persona back into any sort of alignment. We could have done with Sonja's bravery, to keep the two connected throughout. Now – having read the book – I see that self-realisation can be aspired to at the same time and by means of self-representation, and that if you can manage it, new forms of civic action become possible.

It's called 'Intimate Citizenship 3.0'. I wish I'd known!

Well, 'we're both quite strong' now, but one question remains: *who taught her to write like that*? She conducts the reader through complex materials, controversial arguments and personal-emotional quagmires alike with assurance and grace. Something has taken flight in this book. Arriving at Intimate Citizenship 3.0 is not just an intellectual, personal and civic achievement. It's a fine bit of storytelling too.

John Hartley
John Curtin Distinguished Professor, Curtin University
Professor of Journalism Media and Cultural Studies,
Cardiff University
February 2015

Preface and Acknowledgements

My interest in activist-oriented digital storytelling, and, in turn, the research that underpins this book, was sparked by my journey as a filmmaker and as a queer parent. For several years after graduating from film school I worked in social justice contexts, making educational documentaries about and for problematised identity categories. These included Vietnamese drug-dependent parents, youth at risk of suicide, violent young men and their fathers and indigenous women from the stolen generation, among others. Projects like these are often funded by social service providers and aim to re-shape attitudes of relatively small audiences, by raising awareness of the complexities of real-life social issues. Sometimes there is also a vaguely defined, small 'p' political objective, like 'changing the world'. Participants are almost never assigned the right of final cut. However, in examples of best practice, they are consulted throughout production and post-production in the hope that they be relatively satisfied with the way they are represented.

During this early post film-school period I also worked as a project officer at a state-based film corporation, employed at the interfaces between script and documentary development, production and broadcast. I was privy to many boardroom reviews of prospective projects and many discussions with broadcasters, gaining insight into some of the unwritten codes of film financing and distribution, including the inconsistent ones. Interesting characters and a clear dramatic arc are essential ingredients in a documentary treatment but in actuality 'characters' are people that you know, and 'dramatic arcs' are made up of complex and messy real life. Further, while film-financiers and broadcasters wish to support engaging quality content these things are subjective. To assuage these difficult unknowns stakeholders tend to minimise risk by investing in a combination of established filmmaking credentials and content that complies with generic norms and mainstream values. Storytellers who attempt to weave the dramatic fabric of their own lives represent a minefield of difficulties, for investors and audiences and even for the 'characters' in their tales. Their stories are likely to be judged self-indulgent and issues of who controls the narrative loom large. Many projects never make it to a screen.

Despite witnessing these problems I went on to develop an autobiographical cross platform project, composed of an interactive community storytelling website and a linear one-hour documentary. I was encouraged by a wave of user-generated content that reflected participatory production practices, and distribution spaces like YouTube, where diverse and ever-changing tales proliferated. I, indeed, had the naïve hope that my story could contribute to 'changing the world'. I marketed the tale of a queer single mum attempting to conceive a new baby, a challenge to conventional nuclear family units. One of the first interviews I undertook was with my mum who claimed that families couldn't be constructed: 'they just are'. My sister asserted that 'marriage is between a man and a woman'. My path continued to be rife with dramatic obstacles – family court and the antagonistic father of my first child, and a medical system that regarded me as 'socially infertile' by virtue of my sexual preferences. Because I couldn't access IVF, I was on a quest for a known sperm donor that I could trust and, more significantly, a network of supportive friends who would be our 'fairy godfamily'. Despite all the anguish, I persisted because I'd never seen a story like mine on TV. While I was fortunate enough to receive substantial development investment and broadcast interest, for numerous reasons, the project never entered formal production. However, as part of the community storytelling aspect of the project, I investigated digital storytelling, and facilitated a preliminary workshop with a group of GLBTQIS[1] storytellers and family members.

This cross-section of experiences as filmmaker, funding gatekeeper and workshop facilitator was my introduction to the problems of sharing highly personal narratives in public and expression of non-normative or minority voice. In my case I wrangled with how to represent those who were antipathetic to my identity and family, while attempting functional relationships. How would I protect my kids from the consequences of making us visible, including schoolyard homophobia? If making stories like these invite negative ramifications from multiple unknown publics, is it worth it? How can I expect others to negotiate these risks? Fundamentally, if the costs of speaking out are so great, how will the world ever become more accepting of difference?

Conundrums around access/opportunity and representation are difficult to untangle, on every level. Films cost money to make and market. Broadcasters are dependent on ratings to secure advertising and they are entitled to postulate what audiences will want to watch. But there are no guarantees of securing 'bums on seats', even on alternative broadcasting platforms like YouTube. Amid a preponderance of choices, audiences are often more sympathetic to slick and entertaining documentaries narrated by an authority than experimental genres with multiple points of view or self-reflexive narratives. Further, tech-heavy logistics guarantee that *most* people (and certainly most self-defined minorities) lack the resources, skills and social capital to attempt self-representation in either mainstream broadcast media or more accessible online spaces.

Many years later, having reconciled with family and returned to academia, I found that the same ethical and theoretical issues plagued my research, just as they had my production practice. For example, how does one undertake research that can do justice to the complex lived experiences of divergent marginalised voices? How do I know that I'm asking the right questions; that what I am hearing is not just what I expect to hear? How dare I represent another? From filmmaker to researcher, the same questions... Eventually I settled into the mixed methods of cultural studies and grounded ethnography, formulating questions that emerged from situated awareness as a filmmaker, digital storyteller, workshop facilitator and queer everyday activist. I employed a research framework centred on storytellers, facilitators, host institutions and their interactions. I designed and implemented three case studies that systematically evaluated digital stories and digital storytelling practice, engaging with a collection of GLBTQIS participants.

This book is somewhat like a digital story, being the synthesis of much listening and interpretation. It is a representation of many years of networked identity work as I travelled from disillusioned filmmaker, through terrified and tentative would-be scholar, to an identity that I'm proud to own – somebody with a few ideas to share. Many people, constituting familiar, intimate and unknown networked publics, have helped me along the way. My colleague John Hartley (who gave the excellent and reassuring advice to 'fake it till you make it') and, in the final stages, Alan McKee (who offered many provocations in refusing to be entertained by digital stories) have shaped the scholar I have become. Jean Burgess consistently raised the bar a little higher, alternating between stern appraisals and encouragement. Their work, and their critiques of my work, has been an unfailing inspiration to think more carefully and communicate better. 'Thank you' seems an inadequate expression of my gratitude for such priceless mentorship.

Queensland University of Technology (QUT) and the Centre of Excellence for Creative Industries and Innovation (CCi) supported me to attend many emerging scholar workshops and symposiums as well as the excellent Oxford Internet Institute Summer Doctoral Programme (OII SDP). I have been fortunate enough to publish some of this research and, in every case, the anonymous reviewers have substantially contributed to the development of my analysis and the presentation of ideas. Thank you also to the many steering committee members, editors, photographers, sound recordists, co-facilitators, workbook designers and web curators who were involved in the three case studies. Of course none of this could have happened without the 25 storytellers who participated, taking a massive leap of faith, in every case offering up precious and painful memories, vulnerable identities and dangerous dreams, for public consumption. In this book I offer recognition and respect for their efforts to distil their stories, and I empathise with the hopes and fears they express about sharing these stories with a variety of imagined audiences. Our stories are gifts. Ripples in the pond maybe, but I believe they have already changed the world.

Finally, thanks to my family and the 'subjects' of my digital stories... Rosie and Ari, who put up with my crankiness and absence, while my mind was elsewhere. Gill, who offered unfailing support. An extended network of 'chosen' family, our fairy godparents, who had faith in me when I had none. My sister, who judiciously avoids asking about 'my work' while accepting that our lives are an enormous part of it. And Mum and Dad. I don't think I ever would have set out on these convoluted non-linear and intersecting paths, if I hadn't sought your acceptance, and hoped to make you proud of all of the contradictory little bits of me.

1
Introduction

Access to and capacity for public self-representation have become markers of civic engagement and social wellbeing in Western democratic societies. Digital tools and platforms have extended opportunity for self-representation to many marginalised groups. Nevertheless, inequities persist. Barriers to social participation and adequate self-expression are similar to, but also different from, those experienced prior to widespread digitally mediated communication.

Digital storytelling is a workshop-based participatory media practice focussed on self-representation. In a variety of forms and over the last 25 years, it has come to play a substantial role in many development, empowerment and educative contexts. Meanwhile, everyday activists, including those campaigning for recognition of alternate family structures, same-sex marriage and non-normative gender representation, have seized upon the potential for digitally disseminated personal stories to catalyse various kinds of social change. This book uses the term 'everyday activism' – the sharing of personal stories in public spaces with the aim of challenging the status quo – as an expansion on existing definitions of organised, strategic and intentional activism. I contend that this domestic iteration of activism contributes to 'erosive social change': changes in attitude that take place slowly over extended time frames, profoundly reshaping social norms as they diffuse among networked publics. This kind of change can manifest in multiple forms and is therefore difficult to quantify or correlate with a specific cause.

Whereas previous scholarly work has focussed on digital storytelling as an *institutionally mediated practice* with *limited distribution*, I extend this research to consider *individually motivated* activist-oriented storytelling that actively engages with *online distribution*. Between 2009 and 2013, I worked with GLBTQIS storytellers and their advocates in three interwoven case studies that took place in Adelaide, Australia.

What's Your Story? and *Positive Stories* were digital storytelling initiatives that were supported by social service institutions SHine SA[1] and ACSA,[2] respectively. The third case study, *Rainbow Family Tree*, was and remains an independent online community of queer activist-oriented digital storytellers and their friends and family members. My engagement in all three case studies was as queer digital storyteller, workshop facilitator, web curator and researcher. All three case studies experimented with different forms of online and face-to-face practice over extended time frames. Over a three-and-a-half-year period, I adopted the role of 'observant participant' of storyteller practice and online participation. I conducted in-depth semi-structured interviews, questionnaires and a focus group with a small group of 25 participants. I analysed a total of 33 digital stories and scrutinise 24 in this book.

I describe case studies by privileging the experiences of storytellers and the stories they produce. As a means of allowing the research story to unfold I start first with a *micro* examination of individual experiences of co-creating queer identity, pulling out to a *meso* analysis of both personal and institutional processes of mediating voice, before considering the *macro* landscape of imagined networked publics. This might be regarded as a movement from considerations of 'me', on to 'us', and finally through to 'me, us and the world'. I interweave descriptions of story content and/or process with theory throughout and use sub-headings to highlight thematic concerns.

Queer[3] identity stories are of particular research interest because they are shared in potentially hostile environments and invoke a need for privacy. Further, the very definitions of these collective identities are in flux. Despite fears of homophobic or transphobic ramifications (for themselves, their friends and their family members), queer digital storytellers co-create new, increasingly complex identities with a variety of networked publics that they consider themselves to be *a part of* and/or *apart from*. In the hope of generating empathy and eventually greater social acceptance, storytellers *speak and listen across differences* between face-to-face and online publics, both real and imagined. My participants engaged in specific pre-production, production and distribution practices as a means of maintaining a degree of control over privacy and publicness. I identify three textual approaches (visible, bounded and pseudonymous) and three modes of sharing (targeted, ad hoc and proxy) and characterise these in a typology of *outness* and *otherness*.

In this book, I argue that this attenuated approach to privacy and publicness constitutes a sophisticated form of *digitally mediated civic engagement*. On a broader social canvas, these strategies for self-representation can also be mapped back to identity management practices undertaken by a broader population across a range of social and networked media. In the final chapters of the book I consider how what I have come to call *Intimate Citizenship 3.0* stakes out new territory in participatory culture for everyone, including the most socially at-risk identities.

While it is difficult to evaluate the extent to which the everyday activism of the storytellers I work with achieves the social change they hope for, the capacity for Intimate Citizenship 3.0 to generate ripples in the pond of cultural renewal nevertheless emerges with clarity. In conclusion, this book offers support for the notion that, despite numerous obstacles, the cumulative influence of diverse voices dispersed among networked publics can provoke subtle and profound shifts in values, thereby constituting new cultural norms.

What is a digital story?

Digital stories are short (3-5 min) rich media autobiographical videos, combining personal photographs and/or artworks, narration and music. They are traditionally created in a workshop context that takes place over 3-4 days and includes a story circle, technical instruction and celebratory screening for fellow storytellers and invited guests. 'Digital' refers to the digital tools used by storytellers for production (computers, digital cameras, editing software, etc.) and in some cases the digital distribution mediums (ranging from DVD to the internet).

In colloquial usage, 'digital storytelling' can refer to blogs, vlogs, digital special effects, hypertext fiction and so on, but these are not my focus. In this book, I examine three stages of digital storytelling that I categorise as pre-production, production and distribution. 'Preproduction' refers to the frequently under-examined prerequisites to becoming a digital storyteller including the cultural capital and agency necessary to engage in storytelling. There must also be some affinity with workshop criteria that affords resonance between individual and group identity. 'Production' refers to all aspects of the production process, from assessing which story to tell and how to tell it, to, mastering digital tools and negotiating with the numerous friends and family who are implicitly part of the story as to how they will be represented. 'Distribution' refers to the processes storytellers undertake to distribute their stories to an audience, whether in a face-to-face theatrical screening or viral circulation via a variety of online platforms. Digital storytelling has been lauded as an exemplar of digital emancipation (Lambert, 2002; Meadows & Kidd, 2009). As a cultural form of self-expression, it parallels other forms of personal storytelling undertaken for social change including certain forms of public speaking (witnessing), life writing, blogging and autobiographical filmmaking.

Everyday activism and social change

Digital storytellers typically regard themselves as 'ordinary people',[4] and apprentices in formal media production. Sometimes they are motivated to share their personal stories in public spaces in order to catalyse social change. I call the people in my case studies 'everyday activists' because they are not strategic or organised but are called upon in everyday life to use their personal stories in mundane environments to challenge social norms. They have varied political viewpoints, ideological beliefs and values. Like the 'grassroots, non-party political activists' in a case study by Chatterton and Pickerill, my research cohort 'articulate(d) their engagement in political projects through messy, complex and multiple identities – always in the process of becoming and moving forward through experimentation and negotiation' (Chatterton & Pickerill, 2010). Mansbridge and Flaster define everyday activists as individuals who 'may not interact with the formal world of politics, but they take actions in their own lives to redress injustices' (Mansbridge & Flaster, 2007, p. 627).

An anecdote helps illustrate everyday activism. A friend of mine was at the checkout at a major hardware chain buying sacks of heavy potting mix with her twin eight-year-old boys. The shop assistant exclaimed, 'I hope Dad's going to help you with these when you get home!', to which one of the boys responded, 'We don't have a dad!'. The shop assistant looked embarrassed and the other boy announced proudly, 'We've got two mums!'. The shop assistant squirmed and my friend said reassuringly, 'It's OK; we're both quite strong'.

The social context in Australia in 2012 was one in which politicians, the religious right and general public hotly debated gay marriage and legal recognition of same-sex parents and partnerships. In the years in which I gathered data, I read many weekend newspaper editorials that debated whether being gay is a moral blight or something to tolerate. Online polls and 'have your say' spaces were filled with comments ranging from hateful and inflammatory to 'what's the problem, they're normal, just like us!'. The GLBTQIS community is also riven by debates over who can be included among the ranks of 'other' and whether wanting to be 'equal' equates to wanting to be the 'same' as witnessed on mailing lists and newsgroups like 'ausqueer' ('ausqueer: yahoo group', 2012).

My aforementioned friend doesn't have much interest in politics but is passionate about her kids' right to attend school free of homophobic harassment and bullying. At times this brings her into conflict with the school and school community. She wants her kids to be proud of their family circumstances when other people may prefer that they be discreet. She feels duty-bound to model openness and pride despite the awkward social moments it sometimes generates. The family marches with the 'Pink Parents'[5] group in the annual pride march although, as her kids have gotten older, my friend has become increasingly concerned that they may be upset and shamed by the religious protests and homophobic commentators that often frequent the parade. She experiences conflict between wanting to protect her children while helping them be proud, engaged citizens of the world.

Foucault draws on ancient Greek and Roman literature to explore the concept of truth telling as 'parrhesia'. He characterises parrhesia as 'a verbal activity in which a speaker expresses his personal relationship to truth, and risks his life because he recognises truth telling as a duty to improve or help other people (as well as himself)' (Foucault, 2001, p. 19). He outlines several critical qualities in the parrhesiastes. The message must constitute the speaker's own opinion and be expressed in a fashion that makes no rhetorical effort to veil what he thinks. There must be an alignment between 'belief' and 'truth'. While Foucault does not dwell upon 'what is truth?' (in the Cartesian sense) he imputes that the parrhesiastes, in speaking his personal truth in order to criticise someone or something more powerful than himself, takes a considerable personal risk and does so voluntarily, out of a sense of duty:

> when a philosopher addresses himself to a sovereign, to a tyrant, and tells him that his tyranny is disturbing and unpleasant because tyranny is incompatible with justice, then the philosopher speaks the truth, believes he is speaking the truth and, more than that, also takes a risk... In parrhesia, the speaker uses his freedom and chooses frankness instead of persuasion, truth instead of falsehood or silence, the risk of death instead of life and security, criticism instead of flattery, and moral duty instead of self-interest and moral apathy.
> (Foucault, 2001, pp. 16–20)

A substantial qualifier is present in Foucault's description of parrhesia and follows in my definition of everyday activism. Foucault says: 'the speaker uses his freedom and chooses', thereby highlighting the prerequisite social agency that is central to activist-oriented self-expression.

The question of choice is also implicit in the previous anecdote when my friend, the lesbian mum, makes a choice as to whether she'll correct the presumptions of the shop assistant. Like the parrhesiastes she elects 'frankness instead of persuasion, truth instead of falsehood or silence'. While it is a choice it is nevertheless a limited one – as a parent she wishes her children to grow up proud of their family so she is impelled to model this behaviour in the face of powerful normative values that depict 'family' as heterosexual and nuclear. She responds to a social 'injunction' – defined by Riggs and Willing in research with lesbian mothers, as an 'unreasonable' expectation, 'not of their making', to live with and manage heteronormativity (Riggs & Willing, 2013, p. 7). In this way lesbian mums, like other everyday activists, are summoned by social norms that simultaneously limit their choices and freedom. In my case studies, while participants were often 'called upon' (sometimes by an institutional recruitment drive), their civic engagement was not diminished. Storytellers have many reasons for becoming involved in digital storytelling; however, they invariably describe a desire to 'contribute in some way' or 'make a difference'.

Everyday activists speak their personal truths to socially legitimised power despite risk of significant ramifications. For digital storytellers the consequences of truth telling can include falling out with family members who don't share their representation of family history. For socially maligned identities, consequences may be even more severe. An HIV-positive storyteller fears losing his job in a small rural community should his health status become public knowledge. Another storyteller fears that his nephews and nieces will be hassled at school. Transgender storytellers may not choose to share their biological history with everyone they meet. Parents of transgender children face tough choices between wanting to change the world their children are growing up in and needing to protect their privacy. Storytellers who are very concerned about privacy may simply choose to withhold personal information or share it only with people they know and can see (Hogan, 2010). However, the more personal the story, and the more revealing of unique idiosyncratic identity, the more vulnerable storytellers are to judgment. Despite this, many of my research participants speak of 'becoming empowered', or acquiring agency through digital storytelling that in turn facilitates further active civic engagement. The question of how storytellers maintain safety (ostensibly via carefully managed privacy) while harnessing the potentials of online communication (and a degree of publicness) is a central concern of this book.

While, for various reasons, my aforementioned friend has not made a digital story herself, the lesbian parents in this study (alongside other queer identities with divergent preferred nominalisations) seized the opportunity to amplify their everyday activism in digital story form. Unlike face-to-face everyday activism (that requires being 'out' or identifiable), the digitally mediated equivalent affords an opportunity to strike a balance between privacy and publicness; often perceived as safety and risk. For those who wish to preserve a level of pseudonymity, their digital stories stand in for them as proxies. Their archived and distributed stories have potential to reach many more people, and for a greater length of time, than their face-to-face exertions.

Nevertheless, the obstacles to adequate, congruent digitally mediated self-expression are many. These include: (1) social convergence of familiar and unknown publics, (2) insufficient social capital or technical aptitude and (3) everyday difficulties like time, money and emotional energy (Livingstone, 2005). When a storyteller is co-present with their audience, they can tweak their performance according to audience response, but mediating technologies – (from telephones to television to social media) – cause storytellers to *imagine* the audience's responses. They consider 'what will they think of me?' and shape their stories in anticipation. They manipulate tone and pacing and emphasise turning points where underlying themes are overt or implicit. Online distribution also renders stories persistent and searchable (boyd, 2008a) to unintended audiences and publics that may simultaneously include family and strangers, friends and enemies.

Everyday activism is not a term that my participants typically used to describe themselves and few research participants thought of themselves as activists in the traditional sense:

> I thought to be radical you had to [be] standing on the barricades or hanging huge screaming signs off the top of the Sydney opera house [sic].
>
> (Sarah, private correspondence, 2011)

However, as we discussed daily social behaviour and motivations during workshops and interviews, some central themes emerged – many people calculated risks before engaging with social presumptions. They nevertheless favoured truthful, utilitarian and opportunistic responses, and simply managed their ensuing personal vulnerability. The concept of 'everyday activism' therefore had wide resonance with participants. General discussion of the term helped situate both participants and digital storytelling in social context. Those that were inclined to think of the practice as a little self-indulgent began to think more about the publics, real and imagined, that they hoped to address. My role, as storyteller, facilitator and scholar, brought participants' awareness to the mediation of their voices and the social-construction of identity. I was privileged to observe the nuanced ways in which they negotiated self-representation. Throughout this book I acknowledge the highly partisan part I myself play in framing and mediating voice and argue that this subjectivity affords privileged, yet qualified, insights. In interviews, participants were able to reflect upon their own motivations and negotiations without needing to defend their self-defined marginalised status. The similarities between us, as people who are accustomed to negotiating visible identity in a range of social contexts, afforded a certain trust that in turn allowed gentle probing into new understandings of privacy and publicness. On the other hand, as an embedded observant participant, I needed to utilise methods that checked my implicit assumptions.

Meanwhile, several normative assumptions underpin the use of personal stories as activist tools in everyday life. Many digital storytellers express a belief that sharing personal stories evokes empathy where stating facts of discrimination does not. Establishing a causal relationship between compassion and social change is nevertheless problematic, in part because definitions of 'social change' are so numerous. *What* is the qualitative nature of change? Any given frame of analysis may spin change as positive or negative determined by moral values and ideas like 'progress'. *Where* does the change take place – perhaps in the home, the school community, broadcast media or parliament? *Who* is involved in the change – friends, strangers, one or many? *When* does it take place – in a re-evaluation of the past, in the present or the future?

While some of my participants understood social change as specific law reform, others aspired to change systemic education and anti-discrimination policies on sexuality and gender, and most participants coalesced around generalised aspirations for a more accepting, less judgemental society. It is possible to distinguish six kinds of prospective social change that may be catalysed by digital storytelling, represented in Figure 1.1. These are situated in a framework in which storytellers consider themselves to be 'a part of' or 'apart from'. Working from micro to meso to macro (as I do throughout this book), there is *firstly* the form of social change that unfolds from the therapeutic belief that, as an individual, one has a story worth sharing. This shift in personal awareness often precedes a *second* form of social change among intimate publics (including family, close friends and acquaintances on and offline) referred to here as 'familiars'. As McKee points out, 'people respond well to videos made by people they know. There is always a pre-existing interest that doesn't exist with unknown publics' (McKee,

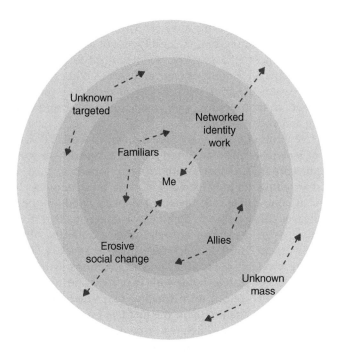

Figure 1.1 Intimate Citizenship 3.0 – The sharing of private stories with networked publics as everyday activism

personal correspondence, 2012). The *third* form of social change happens as a result of mutual support among workshop participants and members of the online storytelling community, referred to as 'allies'. These are people the storyteller gets to know (and influence) through the process of making and sharing a story.

A *fourth* kind of change is possible at the meso level when a specific unknown audience is targeted for their position of influence and the duty of care that requires them to listen ('unknown targeted'). They are teachers, politicians, human resource and professional development people, social service providers and law and policy makers. With a mandate to consider equity and diversity they have a vested interest in watching material created by their constituency. I offer evidence of social changes that have manifested in this fourth form in Chapter 4. The *fifth* form of social change is the most problematic, occurring among antipathetic audiences and/or among a mass of unknown people ('unknown mass'). While storytellers often hope to catalyse this form of widespread change (and viral distribution of their stories), it is not supported by evidence in this research. The second half of Chapter 4 explores related questions of how socially provocative messages are best conveyed to a mass audience (e.g. do they need to be 'entertaining' to win the hearts and minds of large audiences? What rhetorical tone is most successful?). Efforts to speak across difference provoke questions around communication style, mediating voices and difficulties predicting audience reception.

These five forms of social change are frequently conflated in the aspirations of storytellers who are often more concerned with sculpting a congruent story that resonates with different aspects of their identity. Digital storytelling not only increases personal awareness but also facilitates social connection with divergent publics, building bridges that model engaged listening across difference. For marginalised storytellers, declaring a 'preferred identity' actively stakes a claim to public space, and thereby creates further space for others to speak. I characterise the resulting production processes and negotiations as Intimate Citizenship 3.0 (a conceptual framework that I expand upon briefly in Chapter 2 and then return to in Chapter 6). I argue that this results in a *sixth* complex variation upon the first five forms of social change. Rather than the rapid and widespread viral distribution, this sixth form of change might be better characterised as 'erosive' – still transmitted, metaphorically, from one person to the next, however in a slow, almost imperceptible, fashion. Erosion gnaws away at monolithic structures in ways that are not entirely predictable, invariably sculpting a new form, previously unimaginable. Digital storytelling and networked identity work are examples of Intimate Citizenship 3.0 that slowly gnaw away at established resistance and social norms, revealing unanticipated ways of being. Of course I don't think that digital stories stand alone in catalysing these social changes – they are just one tool among many – but greater audience acceptance of YouTube aesthetics and proliferations of autobiographical content on Facebook have established new platforms for everyday activists.

Participatory culture and the digital divide

Digital stories are significant because (like blogs and other social media platforms) they offer an opportunity for marginalised people to represent themselves, where previous representations in cinema, television and the press have historically run the gamut from victims and freaks to abnormal social rejects (Dolan, 2001; Halberstam, 2005; Keller, 2002). Iris Marion Young uses the concept of 'cultural imperialism' to describe how minority voices have traditionally been excluded from discussion in the public sphere:

> To experience cultural imperialism means to experience how the dominant meanings of a society render the particular perspective of one's own group invisible at the same time as they stereotype one's group and mark it out as other.
>
> (Young, 2011, p. 58)

While there is certainly a lengthy tradition of alternative, identity-based fiction, cinema, television and so on, much of it is still mediated by the normative arbiters of funding and broadcast agencies. Although the technology for amateur production has existed for some time, as Patty Zimmerman argues, 'ideological, technical, and social constraints have stunted amateur film's potential for extending media production beyond corporate monopolies and into the hands of everyday people' (Zimmermann, 1995). Digital storytelling, on the other hand, is grounded in self-representation by everyday people. Amplified by accessible online distribution via platforms like YouTube and Facebook (Burgess & Green, 2009; Milliken, Gibson & O'Donnell, 2008; Thorson, Ekdale, Borah, Namkoong, & Shah, 2010), digital storytelling offers a new iteration of self-broadcast, and is consequently an exemplar of what Henry Jenkins calls 'participatory culture':

> A participatory culture is a culture with relatively low barriers to artistic expression and civic engagement, strong support for creating and sharing one's creations, and some type of informal mentorship whereby what is known by the most experienced is passed along to novices. A participatory culture is also one in which members believe their contributions matter, and feel some degree of social connection with one another (at the least they care what other people think about what they have created).
>
> (Jenkins, Clinton, Purushotma, Robinson & Weigel, 2006, p. 7)

Digital storytelling lowers the bar to participation – that is, theoretically, anyone can do it at their 'kitchen table' (Meadows & Kidd) – and offers a collaborative workshop context in which 'informal mentorship' thrives and the asymmetrical expertise of storytellers and facilitators can be acknowledged in co-creative practice. The kind of civic participation that Jenkins refers to also constitutes a shift away from traditional notions of the public sphere as 'rational deliberation within representative democracy... Towards digitally enabled civic habits in which we find alternative formats for information and opinion exchange' (Papacharissi, 2010, p. 20).

Advocates for digital storytelling draw attention to the significance of the workshop story circle. This is a time and space where participants develop affinity with one another and confidence in the telling of their stories. Evidencing the second and third forms of social change outlined above, this affinity building occurs in several ways; between workshop participants and, on another level, between storytellers and the many people who are imbricated in their stories. Networked identity work occurs across a range of networked publics – real and imagined, familiar and unknown, on and offline, now and in the future. While digital stories themselves may circulate in contexts that enhance feelings of social connectedness, it is the networked identity work implicit in the digital storytelling process that affords a sense of participating collectively and creatively in a cultural space that is greater than the individual.

While digital storytelling has no doubt enabled a great number of marginalised individuals to participate in the shaping of culture, critics of the claim 'anyone can do it' have outlined a number of obstacles. Democratic participation is thwarted by uneven access to both information and communication technologies (ICTs) and workshop practice. Digital storytelling in development contexts simultaneously critiques and endorses simplistic understandings of the digital divide and social inclusion. These issues are no less relevant in the West. Many scholars argue that the digital divide extends beyond *consumption* of new technologies to the *production* of digital content (Schradie, 2009). While digital storytelling can address uneven access to digital production tools (Burgess, 2006; Jenkins, 2006; Tacchi, 2006), much of current scholarship stops short of nuanced analysis, particularly of the terms of participation and ownership of stories that are distributed online and enduring in perpetuity. Similarly, the question of how people specifically manage privacy and publicness in digital stories constitutes a gap in the field of digital storytelling literature but maps onto burgeoning interest in the wider field of internet studies.

Social convergence: Publicness and privacy

The rise in popularity of social network spaces, like Facebook, has increased awareness of the potentially negative ramifications of public sharing of personal stories. Any young adult looking for employment will have heard horror stories of prospective employers searching the internet for drunken party photos that are liable to be interpreted as evidence of unstable and unreliable risk-taking behaviour. boyd describes social convergence in this way:

> Social convergence occurs when disparate social contexts are collapsed into one. Even in public settings, people are accustomed to maintaining discrete social contexts separated by space. How one behaves is typically dependent on the norms in a given social context. How one behaves in a pub differs from how one behaves in a family park, even though both are ostensibly public. Social convergence requires people to handle disparate audiences simultaneously without a social script. While social convergence allows information to be spread more efficiently, this is not always what people desire.
> (boyd, 2008b, p. 19)

Social convergence complicates digital storytelling when participants are encouraged to consider the privacy concerns of third parties – the friends and family members who are implicated in their stories. Storytellers decide whether to render them identifiable and also consider whether their construction resonates 'truthfully' for all the disparate viewers of their story.

Networked identity work involves extensive reflection (with friends and family as well as imagined publics) upon the cultural parameters of privacy and publicness or what constitutes 'over sharing'. Weintraub argues that, while the dichotomy of public/private offers a useful mechanism for analysis of our social universe, these categories are nevertheless complicated:

> at the deepest and most general level, lying behind the different forms of public/private distinction are (at least) two fundamental, and analytically quite distinct, kinds of imagery in terms of which 'private' can be contrasted with 'public':
> 1. What is hidden or withdrawn versus what is open, revealed, or accessible.
> 2. What is individual, or pertains only to an individual, versus what is collective, or affects the interests of a collectivity of individuals.
> (Weintraub, 1997, pp. 4–5)

While many social theorists explore privacy and publicness as dimensions of self-representation (Giddens, 1991; Goffman, 1963), the discussion has taken on new dimensions as online communication affords disembodied, interactive, non-linear and persistent expressions of fluid identities.

Queer community voice and intimate citizenship

Marginalised communities (and, in some cases, individuals) are split by conflicting desires to blend with a perceived mainstream, versus maintaining a sense of 'difference' or 'otherness'. This dualism of visibility/invisibility is a feature of identity categories that are, firstly, not easily discernible and, secondly, socially maligned.

On the first point, everyday activists have a tendency to make important self-descriptors material. My friend's experience as a queer parent, though not representative, is typical. When confronted with questions about her sons' father, she can be either vague and dismissive, using the male pronoun (as in 'he's not around'), or explicit (as in 'my children were conceived with donor sperm... and they have two mums'), thereby making their family visible. When she takes the latter path, whether cognisant or not, she is enacting a form of everyday activism in which she names a non-normative identity (lesbian parent) that also challenges popular stereotypes (lesbians don't have children). When she consciously undertakes such activity in front of audiences she knows may not approve, she seeks to catalyse social change. Queer everyday activists knowingly amplify an already complex set of risks around self-disclosure. Digital storytelling as a genre is self-revelatory in many explicit ways, causing queer everyday activists who wish to maintain privacy to explore a range of creative storytelling alternatives.

On the second inextricably related point, queer identities are frequently not socially sanctioned. As Goffman (1963) points out in his exploration of stigma, people who perceive their identity to be socially unacceptable may conceal these aspects from public judgement. Sharing queer stories in public involves a risk of homophobic or transphobic repercussions. Same-sex attracted people are over-represented in statistics on suicide, homelessness, drug abuse and frequently subject to both street violence and schoolyard bullying not to mention just feeling uncomfortable every time they hear the ubiquitous expression of 'that's so gay!'. As Gross points out, 'Queer folk are past masters at this [performativity] game... most of us survived society's sexual boot camp – high school – either by masquerading and passing, or living on the margins' (Gross, 2007). While there are homologies between the ways queer everyday activists create and share their digital stories of self and the ways they perform identity in everyday life, digital tools remediate their stories and performances of identity (Gray, 2009) as well as their duelling needs for privacy and publicness. The mechanisms by which queer activists reconcile these needs can be mapped onto other socially maligned minorities participating in public spaces. Conversely, through fine-grained examination of queer activist-oriented digital storytelling, the nuanced particularities of digitally mediated personal sharing by mainstream users become apparent. Further, whether queer or not, a postmodern rendering of identity as situated, fluid and evolving poses corresponding difficulties for any persistent and searchable rendition of identity.

The participants in this research, while unified by their common interest in digital storytelling, were diverse in age, social class, ethnicity, race and religion. The youngest participant was 17, the oldest approximately 50; some had experienced relatively affluent and secure upbringings, while others had experienced extreme poverty and a lack of childhood nurturing. There were several indigenous participants, one from a non-English speaking background, and spiritual beliefs ranged from atheist to Christian, Jewish and Islamic. While I have not attempted to analyse these distinct socioeconomic contexts as the basis of different approaches to self-representation, I take a storyteller-centred approach in which I privilege their reflections upon motivations, agency and ownership. The data I collected, being a very limited sample from a small community, does not substantiate claims to different generational, spiritual, economic or other approaches to self-representation. Of greater concern were questions regarding the degree to which each individual initially felt entitled to share a story, their self-defined technical and creative aptitude and their concerns over publicness and privacy in both face-to-face and online contexts.

Roadmap

Chapter 2 offers an overview of digital storytelling among other autobiographical genres, as tools for everyday activism. I canvas some of the changes wrought by digital technologies and consider some of the heretofore disregarded potentials and problems of digital storytelling in online spaces.

In the formative Chapters 3, 4 and 5, I describe my case studies, with particular attention given to the experiences of storytellers and the stories they produce. As a means of allowing the story of the research to unfold, I have chosen to start first with a *micro* examination of individual experiences of co-creating queer identity, pulling out to a *meso* analysis of both personal and institutional processes of mediating voice, before considering the *macro* landscape of imagined networked publics. This might be regarded as a movement from considerations of 'me', on to 'us', and finally through to 'me, us and the world'. Throughout these chapters, I interweave descriptions of text and/or process with theory, using headings to highlight thematic concerns.

In Chapter 3, I consider how individuals make meaning out of understandings and performances of identity. Identity is employed as a term that evokes the description and performance of self in a social context. In particular, I examine Goffman's ideas of performing identity front and back stage (Goffman, 1959) and Butler's notions of performativity (Butler, 1990) as well as her analysis of the difficulties of 'giving an account of oneself' (Butler, 2005). I consider how and when these philosophical understandings of identity align and diverge from the vernacular understandings articulated by participants. In particular, I examine difficulties with nominalising queer identities and the everyday disruption of categories undertaken by storytellers. The second section of this chapter analyses the problems posed by narrative coherence, partial self-awareness and/or opacity and the limitations of language. I argue that efforts to craft authenticity[6] should be reconstituted as a move away from social expectations of coherence towards self-ascribed congruence – reflecting, in turn, agency (in storytelling) and ownership (of contextually located stories).

Chapter 4 is divided into two sections in which I consider the facilitation of voice at institutional levels (how can speaking be supported?) and the orchestration of voices at personal levels (for whom do I speak?). The term voice is used to encompass discussions around how marginalised individuals find the confidence (or agency) and the means (or access) to articulate personal stories. In the first section I detail strategies in each of the three case studies, *What's Your Story?*, *Positive Stories* and *Rainbow Family Tree*. In the second section, I consider how storytellers give voice to family members or groups and other collective identity categories. In this section, voice is also used literally – in various analyses of how digital storytellers use their voices to strategically convey their messages. I draw on political philosophy and social movement theory to consider strategies for speaking across difference. The cultural nuances of speaking (who speaks, when and where?) and listening (what constitutes 'good' listening? how is it modelled and by whom?) are examined further.

In Chapter 5, I consider *to whom* and *with whom* storytellers speak. Creating digital stories intended for online distribution means accommodating multiple audiences in multiple locations and time frames, referred to as 'social convergence' (boyd, 2008b). I explore understandings of publics – familiar, intimate and unknown. I consider how storytellers imagine various audiences or publics with particular reference to the work of Berlant (1997) on 'intimate publics', Warner (2005) on 'counterpublics', and boyd (2011) and Papacharissi (2010) on 'networked publics'. The ways that storytellers constitute themselves as a part of or apart from specific imagined publics also have ramifications for our understandings of private and publicness. I explore intersections between textual approaches to identity construction and modes of content sharing and categorise these processes in a typology of otherness and outness. I discuss *visible, bounded* and *pseudonymous* approaches to self-representation and offer several examples in each category. I illustrate three modes of content sharing – *targeted, ad hoc* and *proxy*. I unpack the notion of networked identity work and argue that by undertaking this labour storytellers actively bridge the boundaries between visible/hidden and individual/collective constructions of identity both face-to-face and online. I consolidate these concepts in a further description of empowered agency and ownership.

In Chapter 6, I discuss specific issues for digital storytelling practice at *micro*, *meso* and *macro* levels. While there is no doubt that digital technology facilitates the articulation of marginalised voices in public, there remain many difficulties. Some may be addressed by breaking down tangible obstacles to access; other problems are rooted in social understandings of identity construction, dynamics of power and communication paradigms that are perpetuated in online realms. However, while the networked identity work of digital storytelling is hard labour and clearly a deterrent to everyday activism, I argue that it is also the source of personal and social transformation and constitutes evidence of Intimate Citizenship 3.0.

Finally, in Chapter 7, I discuss my findings across the three case studies and argue that a more nuanced understanding of the intertwined complexities of voice, identity and networked publics may result in better design of face-to-face and online initiatives, both formal and uncoordinated. Further, my findings map onto generic experiences of managing privacy and publicness in an era of ubiquitous social media, and offer insight for anyone engaging in identity curation as a pathway to active and fulfilling citizenship.

2
The 'Social' in Storytelling

This chapter is divided into three main sections that position digital storytelling within a historical and social context. Firstly I discuss what constitutes a 'personal story' and then move on to consider how this rhetorical form has functioned in a cultural context in relation to social change. I argue that digital storytelling inhabits a particular space that sits on the brink of further metamorphosis should it adapt to some of the idiosyncrasies of online realms. I do not ascribe agency to digital storytelling itself, rather to the people and institutions that employ it as a tool. In the second section I describe the emergence of digital storytelling and its uses for personal empowerment, archiving social history, community development, education and social advocacy. I follow this overview with discussion of the cultural significance and critical problems that frequently emerge in scholarly literature on digital storytelling, in particular ordinary people and broadcast access, listening and development, expertise and sustainability and the ways in which context shapes production (coaxing a supposedly authentic voice) and consumption (framing the way that stories are interpreted by audiences). Finally, in the third section, I consider some examples of personal online storytelling in multiple forms including personal blogs ('Same Plus'), collective themed blogs ('Born This Way') and affirmational vlogs ('It Gets Better') before moving on to discussion of specific possibilities for digital storytelling in online spaces.

Personal storytelling for social change

Personal stories are shared in a variety of contexts for a variety of purposes. Public speakers, ranging from politicians to stand-up comedians, use both self-deprecating and triumphant anecdotes to connect with an audience, inviting empathy. The 'personal' dimension is intimate, not something that would otherwise be commonly known, and frequently revealing of a small or significant vulnerability. This makes the speaker appear human rather than remote and overly powerful. Thompson calls this the 'new transparency' and argues that the blending of personal and public is a constitutive aspect of public life in a hypermediated age (Thompson, 2000).

Personal storytelling also takes many forms, ranging from semi-autobiographical novellas, broadcast documentaries, poems and music through to aphorisms shared at the check-out. Autobiographical stories differ from fiction in that they are narrated in the first person and purport to be factual. Philippe Lejeune defines autobiography as a 'retrospective prose narrative that someone writes concerning his own existence, where the focus is his individual life, in particular the story of his personality' (Lejeune, 1989, p. 14). Further, Lejeune argues that autobiographical texts rely upon a pact between author and audience whereby both agree that the content of the narrative is truthful. While Lejeune acknowledges the subjective nature of memory, self-representation and truth, he nevertheless regards this author–audience pact as a measure that distinguishes the respective authority and authenticity of factual versus fictional texts. While audiences tend to regard autobiographical stories as real, biographies on the other hand are conferred authority by the reputation of the author as a researcher or by their proximity to their subject, who is regarded as the ultimate source of truthful insight on their existence (Lejeune, 1989). Popular discourse also links the physical presence of a subject in front of a camera with actuality.

> Written texts and sound/image texts diverge at the semiotic level. Written texts are an arbitrary sign system. That is, their material signs, written words, have no physical connection to the real thing that they represent. One does not need the actual thing to represent it in written words. Sound/image texts are a motivated, existential sign system. That is, their material signs, the cinematic sound and image, have a physical connection to the real thing that they represent. The filmmaker needs the actual thing to represent it cinematically.
> (Lane, 2002, p. 5)

Lane raises a distinction between autobiographical forms that position audio-visual representations as more 'authentic' or 'truthful' than text. However, audiences and readers, via post-modernism and increasingly sophisticated media literacy are very aware of the many ways this 'actuality' can be constructed by filmmakers, journalists and storytellers. In an autobiographical film, the presence of the author on screen, flags the mediating influence of a camera operator and quite possibly a sound recordist.

> In literary autobiographies, author, narrator, and protagonist coincide; the author's signature frequently operates as the guarantee of identity. Defining films and videos as autobiographical is more tricky because, as Elizabeth Bruss cautions, one must distinguish between cinema 'eye' (the body behind the camera) and cinema 'I' (the body in the film), and differentiate between (usually) single author of a book and (often) collective 'auteur' of a film.
>
> (Holmlund & Fuchs, 1997, p. 128)

Regardless of form (public speaking, print, broadcast by radio, television or internet) first-person storytelling requires an enactment of identity, or what Goffman (1959) calls 'performance'. While individual audience members inevitably respond differently to the same presentation (see the expansive field of 'audience-reception' literature, beginning with Stuart Hall, 1980) context also influences interpretation.

Public speaking clearly results in a different kind of engagement with an audience, who are physically co-present in time and space, to that afforded by a written text or possibly an audio-visual document:

> Embodiment – among the most widely explored elements in feminist scholarship today – creates a different sort of intimacy between narrator and listener than that experienced by a reader.
>
> (Fosl, 2008, p. 221)

Testimony of personal experience, or witnessing, is highlighted in social movement theory as an influential means of engaging an audience in political thinking. Fosl examines the empowerment narratives of three activists who use personal storytelling to build collective identity, a fundamental tenet of any social movement. Each of the speakers narrates a story whence they were unquestioning members of a silent majority, before experiencing a moment of enlightenment and 'discovering' a distinctive voice:

> ... each experienced a figurative death and rebirth within a more collective [and empowered] identity. Telling that story over and over

became a source of renewed commitment, with the self reconstructed repeatedly in front of others who were or might become similarly committed and thus widening the collective.

(Fosl, 2008, p. 225)

A speaker who shares a personal story in public (whether that be in person, in text or on screen) does so for a reason. Although this may not always be pre-meditated, it frequently is – the aforementioned politician hopes to win votes, the comedian hopes to win laughs, the activist hopes to win allegiance – all, effectively, hope to win approval. The strategic manner in which a speaker formulates a goal for communication sheds light on their motivation. Many of the storytellers I discuss engage in emotional catharsis more than calculated political strategising, and while these are clearly quite different agendas, they may nevertheless be interconnected:

> By placing her individual plot at the center of what is, for the most part, an essentially political action, each of the narrators considered here also asserts the implicit claim, 'I matter', or 'My story is worth hearing'... In the telling and re-telling of their empowerment journeys, each of the three was also defining and re-defining, herself.
>
> (Fosl, 2008, p. 224)

While some digital storytellers engage in personal sharing as therapeutic catharsis and others consciously perform vulnerability as a strategy for winning audience approval, the social consequence of autobiographical storytelling is most pertinent to everyday activism. As such, activist storytellers are likely to consider what form is most appropriate for communicating their message in public.

Put simply, if an activist wishes to catalyse social change through the articulation of a personal story, she may do so by taking up a soap box in the corner of a park (public speaking) or she may consider reaching a wider audience by writing her story down and disseminating leaflets or autobiographical books (in which case she also needs either a photocopier or publisher). She may reach an even wider audience by sharing her story on a talk show, or engaging a film crew or buying a webcam. These distinctions between forms of autobiography have become increasingly blurred as communication technologies transformed printing press into photocopier, amplified a loud voice via microphone and reduced traditional heavy film cameras to increasingly mobile forms, including the ubiquitous smart camera phone. Arguments about the democratisation of media also highlight the increasing affordability of various communication technologies, theoretically making it more accessible to the masses. Later I discuss how relative access to the means of production and distribution, and the influence of mediating technologies, impacts upon the democratic expression of voice.

Meanwhile, Lane, in his historical overview of North American autobiographical documentary, argues that linking the 'everyday to the broader social order' has resulted in a 'potent site of American cultural production' (Lane, 2002, p. 5). Cole et al. argue that autobiographical narratives (documentaries in particular) do this in three ways – by transcending stereotypical plotlines, by embracing everyday experiences, and by using means of production that disrupt formulaic descriptions (Cole, Quinlan & Hayward, 2009, pp. 86–87). In a similar vein, Holmlund and Fuchs (1997) argue that autobiography as a genre plays a very particular role in the history of queer cultural activism. In examples from the 1980s and 1990s, filmmakers like Sadie Benning and Su Friedrich used available technologies (in Benning's case a children's black and white PixelVision camera) and self-reflexive narratives to articulate a marginalised experience of sexual identity. Holmlund and Fuchs argue that a queer approach to self-representation epitomises complex intersections between visibility and social participation:

> ...to see and be seen is a matter not only of visual representations but also of social acceptance and political clout. Increasingly, queer media makers and queer critics also take up questioning of communication and translation, reconsidering how speaking and naming, silence and suggestion, are expressed and experienced.
> (Holmlund & Fuchs, 1997, p. 2)

Approaching the same issue from a different theoretical perspective, public sphere and social movement scholars argue the merit of storytelling as a more inclusive mode of social and political discourse. Iris Marion Young regards Habermasian models of deliberative democracy as discussion that is expressed in a very particular fashion, taking place in particular spaces and consequently argues for a more 'communicative' and inclusive model:

> ...storytelling complements arguments in a communicative democracy because it tends to be more egalitarian than deliberative

processes.... deliberation can privilege the dispassionate, the educated, or those who feel they have a right to assert. Because everyone has stories to tell, with different styles and meanings, and because each can tell her story with equal authority, the stories have equal value in the communicative situation.

(Young, 1997, p. 73)

Aside from their role as a strictly 'political' tool, autobiographical stories play a vital cultural role in shaping meaning, arguably more significant than their service as supposedly truthful reflections of reality.

More than merely self-recognition, self-definition is made possible by means of such [public] showings [of stories], for their content may state not only what people think they are but what they should have been or may not be. Evidently, interpretive statements are mirrors for collectives to hold up to themselves; like mirrors, such statements may lie, reverse, and distort the images they carry, and they need not be isomorphic with 'nature'.

(Myerhoff, 1986, pp. 261–262)

Myerhoff notes the significance of storytelling as self-definition while highlighting that self-representations need not necessarily be accurate or 'authentic' (as digital stories are so often proclaimed to be). Whether embodied or symbolic, realistic or impressionistic, the social history of autobiography is pertinent to digital storytelling, which is effectively a narrative mash-up of domestic snapshots and highly scripted voiceover.

Poletta (2006) acknowledges that storytelling is of value to disadvantaged groups but disputes what she sees as two common claims in contemporary scholarship on storytelling in protest and politics. Firstly, she highlights the risks involved as well as the benefits. Secondly, she maintains these risks come about 'as much from the norms of narrative's use and interpretation as they do from the norm of its content... Stories are differently intelligible, useful, and authoritative depending on who tells them, when, for what purpose, and in what setting' (Poletta, 2006, p. 3). This analysis is pertinent to the use of digital stories as tools for everyday activism because focusing only on narrative's *potential* misses various problems: the possibility that an audience might be moved by a story yet remain unmoved to take action; or that they may be required to empathise with a point of view far removed from their own; and finally that a badly told story may discourage rather than reinforce emotional identification. Poletta calls for scholarly analysis of 'the distribution of storytelling authority [and] identifying the social epistemologies of storytelling that guide its use' (2006, p. 168). She points out that familiar stories can reinforce social norms and dualities like dependent/independent, victimised/empowered, etc., and argues that the 'discursive mechanisms of canonical stories' themselves afford insight into the conventions around when and how stories are told. It is in deference to this established wisdom, that focuses on the context of storytelling as much as the content of the story itself, that I employed a situated methodology for the case studies that underpin this book.

The emergence of digital storytelling

This section traces some of the highlights in the history of digital storytelling (from The Center for Digital Storytelling, to Capture Wales, to the Australian Centre for the Moving Image, and Queensland University of Technology) and overviews a traditional digital storytelling workshop. I canvas some of the diverse motivations for undertaking digital storytelling from individual and organisational perspectives and discuss obstacles that complicate some of the claims made by digital storytelling enthusiasts.

Digital storytelling as a cultural movement has its roots in the storytelling traditions of community arts practice. Dana Atchley, an American artist and educator who died in 2000, is generally acknowledged to be one of the pioneers of digital storytelling. His first experiment in combining autobiographical narration and personal archival photography was 'Next Exit' performed for the first time in 1988 as a personal interactive theatrical piece set at a 'digital campfire'. This was also his first collaboration with Joe Lambert and Nina Mullen, and together they established the San Francisco Digital Media Centre (SFDMC) in 1994. They created a range of interactive new media projects and digital storytelling training initiatives and in 1998, they were joined by Denise Aungst and relocated to the University of California at Berkeley's School of Education. Here they established the Center for Digital Storytelling (CDS) that went on to become one of the major global hubs of digital storytelling practice. With different backgrounds and aspirations for digital storytelling practice, they collectively drew inspiration from 'numerous artistic movements...that celebrated the creative expression of "common folk" – that is, the creativity of the non-professional artist' (Lambert, 2009, p. 79). While Atchley went on to consult for corporate clients who used the medium as a means of developing brand identities, Lambert's approach was more oriented towards self-empowerment and social change. In 2001, CDS staff travelled to New Zealand, Australia and the United Kingdom where they facilitated workshops and trained staff at Evision, Australian Centre for the Moving Image (ACMI) and BBC Wales, respectively.

As the practice was further promulgated worldwide, advocates focused on a variety of democratic potentials. Daniel Meadows, as the chief proponent of the BBC's *Capture Wales* initiative states:

> I believed that the new tools of digital production could and should be used to open up the airwaves for a wide range of new users; in short, to give voice to all of us who are accustomed to thinking of ourselves – in a broadcast context, anyway – only as audience. [Digital storytelling] can be done on the kitchen table using off-the-shelf software and home computers... (it) can be mastered by people of differing abilities and from all walks of life.
>
> (Meadows, 2009, p. 91)

Capture Wales brought digital storytelling to national television screens in the UK; other initiatives and institutions, like ACMI in Melbourne, have brought the practice into the public eye by positioning digital stories alongside more expertly produced media works in cultural archives and galleries. Tertiary institutions like Queensland University of Technology (QUT) have also contributed to the dissemination of digital storytelling practice by encouraging the development of discursive analysis of the form and its cultural significance.

CDS (and many other proponents of the practice) advocate for digital storytelling with the logline 'everyone has a story to tell' and they develop this premise further into five basic principles. These are broadly summarised as: digital storytelling practice *supports people in recognising the significance of their own personal stories* in part by *providing a safe space in which they can open up and be heard.* Third, while a narrative framework is offered to assist people in organising their stories, it is recognised that there is *no formula for making a great story.* Fourth, the process helps participants overcome feelings of inadequacy by *confronting notions that creative activity is the 'province of experts'.* Finally, 'digital literacy begins with a faith that *people can work around the never ending complexities of their computer devices*' (Lambert, 2009, p. 87).

In *The Digital Storytelling Cookbook* Joe Lambert elaborates in further detail, outlining seven fundamental story elements he regards as being at the heart of digital storytelling practice. These are:

1. Point (of View) or what is it that you are trying to communicate?
2. The Dramatic Question or how does the central conflict get resolved? Does the girl get the guy? Does the hero reach the goal? Who is the protagonist and what is the obstacle they need to overcome to reach their dream?
3. Emotional Content or be brave and speak honestly.
4. The Gift of your Voice – natural inflections and speech idiosyncrasies help tell the story – don't hide them and try not to sound like you're reading.
5. The Power of the Soundtrack – an instrumental soundtrack is often more effective; if you use lyrics make sure they're appropriate and don't get in the way of the narration.
6. Economy – keep it simple and brief, allowing space for the audience to fill in the gaps.
7. *Pacing – changing pace can be dramatic and very effective, helping to sustain an audience's interest.*

These seven points canvas similar territory to many other instructional storytelling guides. However, within the digital storytelling movement, they have taken on almost canonical status and are frequently referred to in secondary sources.

Traditionally, digital storytelling workshops take place over three or four days, starting initially with 'getting to know you' games that establish trust between group members and facilitators. On this first day participants will most frequently discuss some of the above elements of storytelling and watch some examples of digital stories. Sitting in a story circle they share their first thoughts on a life experience, place or person they might like to tell a story about. Sometimes participants are asked to bring a symbolic object. This particular exercise can encourage a degree of externalisation – a practice used in narrative therapy (and described further later) that supports participants in thinking of life experiences as separate from identity, as in the phrase 'I am not the problem; the problem is the problem' (White & Epston, 1990). They are encouraged to be self-aware as they respond to each other's stories. As homework participants gather together the assets – photographs, art works, musical inspirations, etc.– that will make up their story.

A second day will often start with sharing draft scripts, distilled to about 250 words of narration. Feedback might include what aspects of the story were emotionally moving, and what might be considered unnecessary detail. Group tuition on edit software follows, ideally with a high ratio of workstations and facilitators to participants. Workshops may be offered with a variety of hardware/software configurations. PC based workshops may utilise editing software like Movie Maker, Sony Vegas or Adobe Premiere while Macintosh based workshops may use iMovie or Final Cut Pro. Cheaper consumer-end edit platforms may need to be supplemented with additional software for photo editing (Photoshop, etc.) and sound recording and/or mixing (Audacity, etc.). The more expensive high-end edit programmes offer greater flexibility in work process but are also more complicated to learn and operate effectively.

The final day of a workshop is frequently spent in a frenzy of editing with facilitators resolving a variety of technical glitches and creative challenges. A workshop often culminates in a screening of (hopefully finished) projects for participants and invited friends and family members.

Cultural significance, critical problems

Digital storytelling initiatives are undertaken for a range of objectives including personal empowerment; archiving social history; community development; education; and social advocacy. In a typical example, a worker in a social-service, arts or educational agency hears about workshops or sees stories online and seeks to fit the practice into their particular institutional itinerary, whether that be a health, education, cultural-preservation or social-advocacy agenda. Individuals who choose to become participants have a similarly diverse range of expectations. In some cases these match the host institution's agenda, sometimes not.

Lambert established the CDS with a focus on community arts practice and activism:

> ...providing people with convivial tools, such as the methods of digital storytelling practice (as opposed to the mass media's 'industrial production'), enables 'autonomous and creative intercourse among persons', which is a precondition for social change.
>
> (Lambert, 2009, p. 82)

Despite this beguiling premise digital storytelling involves nuanced interaction between host institution, facilitators and storytellers, providing interesting examples of co-creative enterprise located in asymmetrical power dynamics.

Opportunities for participation

Hartley outlines digital storytelling's potential to engage 'ordinary people' in self-representation by moving beyond what he calls 'the expert paradigm' as it is traditionally manifest in broadcast media:

> The shift from broadcast to interactive media in particular has democratised self-expression and complicated the entire edifice of 'representation' in both symbolic and political communication. We are no longer satisfied with deferring to representatives; we want direct voice, action, creative expression – and, increasingly, knowledge.
>
> (Hartley, 2008, p. 209)

'Big media' (a term used by Daniel Meadows to describe large commercial or government run broadcasting institutions, publishing houses and film production companies) generally denies access to untrained or inexperienced storytellers (unless they are shepherded by an experienced mentor or supported by an 'emerging filmmaker' initiative) in the name of quality control. Since more affordable technology has extended access to the tools of video production, and the internet has provided an accessible publishing platform, there has been a groundswell of vernacular creativity in a variety of forms (Burgess, 2006). Digital storytelling has arguably found its place, alongside vlogging and experimental home movies uploaded to YouTube, as a medium in which ordinary people, with varying degrees of technical expertise and creative innovation, can represent themselves.

Despite these opportunities for creative participation in public spaces the fact is that digital storytelling remains firmly rooted in workshop process that is resource consuming (cost of hardware, software, facilitators, etc.). Even in the case of CDS, funding comes from a broad cross section of government, business and philanthropic sources and presumably, while these funders contribute on the basis of CDS's stated values, they nevertheless need outcomes that substantiate their investment in individual initiatives. Discordant motivations and objectives on the part of host institution and/or facilitator and participants

can create interesting disturbances that highlight inequitable power relationships.
Workshops also typically involve skilled facilitators teaching unskilled participants. Hartley sees this as a new manifestation of 'the expert paradigm' but argues there is no inherent problem in the asymmetrical relationship between facilitator and participant (on the condition that the terms of collaboration are clearly negotiated). In order that digital storytelling fulfil its potential to play a significant role in public culture he suggests:

> Instead of choosing between the expert paradigm and self-expression, objective and subjective knowledge, it would be preferable to hold fast to both. To do that, it is necessary to abandon the linear model of communication and to replace it with one founded in dialogue.
> (Hartley, 2008, p. 204)

This '"dialogic" development of expertise among users' (Hartley, 2008, p. 206) is increasingly referred to in community media contexts as 'co-creativity' (Edmond & Spurgeon, 2013). By acknowledging the cultural capital that participants bring to the table (as expert storytellers of their own life narratives) Burgess and Klaebe posit that digital storytelling can be re-framed as a mediation of 'vernacular practices that are already in place' rather than 'enabling' creative expression (Burgess & Klaebe, 2009, p. 162).

Despite this reframe, the prohibitive expense of workshops means that a finite number of participants (complicated by questions of who is 'recruited' and why) can be engaged in a finite number of initiatives. Furthermore, how can the technical skills and cultural capacity developed by select digital storytellers extend beyond the parameters of a workshop?

> If Digital Storytelling is to gather momentum and to play a significant role in public culture, the next step is to move beyond the focus on production at the local level ... Digital Storytelling needs to address the question of how to scale up content for audiences, and how to propagate the method as part of universal education.
> (Hartley, 2008, p. 202)

Hartley raises the spectre of propagating digital literacy and building audiences without addressing who might do this or how. Should it be the traditional digital storytelling movement, community arts or public education? Couldry also uses a theoretical and speculative frame, rather than one grounded in practice, to discuss digital storytelling's relevance to a broader cultural landscape:

> ...if we are to take Lambert's vision of digital storytelling's potential contribution to democracy seriously, as I believe we should – (we need) to follow closely not just the forms and styles of digital storytelling and not just who is involved in what locations in digital storytelling, and where, but in what wider contexts and under what conditions digital stories are exchanged, referred to, treated as a resource, and given recognition and authority.
> (Couldry, 2008, p. 56)

Couldry imputes that it is recognition of the form that serves as the best measure of its democratic success, however does digital storytelling (or any new media) require endorsement from governmental and/or educational and/or broadcast media institutions to have authority? Do YouTube recommendations (or 'likes') that vastly increase audience size count or is this the same as referring to ratings as a measure of a documentary's social impact?

Consideration of 'who is speaking' and 'who is listening' continue in ICT4D (Information and Communication Technology for Development), as played out in a variety of co-creative media practices, including digital storytelling, in developing countries. Tacchi points out how opportunities for participation are framed by local context. Regardless of the health, wealth, ethnicity or disenfranchised status of the community in question, a preliminary survey by individuals or agencies with a degree of power (cultural and fiscal) generally determines what the community in question needs. Several issues commonly emerge, suggesting that digital storytelling is perhaps not as democratic as it may appear.

> ...voicing may be encouraged but nevertheless not be heard. Participatory approaches may themselves turn out to constitute 'top-down participation,' where participation simply constitutes 'insider' learning what 'outsiders' want to hear, or simply an exercise in administrative task-sharing or the necessary rhetoric to win funding...
> (Tacchi, 2009, p. 170)

Regardless of mechanisms for engagement or an analytical shift from voice to listening, there remain concerns about how digital storytelling might develop into a participatory medium outside of the heavily mediated context of workshops.

Context shapes production

A substantial body of literature on digital storytelling practice examines the constitutive influence of facilitator and host institution upon workshop process and the resulting story products (Burgess & Klaebe, 2009; Goldman, Booker & McDermott, 2008; Hull & Katz, 2006). Lambert acknowledges the impact of his role as a facilitator thus:

> At the CDS we understand that the choices we make in sharing stories as examples, in how we guide the considerations on meaning, of making connections to the social construct, are not meant to be balanced... Even if our efforts are just showing people a way to take responsibility for their own lives, their own stories, as the first step to larger awareness, all our choices are informed with a touch of the subversive.
>
> (Lambert, 2009, p. 82)

Activist-oriented storytelling has roots in propaganda filmmaking that in turn derives marketing strategies from advertising. While Lambert pursues a social-change agenda, other scholars have drawn attention to digital storytelling's application in commercial contexts.

> On the Coca Cola website, personal stories, activism and corporate big business converge to appear in the same cultural digital space. Coca Cola's online 'Heritage' section includes a collection of personal stories, thereby lending Coca Cola cultural cache. The 'Coca Cola Stories,' approximately 300 of them, are 'browse-able' by category. Some examples include Romance: 'Coke was sacred to our family'; Military: 'when you're at war and haven't had a Coke [a month] seems like forever'; or Childhood Memories: 'I had my first Coke when I was seven years old.'
>
> (Springate, 2006, pp. 5–6)

Digital storytellers who are motivated to transform personal anecdotes into persuasive advocacy may, either intuitively or consciously, and with varying degrees of success, adopt what are essentially marketing strategies in an effort to communicate their message. While Lambert insists on complete freedom of expression and encourages participants to create stories about whatever it is that they think is most significant in their lives, digital storytelling is also frequently used by social service providers either to educate or catalyse discussion around social issues.

Springate examines a South African based digital storytelling initiative with a particular HIV/AIDS activist agenda:

> Activists who seek to make their experiences 'visible' and participate in movements may be telling their stories for the first time. They may seek, through personal and specific details, to articulate a more collective experience and to highlight even broader social and political issues. When digital stories constellate around such issues, they constitute organised political activity. As such there is some expectation for their digital productions to enable new ways of advocating for social change – to do pedagogical work, to raise consciousness, to make claims for justices, to function towards epistemological questioning, and engage in structural and social critique.
>
> (Springate, 2006, p. 4)

How one communicates one's story and to whom is a central theme in much digital storytelling literature. Conveying sentiments, aspirations or complicated ideas can present many challenges. Hull and Nelson suggest that, partly as a result of the multimodal composition process intrinsic to digital storytelling, there can be a tendency for storytellers to default to 'conventionalised forms of self-presentation over inventive and idiosyncratic forms' (Nelson & Hull, 2008, p. 124). Facilitation also influences tropes of self-expression producing an archetypical digital story genre. Many stories follow a linear narrative arc – from childhood to adulthood, from adversity to triumph – in a fashion that resonates with Joseph Campbell's seminal 'hero's journey' (Campbell, 1949). Meanwhile Hull and Nelson draw on Bakhtin to elucidate 'overpopulated intentions' (particularly apparent in digital story texts):

> According to Bakhtin, one cannot truly 'speak' without orientating toward an addressee, even in the case that one is addressing oneself. And one cannot but speak in a variety of 'languages' and a chorus of 'voices', for oral and written language and all other semiotic modes, we submit, are not neutral [media] that [pass] freely and easily into the private property of the speaker's intentions; [they are] populated – overpopulated – with the intentions of others.
>
> (Nelson & Hull, 2008, p. 138)

Taub-Pervizpour situates these concerns in digital storytelling workshop practice, questioning: 'how we position ourselves in relation to the stories that emerge in our workshops and programs, and how who we are informs which stories get told, by whom, and for whom' (Taub-Pervizpour, 2009, p. 246). Digital storytelling is often lauded as an expression of 'authentic voice'. However, Hertzberg Kaare and Lundby (2008) critique these notions. In their analysis of a Norwegian faith-oriented digital storytelling initiative, they use qualitative interviews with young storytellers to reveal the gap between popular notions of authenticity as 'the degree to which one is true to one's own personality or identity' (Guignon, 2004, p. 126) and the influence of workshop context in shaping digital stories. The young people they interviewed were clearly influenced by the sample digital stories they were shown as well as what they perceived to be group expectations. These factors had at least as much significance as the true-life anecdotes they drew upon in framing their digital narratives.

Context shapes consumption

The cataloguing of digital story 'artefacts', or the context in which they are presented, goes further than a nonpartisan gathering of historical accounts.

> Cataloguing archival material – in this case digital stories – is not a neutral act, for the way in which material is categorised informs and shapes research, public viewing, relevance, and access. Cataloguing is thereby an ethical issue. Who decides on the themes and categories by which archival material is grouped? And by what criteria are these decisions made? Selection and categorization of material also functions to define what counts and for whom. As such, it defines who will find it and how.
>
> (Springate, 2006, p. 7)

Just as Springate highlights the subjective evaluation of story content that determines how they are archived, the institutions that display, distribute or broadcast digital stories undertake a similar appraisal of 'quality'. Thumim analyses these cultural tensions in her survey of participants in the *London's Voices 16–19* initiative. Here, storytellers speak about how their work was presented to audiences in the Museum of London:

> Interviewer: And whereabouts in the museum was it, when you come in the museum?
> Kimberley: In the corridor like no one even cared about us. They didn't even put us in properly, just in the corridor.

Clifford: I thought our pictures were going to be on the wall...

(Thumim, 2008, p. 98)

How can this shaping of the production and consumption of identity narratives avoid a constitutive effect on everyday performances of identity? Notions of performativity (Butler, 1990) trouble understandings of truth, fiction and authenticity by acknowledging that individuals routinely modify aspects of their identity according to social context. Analytical tools derived from queer theory are brought to bear in a more detailed exploration of identity construction in digital stories in Chapter 3.

Digital storytellers must also consider what their prospective audiences may choose to watch and this presents multiple issues of how to reach audiences and how to market stories in order to attract audience attention (and, in online realms, 'views'). As Ken Plummer points out in the seminal 'Telling Sexual Stories':

> Stories get told and read in different ways in different contexts. The consuming of a tale centres upon the different *social worlds* and *interpretive communities* who can hear the story in certain ways and hence not others and who may come to produce their own shared 'memories'... Stories feed into different communities, evoking contrasting responses. The stories of people with HIV infection feed into some communities where support, love and care is offered; but into others where exclusion, stigma and fear is the interpretive frame... More, such communities are not permanent and fixed: when for instance, the US basketball player Magic Johnson announced his HIV status in 1991, his story became accepted in the same youthful communities (where he was an established hero) that had previously shown enmity to Aids stories.
>
> (Plummer, 2002, p. 22)

Plummer draws attention to the structural and discursive prerequisites to both *production* and *consumption* of stories (in particular sexual stories, taboo in previous times) and highlights the evolving interaction between producers, coaxers (in other words, facilitators) and consumers that influence the continually shifting meaning of stories. Further, he considers the sharing of stories as the moral foundation of communities in which rights and responsibilities are invented through human activity: 'The nature of our communities – the languages they use, the stories they harbour, the identities they construct, the moral/political codes they champion – move to the centre stage of political thinking' (Plummer, 2002, p. 150).

Writing about a pilot digital storytelling workshop I facilitated in 2009 for a community of 'Pink Parents', Julia Erhart explores the capacity of 'digidocs' to 'get their message out, loudly and clearly, powerfully and memorably, to the widest audience possible' (Erhart, 2009, p. 48). However she also notes an inherent conflict between privacy and publicness. On the one hand there is a desire to speak out on behalf of families that have little or no visible public profile, while on the other hand there is a need 'to safeguard the interests of children who may neither yet know what it means to be "out" nor may in the future wish to have been "outed" ' (ibid., p. 48). Of all the stated objectives for digital storytelling it is this area of social activism that is least scrutinised in the existing literature, partly because, as I mentioned earlier, measures of 'social change' can be subjective and partly because the practical mechanisms of managing privacy and publicness is complex.

The final section of this chapter explores the potential of personal stories that reach people online, while the issue of appealing to audiences is discussed further in the second half of Chapter 4.

Potentials of online storytelling

New technology has borne forth new forms of self-reflexive narrative like blogs (Karlsson, 2004; Tremayne, 2007; Walker, 2004) and vlogs (Burgess & Green, 2009; Raun, 2010a; Thorson et al., 2010). While these forms bear some resemblance to life-writing, autobiographical documentary and digital storytelling, perhaps the biggest distinction is their episodic, organically unfolding nature, affording representation of fluid and complex identities. For example, YouTube plays host to a vlog genre of intentional body transformation, ranging from weight loss to gender transition. In the particular case of gender transition, video diaries serve as a means of cataloguing transformation, refining gender performance (including mannerisms, vocal pitch and speech patterns) and connecting with a like-minded community of supporters. While there is potential for both positive and negative feedback, derogatory comments are often countered by affirming voices. For socially maligned identities vlogs offer safe spaces (both in the location of their recording and consumption, most often bedrooms). Virtual audiences provide rehearsal opportunities for later face-to-face encounters. While many vlogs are open to an unrestricted public audience they nevertheless function as semi-private spaces in that they are created for an imagined intimate public of supporters or counter-public (Berlant, 1997; Raun, 2010b; Warner, 2005). As activist tools, blogs and vlogs also take many forms. They range from journal-like entries that catalogue face-to-face activist encounters, through to intimate personal reflections that, while not overtly political in their stated intent, nevertheless contribute to a cultural public sphere in challenging mainstream values. In the section that follows I reflect upon examples of queer activist uses of online spaces for sharing personal narratives – Jacqui Tomlins 'SAME + blog'; 'Born This Way'; 'It Gets Better'; and 'Make It Better'.

Jacqui Tomlins is an Australian activist, mother and blogger who has been involved in several queer community campaigns for legislative reform. The first, 'Love Makes a Family', was launched in 2004 and coordinated by the volunteer-based 'Rainbow Families Council' to increase awareness around issues of equal access to Assisted Reproductive Technologies and Adoption in Victoria. The group established a website and Yahoo! group and called for community members to share their personal stories of family with politicians, policymakers and friends in the general community. The website featured real-life family portraits and there were regular call-outs for people who might be happy to speak to the media in features about their alternative family structures and conception processes. People were encouraged to report back to the community about their experiences of everyday activism, including anecdotes about visiting members of parliament. As parliamentary debate drew closer, community members were encouraged to recruit heterosexual family members and teachers, childcare workers, doctors and acquaintances to write letters of support to their local members or visit them in person. During the parliamentary debate, families visited with their children and sat in the public gallery.

> ... because it's not like being black or disabled which are very identifiable visible things... as queer, you can go through life and nobody would know... that's the particular interesting thing, this notion of visibility for our community, the parallels between 'coming out' and [moves forward in] gay and civil rights... that's where, on a small scale, Sarah and I, and 'Love Makes a Family' and other campaigns we've been doing [are significant]... Now the notion that there are families with two mums or two dads is not a revelation to most people...
>
> (Tomlins, interview, 2010)

Tomlins also acknowledges the significance of the e-list as a mechanism for rallying community energies and coordinating face-to-face actions in the campaign that followed.

In 2003, Jacqui and her female partner got married in Canada and when they returned to Australia they lodged an application in the family court to establish the legal validity of their marriage. It was this action that prompted the Howard government to amend the Marriage Act to define marriage specifically as 'the union between one man and one woman' (Tomlins, SAME + blog, 2011). Following the 2009 federal election and a change of government the issue of same-sex marriage became increasingly significant for politicians as it was widely debated in the media and in public. In 2010 Jacqui established her Same + blog and e-list as a tool for engaging with the wider gay and straight communities and continues to publish updates every couple of weeks on her personal lobby for marriage recognition. She reflects on the issue of visibility and the risk this entails for her and her family:

> ...there's that famous quote... 'in order for evil to thrive it just needs good people to be silent...' you know we could just let this go and that's not good for our kids either. I've always felt a strong responsibility to attempt to affect change if we can, partly because we are very protected...privileged...we are white, middle class, affluent, educated...all those things. We're not vulnerable. Not to say on a daily basis I don't feel discriminated against...but there's a lot of people out there whose lives are a million times worse than mine, I don't have much to complain about...I'm in a safe position to put myself out there...
>
> (Tomlins, interview, 2010)

As corresponding issues of queer visibility, homophobia and same-sex marriage are debated in the United States many interesting online projects have emerged featuring personal storytelling as a tool for catalysing social change.

The 'Born This Way' blog, established in 2011, features contributions from queer adults who submit short 250 to 300 word reflections and a photo on 'growing up gay'. The background information on the site clearly states that, while some stories feature girls with masculine traits and boys with feminine traits, these stories do not represent the entire community and each individual has selected their own photograph 'with no form of encouragement for a certain "type" of pic' (Paul V, Born This Way Blog, 2012). The blog was voted 'best google blog' in the about.com People's Choice award in 2011. Paul V., a Los Angeles-based DJ and the blog curator, states:

> My ultimate goal with the blog is to help chip away the stone of homophobia, show that being gay has never been a choice, and to help humanise, personalise, and globalise what our experiences are/were as children growing up LGBTQ.
>
> (Paul V, Born This Way Blog, 2012)

While the blog doesn't have an explicit agenda regarding law reform it is clear that its creator aspires to contribute to social change by offering a 'safe space' for people to share their stories. It also serves as an outward-facing curated collection of self-representations for a wider readership. The identity discourse articulated by the blog, one of innate queerness, is both shaped by discourses in popular culture (including the massively popular Lady Gaga hit 'Born This Way' which has also spawned a philanthropic foundation by the same name) and a normative shaping influence itself.

The 'It Gets Better' project offers another example of personal storytelling shared in online space ('It Gets Better Project | Give hope to LGBT youth,' 2012). Established in 2010 by Seattle based columnist and media pundit Dan Savage and husband Terry Miller, the site was a response to a wave of gay youth suicides. Over 200 videos were uploaded in the first week. Most clips are between 3 and 10 minutes and feature individuals speaking directly to camera about personal experiences of surviving teenage bullying. While initially queer adults created these videos, later contributions feature heterosexual people, celebrities and young people (both gay and straight). At the time of writing the site hosted 30,000 videos and has had in the vicinity of 40 million views.

While youth suicide continues to be a problem in the United States, scholars are starting to question whether the discourse of 'getting better' in some way contributes to the problem (boyd, 2012; Gray, 2012). Notably, in September 2011, 14-year-old Jamey Rodemeyer took his life after creating his own supportive 'It Gets Better' message in May that year. While not referring specifically to the 'It Gets Better' project, Waidzunas reflects upon the 'ironic consequences' of widely circulating statistics on gay teen suicide: 'including the fostering of gay youth identification with suicide as a potential correlate of their identity. They have also led to a reaction in the form of 'resilience' narratives' (Waidzunas, 2011, p. 1). The 'Make It Better Project' attempts to address these issues by offering tangible strategies for overcoming bullying and harassment including active involvement in youth gay–straight alliances (for students) and a personal storytelling letter writing campaign (for adults). Their site offers further clarification:

> 'It Gets Better' is a powerful story-telling campaign, which imparts hope by showing the difference between 'now' and 'then.' Its arc is: 1. Life was tough. 2. Time passed. 3. Life is better. The Make It Better Project complements the It Gets Better Project by filling in the gaps – and the action – of that story, fleshing out step number two: how you can make it better.
> ('Make It Better Project | LGBT youth should not have to suffer through bullying at school!' 2012)

This contextualised approach to distributed personal narratives and face-to-face interaction is at the core of the most exciting prospects for digital storytelling in online spaces.

Digital storytelling in online spaces

Given the diffusion of activist strategies in multiple forms across online spaces, what potentials has technological innovation afforded for digital storytelling? Digital stories are multimodal in form, but nevertheless linear and static, while contemporary digital cultures allow stories to be presented in contexts that are interactive and dynamic. Not only can storytellers provide viewers with additional information on the story-making process and life updates, they are also able to embed their stories on multiple sites (e.g. Facebook, Myspace, YouTube, Twitter) and distribute their stories in multiple forms (DVD, vodcast, RSS feeds, etc.). They can respond to viewers' comments and support one another on individual storytelling journeys. They can interact with other community members by offering links to archives of photos and music (freely available for use under Creative Commons licenses) or links to other activist-oriented lobby groups and information services. While all of these possibilities exist, the reality is that most digital storytelling practice remains firmly entrenched in face-to-face contexts. Even if they were to take the leap online, difficulties in formation and engagement of online activist communities are well documented (Haythornthwaite, 2009; Ostrom, 2000; Pisano & Verganti, 2008; Preece & Shneiderman, 2009; Shirky, 2009). In the following section I will consider some modifications of the conventional workshop format as facilitated by Creative Narrations (Seattle and San Francisco).

Creative Narrations is a partnership between Seattle based Natasha Freidus and San Francisco based Jen Nowicki-Clark and together they have been facilitating digital storytelling initiatives for over 10 years. They formed Creative Narrations as a small independent multimedia consulting and training organisation with affiliations with Mass Impact and the Centre for Digital Storytelling. They also facilitate a website, 'Stories for Change', that functions as an online archive of digital stories and a space where digital storytellers and facilitators can meet and discuss both practice and products. 'Stories for Change' grew out of the first annual 'Gathering of Community Digital Storytelling' at Massachusetts Institute of Technology in June 2006 and is a collaboration between several educational and social justice organisations. Although the web space has been a success and currently has over 800 members, most stories are uploaded from face-to-face workshops and downloadable resources are also focused primarily on this mode of practice. Conversations between members on the site are also limited.

Creative Narrations see themselves breaking new ground not so much in this space as in their recent experiments with virtual workshop facilitation. Thus far, these have been conducted mostly as train-the-trainer initiatives for large multinational organisations with staff located globally. Everyone logs on at a pre-appointed time to be guided through a live webinar of around 2 to 3 hours in length. Participants engage via virtual whiteboard and shared desktop spaces and can hear one another via conference call facilities. Prior to the workshop, facilitators are provided with brief bios and head shots of participants, and groups are generally small, often around 10 people, sometimes with groups co-located in one office space. PC based edit software like 'Sony Vegas' is most often purchased by the host institution and installed on work based laptops or desktops prior to workshop commencement. When individuals are undertaking training as part of their work commitments, the group workshop is limited to one or two sessions with individual follow up after preliminary scripting and storyboarding. When time limitations are extreme, an external editor may assemble story components (images, music, narration) for participants to review (and eventually approve).

When asked to compare virtual and face-to-face facilitation of workshops, Jen noted that it was equally important to be gentle with egos and make no assumptions around people's technical expertise. However, in an online environment, sometimes explanations needed to be repeated (because physical demonstrations are impossible) forcing a certain artfulness with both technical and creative language.

> My heart is still attached to creating a sacred [physical] space... in our society we do so much multi-tasking already... but if [virtual workshops] help us reach more people and it helps more people acknowledge their own stories and use their stories for greater advocacy and purpose... and it helps bring that process into their multitasking world... then that's where I want to be! The experiences are different...
>
> (Jen, Co-Director of Creative Narrations, personal interview, 2011)

Creative Narrations argue that experiments with workshop form conducted in online spaces can still maintain the integrity of a face-to-face workshop and they build the significance of authorial control and self-expression into their introductory overview.

> Telling your story is essential to having a voice in a democracy, levelling a playing field... all of that... ideally people see the process as connected to a larger process of democracy and civic engagement especially when they're using story in an overtly political way; [however] if it's more of a straight up personal identity story and it doesn't have a clear audience or purpose then I'm not so sure...
>
> (Natasha, Co-Director of Creative Narrations, personal interview, 2011)

Natasha posted the question 'Who's leading virtual workshops?' to a digital storytelling Facebook group and was met by responses like 'How can that be done?' She notes that: 'Digital Storytelling is struggling to define itself - one of the things is "we're not this, we're not that" like "we don't have external editors, otherwise you lose authorial control..." I don't agree...'.

Just as online digital storytelling workshops are few and far between, it seems that little attention has been paid to the potential self-empowerment and civic engagement that might be experienced if storytellers were more engaged in the distribution stage of digital storytelling. Some of the obstacles that are implicit in the form, like difficulties representing complex, fluid identity in brief, self-contained and linear narratives, might well be overcome by better understanding (and analysis) of the complicated and interactive contexts in which the products can be viewed. Alexander and Levine illustrate the expansion of concepts of narrative structure that have been fuelled by Web 2.0:

> A story has a beginning, a middle, and a cleanly wrapped-up ending. Whether told around a campfire, read from a book, or played on a DVD, a story goes from point A to B and then C. It follows a trajectory, a Freytag Pyramid – perhaps the line of a human life or the stages of the hero's journey. A story is told by one person or by a creative team to an audience that is usually quiet, even receptive. Or at least that's what a story used to be, and that's how a story used to be told. Today, with digital networks and social media, this pattern is changing. Stories now are open-ended, branching, hyperlinked, cross-media, participatory, exploratory, and unpredictable. And they are told in new ways: Web 2.0 storytelling picks up these new types of stories and runs with them, accelerating the pace of creation and participation while revealing new directions for narratives to flow.
> (Alexander & Levine, 2008, p. 40)

I consider some of the possibilities and difficulties of sharing digital stories with networked publics and discuss online curation of identity in Chapter 5.

Intimate Citizenship 3.0

While notions of Citizenship have been well canvassed by scholars since Ancient Greece, recent variations complicate a framework of legally affirmed rights and responsibilities. These include online participation as a measure of digital citizenship and to include less tangible measures like the 'sense of belonging' that affirms capacity to contribute to social discourses. In 2003, in the United Kingdom, sociologist Ken Plummer developed a frame for what he called 'Intimate Citizenship'. He perceived increased public awareness and discussion of 'the decisions people have to make over the control (or not) over one's bodies, feelings, relationships; access (or not) to representations, relationships, public spaces etc.; and socially grounded choices (or not) about identities, gender experiences, erotic experiences' (Plummer, 2003, p. 14). He canvassed the identity construction practices of many emergent social identity and/or issue categories – new forms of 'family life', choices around sexuality and gender, IVF, cosmetic surgery, post-human cyborgs and unacceptable approaches to intimacy (e.g. sexual harassment, child-abuse and sex-murders). These non-normative versions of citizenship involve everyday activism that stakes a claim, whether big 'P' political or not, on what kind of world we wish to live in. From Plummer I derive a conceptual research frame that focuses on public encounters over the norms of embodied and bodily intimacy. In the years since 2003 these public encounters invariably include a digital dimension, either mediated by digital tools or disseminated via digital platforms. Further, social networks have converged to include both face-to-face and online publics as communication spaces that are the same yet different: 'always already' interactions that move beyond digital dualisms (Jurgenson, 2011, 2012). Modern intimate citizenship constitutes networked negotiations that intersect across intimacy, privacy, publicness and difference. I add '3.0' to draw attention to the relatively new complexities of managing privacy and publicness when stories are shared among networked publics, making them persistent, replicable, scalable and searchable (boyd, 2011). '3.0' aligns with Tim Berners-Lee's evocation of the semantic web as 'fractal' (Berners-Lee & Kagal, 2008), a conceptual framework that is challenged by vastness, vagueness, uncertainty, inconsistency and deceit (Lukasiewicz & Straccia, 2008). These many variables similarly invoke the uncertainty and inconsistency of navigating digitally amplified self-exposure. It has become apparent that we each have an infinite number of self-representations that we share with an infinite number of audiences for infinite time to come. I return to the conceptual framework of Intimate Citizenship 3.0 in the closing chapter of this book.

This chapter has established a context for the emancipatory claims of digital storytelling within a history of activist-oriented personal storytelling and autobiographical documentary production. I outlined contemporary uses of digital storytelling and problematised the aforementioned claims, with critiques of the paradigms that shape workshop participation, both face-to-face and online. I briefly considered some of the new frontiers of online activist-oriented storytelling ('Born This Way', 'It Gets Better' and 'Make It Better') and explored situated examples of facilitation (Creative Narrations). Just as Plummer drew attention to the wider social circumstances in which intimate sexual stories may be voiced and heard, I have highlighted some of the theoretical possibilities of curating identity stories for networked publics in face-to-face and online spaces, through Intimate Citizenship 3.0.

3
Identity: Nominalisation, Authenticity and Incoherence

In this chapter I start where it all begins – with understandings of identity at a *micro* level. I consider digital stories as sites of active social and political negotiation that enact personal identity. Drawing on textual analysis of stories, interviews with storytellers and observations of identity negotiations in flux, I consider identity from the point of view of individuals actively engaged in asking 'who am I?' and 'how will I represent myself?'. While discussing these generalised processes I consider pertinent theories of identity put forth in popular psychology, post-structuralist philosophy, postmodernism, narrative theory and queer theory.

The chapter is divided into two sections: *Understanding Identity* and *Crafting 'Authenticity'*. In the first section, I consider tensions between philosophical and vernacular understandings of identity and difficulties with nominalising identity categories, queer in particular. I conclude this section with some examples of how storytellers selectively embrace and disrupt a variety of nominalisations. In *Crafting 'Authenticity'*, I consider notions of performance and performativity alongside narrative coherence. I argue that the genre conventions of traditional digital storytelling are problematic for a number of reasons including partial self-awareness, and the limitations of language, and difficulties articulating fluid, complex or transgressive identities in a short, fixed, widely distributed story. I put forward congruence as a more feasible pursuit than coherence or authenticity. Finally I argue that identity can only be understood comprehensively 'in media res', that is, as a work in progress. Combining epistemological and empirical insights, my evaluation of digital stories (content) and digital storytellers (process) spans situated personal, social, technical and political contexts.

Understanding identity in theory and practice

Our lives are made up of a series of incidents, anecdotes and interactions that we parse as insignificant or, alternatively, as moments that merit retelling. Put simply, we make meaning of who we are. We shape stories about work, love, travel, birth and death, often smoothing out inconsistencies and leaving out boring details. Most of us are able to recall turning points or times when a definitive statement or action changed the direction of our lives. Some of these become defining markers of identity. Did a fluke opportunity during high school lead to an unexpected career? Or is the future partially determined – as evidenced by the engineer who was always interested in pulling things apart as a toddler, or the nurse who is always caring for friends in need? Some accounts are collectively authored, shaped by the annotations provided by family, friends and authority figures. Some are individual accounts. Some are disputed but nevertheless widely shared. Audiences arrive at 'first impressions' or 'gut instincts' based on incomplete snippets of story. Others, linked to us by biology, affinity, marriage or business, hear our stories over and over again and nevertheless arrive at their own disparate interpretation of who we are. Our lives are woven of many stories, summarising many meanings and many aspects of self, brought together and encapsulated as 'me' or 'my identity'.

Digital stories are also encapsulated units of identity. For everyday activists, stories are tools that amplify communication and raise social awareness. The creation of these stories is collaborative (involving friends and family members as well as facilitators and editors) and performative (enacting new understandings of self). Here I distinguish between 'self' and 'identity' although in vernacular use the two terms are frequently interchangeable. I take 'self' to refer to indistinct or unexpressed understandings while 'identity' tends to refer to an assemblage of characteristics that are consciously or unconsciously presented to the wider world.

Nature versus nurture: Theoretical frameworks for identity

The phenomenon of 'being' is obfuscated by philosophical and social understandings that contest whether we are biologically determined or socially constructed. The degree to which we have agency to determine the paths our lives take is a question that has been similarly disputed by different epistemological traditions for a very long time. Are we human in some fundamental ways that make us similar to every other human on the planet? Should we therefore be accountable to common moral and ethical standards or norms? Is there an essential inner truth that we should all endeavour to find and be faithful to? Does congruence between perceived inner and outer selves imply an authentic representation of self? Alternately, are we made by the worlds we live in? Or perhaps the iterative force of 'being me' and 'fitting in' shapes the world's expectations of me?

In the dualism of the subtitle, 'nature' represents our biologically determined, essential and largely unalterable qualities, while 'nurture' speaks of behaviours that are socially constructed. Broadly speaking, essentialism holds that we have something at our core that we know to be our self. Classical Humanism presumes that, regardless of race, creed or colour, we share an essential commonality – human nature. These ideas play out in popular psychology and numerous self-help texts where we '...remain attached to the idea of a self that could become authentic – an idea which implies a real self with which one might, with behavioural modifications, more fully accord' (Tregoning, 2006, p. 175). This striving for authenticity, inner truth and honesty, both personal and communal, is rhetoric that is central to the digital storytelling movement (Lambert, 2002). Meanwhile other analyses of nature and nurture focus upon structure (socialisation) and agency (individual autonomy). Epistemologies that emphasise how our identity and actions are shaped by social forces beyond our control draw attention to our limited agency, while those that emphasise our essential human nature tend to diminish the many social structures that operate to limit our autonomy.

Contemporary manifestations of these disputes manifest as binary oppositions like 'I was born this way' versus 'gender and/or sexuality is a social construct'. While on the one hand it seems obvious that we are constructed by heteronormative and gendered social norms, on the other hand, many people deduce an 'inner truth' that is the 'essence' of identity. Being accountable to one fixed truth throughout our lives, and in performances for divergent audiences, is clearly problematic, especially given the enduring, searchable and amplified qualities of self-representation borne forth by social media. After all, few of us choose to remain consistent with our teenage representations of self.

In the late 1970s Foucault argued that social institutions (like prisons and hospitals and schools) influence what behaviours we constitute as 'criminal' or 'perverse' or 'educated' (Foucault, 1979), thereby problematising the prevailing subject-centred existentialism of the 1960s.

Linguists like J. L. Austin (1978) focused upon the way language, in particular 'speech acts' and 'performative utterances', are used not just to state facts or describe things but to actually 'do' things. The way we use language to name things can actually influence the way we experience them – words can have a constitutive effect on actions and social values. Judith Butler later expanded upon Austin's notion of the 'performative utterance' and Foucault's 'regulative discourses' in her analyses of the cultural construction of identity, in particular gender and sexuality (Butler, 1990). She coined the term 'performativity' for '...that reiterative power of discourse to produce the phenomena that it regulates and constrains' (Butler, 1993). Feminism, queer theory and postmodernism have all contributed to an understanding of identity as fluid, complex and located in a social context.

In his foundational essay 'Who Needs Identity?' (Hall, 1996), Stuart Hall summarised a 'discursive explosion' around the concept of identity as it played out across philosophy, psychoanalytically influenced feminism and cultural criticism. Hall argues that two factors sustain the concept of identity. First is the fact that the deconstruction of identity has not resulted in the concept being supplanted by a better or truer concept, rather that it remains 'under erasure'; 'in the interval between reversal and emergence; an idea which cannot be thought in the old way, but without which certain key questions cannot be thought at all' (Hall, 1996, p. 2). He poses the second factor as a question: '...in relation to what set of problems, does the *irreducibility* of the concept, identity, emerge?'. Hall answers with 'It seems to be in the attempt to rearticulate the relationship between subjects and discursive practices... or the question of *identification*' (Hall, 1996, p. 2). Hall goes on to describe identification as 'a process of articulation, a suturing, an over-determination not a subsumption' (Hall, 1996, p. 3). He argues that:

> [Identities] arise from the narrativization of the self, but the necessarily fictional nature of this process in no way undermines its discursive, material or political effectivity, even if the belongingness, the 'suturing into the story' through which identities arise is, partly, in the imaginary (as well as the symbolic)...
> (Hall, 1996, p. 4)

This recognition of the subjective nature of personal truth and the fictive nature of personal narrative resonates with deconstructions of autobiography. The concept of 'authorship' has largely replaced mutually exclusive analyses of text or context as a means of revealing situated power. Ahmed argues that any analysis of text must include its context:

> By opening out the process of writing to the contexts of authorship, such a feminist approach would not de-limit or resolve the text, but complicate it. Here, the relation between writing and auto/biography becomes constitutive: the border between work and life is unstable, an instability which points to the contextualisation of the text (the life that is not inside or outside the work) and the textualisation of the context (the work that is not inside or outside the life). The relation between the literary, the embodied subject and the social becomes an issue that troubles the demarcation of one text from another.
>
> (Ahmed, 1998, p. 123)

Similarly, Butler points to the use of the authorial 'I' as a taken-for-granted starting point and argues for recognition of specific 'Is' as situated in and simultaneously constituting history. Nicholson summarises: 'For Butler, the move here is not to reject the idea of the subject nor what it presupposes, such as agency, but rather to question how notions of subjectivity and of agency are used: who, for example, get to become subjects, and what becomes of those excluded from such constructions?' (Nicholson, 1995, p. 5). Butler's critique of the political context of subjectivity and agency has been lauded by some and lambasted by others, particularly as her analysis tends towards abstract rather than pragmatic (Fraser, 1995). This gap between theoretical understandings of identity and popular enactments of self mirrors a fundamental tension in the production of queer activist-oriented digital stories.

While storytellers may not use the language of critical theory to articulate their concerns, the processes by which they enact identity are at the centre of many theoretical debates. McLaughlin proposes mutual consideration and a stronger intertwining of vernacular and critical theory:

> Groups defined by demeaning and dehumanizing mainstream values either do theory or die in spirit. That is, either they internalise those definitions and accept self-hatred, or they recognise that the official version is not the only way of looking at the world. When definitions imposed from above simply don't match daily social

experience, there are two choices: either deny yourself or learn to question authorised versions.

(McLaughlin, 1996, p. 21)

This also resonates as a description of queer activist-oriented digital storytellers who are actively struggling against and yet are simultaneously shaped by social norms around gender, sexuality, race, class and embodiment. As Hall points out:

> Precisely because identities are constructed within, not outside, discourse, we need to understand them as produced in specific historical and institutional sites within specific discursive formations and practices, by specific enunciative strategies. Moreover they emerge within the play of specific modalities of power, and thus are more the product of marking of difference and exclusion, than they are the sign of an identical, naturally constituted unity – an 'identity' in its traditional meaning (that is, an all-inclusive sameness, seamless, without internal differentiation).

(Hall, 2000, p. 4)

Queer digital storytellers articulate their chosen identity (or identification, as Hall prefers) through textual processes (creative and technical) and negotiations with their networked publics. Drawing on their personal and social histories and locations, they make themselves visible by 'marking their difference', however this enunciative process is often complicated and complex as evidenced in the following analysis.

Claiming identity in practice: The problem of visibility

Workshop practice routinely engages storytellers in meaning-making activities. An introductory exercise like the 'name game' can reveal understandings of identity on many levels. While sitting in a circle, participants each tell a short story about their name – how they came by it and what it means to them. Perhaps surprisingly, very few respond with straightforward statements like 'my name is John Smith, it's the name my parents gave me at birth and I don't have any particular feelings about it'. Participants frequently tell well-honed stories about re-inventing themselves with name changes, revealing tensions between nature and nurture; inner and outer selves; public and private selves, and so on, that correlate with more abstract theoretical analyses.

People who are accustomed to 'passing' or 'fitting in' in social contexts (as whatever the prevailing norm may be, often white, middle class, heterosexual) undertake extraordinary considerations when making a digital story. In most cases they must declare their unseen identities, something they frequently refer to as 'standing up', 'coming out' or being 'out and proud'. In the following example, 17-year-old Janaya describes slowly coming to understand her identity in a social context where 'aboriginal' is equated with 'black' and 'girlfriend' means 'female friend' not 'lover'. She does not reflect upon the metaphysics of how or why she came to be who she is but defines, in no uncertain terms, the world she is happy to engage with and how she identifies herself within it.

In *Brown Baby* (Figure 3.1) Janaya remembers being little and, placing her arm next to her papa's, asking 'when am I going to be that colour?'. Over a series of photos of her toddler self, blond and pink skinned, surrounded by dark haired, dark skinned cousins she recalls hearing 'everyone saying to me "You're not Aboriginal! You're not black! You're white, so you can't be!" '. Later she speaks about going to play at other people's houses instead of her own in order to avoid complicated justifications of her mum's live-in girlfriend. Janaya narrates the slow shifts she made as she was growing up, from feeling 'annoyed' and 'upset and frustrated' about social judgements to 'not caring so much about what people think'. She declares 'I don't have that fear anymore' and at the end of her story 'If they do have a problem with it, they will not be a part of my life!'. In this story, Janaya not only comes to terms with her identity, she makes it visible for the world to see. She arrives at her own personal meanings of aboriginality and family and challenges the world to expand its current narrow definitions. These are her terms of engagement.

Stealth Crip (Figure 3.2) provides another example of difficult to categorise hidden and visible identities. Ad'm is a young gay man who has a degenerative neurological condition that was diagnosed in his early teens. In his story, he speaks directly to camera, framed in a medium wide shot that includes his wheelchair. He tells how he modified his name from Adam to Ad'm after being inspired by a Chinese proverb. The ancient story describes a water bearer who carries two pots down the same path every day. The pot on one side is cracked and apologises to the water-bearer about spilling water. The water bearer points out the flowers that blossom on that side of the path. Ad'm also regards himself as 'cracked' and considers his name change to be a significant marker of accepting his disability. Much of Ad'm's story

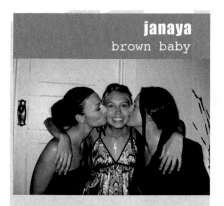

janaya
brown baby

The story I have made means a lot to me. It show's two aspects of my life – one side about being a proud Aboriginal woman and how society and friends react to that, and the other side is about my mum and her being a part of the gay community. These two parts of my life have made me the person I am today.

I made this story because, even if we can't see it, there are a lot of people in my situation and I want to let them know it's normal. You can be proud to just be yourself, to stand up for yourself and your family.

I was inspired to write my story due to the racism and homophobia that are around me constantly. Judgmental attitudes have such a huge impact on me and my family. My mother, step mother and father inspired me to come out and share this story with the community.

I didn't have too many difficulties making this story but I was concerned about presenting my family and friends to the public. I hoped they would be ok about me telling people about them and using their photographs to show what I was feeling.

Hearing all the other stories in the group made me even more open minded. After writing and making mine, I am motivated to do something in society that will make a change… and hope that others can see that everything in my life is normal and we are all equal.

Figure 3.1   Brown Baby

As a disabled man, I have witnessed a lot of ignorance in the queer community. The original idea came from a desire to explore this. For example, as my 'illness' became more visible, a lot of the friends I had when I could walk began to drop away. I felt shunned by potential dates. The story then (somehow) became about disability and identity.

I was very happy with the story, but it didn't actually contain much gay content. I came out to myself when I was fourteen and to my family when I was fifteen. When I was sixteen I was diagnosed with Friedreich's Ataxia (FA). I guess all the gay stuff and disability stuff sorta blurred through an already hazy adolescence. So it's no wonder I see those issues as overlapping facets of me. So my story is a combination of travelling through disabled life and being gay.

It's the story of my personal journey to Ad'm.

Figure 3.2   Stealth Crip

focuses upon the assumptions people make about him when they see his wheelchair and what this means for his sense of identity. When fellow storytellers and facilitators viewed his story at a test screening several people commented on the fact that Ad'm never mentions his sexuality. Ad'm himself was surprised: 'Shit! What have I done?'. He said he'd assumed that the teenage photographs of himself with pink hair made his sexuality visible and, while he didn't want to dramatically rewrite the original story, he was keen to add an ironic layer of reflection. He added subtitles that ran over his narration of discovering disability: 'meanwhile, the whole queer thing took a back seat... although it offered a chance to escape and explore a parallel life'. Later his voiceover continues with: 'I'm disabled by my environment and my society, not my wheelchair... I think every single person is disabled in some way, it doesn't have to be obvious, it doesn't have to be physical...' while the subtitle text runs: 'we've all got unseen identities... for example I forgot to tell you I'm gay)'.

The title 'Stealth Crip' plays on a term used in trans and queer circles – 'Stealth' – for people who 'go undercover', passing as their gender of choice and breaking contact with everyone who knows their biological gender history. For many it imputes secrecy and a degree of personal shame that is presumed to be the antithesis of everyday activism and yet here Ad'm complicates it with a text card that finishes his piece: 'Once upon a time, I was a Stealth Crip. Before that I was undecided, and before that I was unknown. Now, similar to before, I don't know what I am. But throughout it all, I have remained miscellaneous'. Later in an interview, Ad'm told me that he regards disability, as a marginalised state differentiated from 'normal', as a fundamentally 'queer' state of being. 'This whole thing of difference' he laughed 'all you have to do is look at an x-ray of my spine to see how "bent" I am!'. Ad'm makes his own meaning of disability and queerness and takes pleasure in stirring up social expectations of same – as he says with a mischievous smile 'I kind of like having an impact on people!'.

Nominalising queer

The word 'queer' has a convoluted and contested history. While current dictionary definitions of 'queer' firstly offer 'odd' or 'strange', a secondary use is frequently listed as a *derogatory* term for male homosexual. Since the early 1980s however, 'queer' has been reclaimed by the GLBTQIS community as a broad-ranging and multivalent term. It is frequently used as a means of avoiding the previous clumsy acronym and is often deemed to be inclusive of any who regard themselves as outside mainstream sexual or gender identities. Transgender scholar Susan Stryker uses it 'as a term that refers to all identities or practices that cross over, cut across, move between, or otherwise queer socially constructed sex/gender boundaries' (Stryker, 2006, p. 254).

Although identity categories that attempt to nominalise sexual practices, social behaviour and gender representations are too numerous and contested to describe in any depth here, the deep and abiding schism between homosexual and queer categories remains pertinent to digital storytellers because, at the core, it summarises a distinction between finite (homosexual) and fluid (queer). In any case, articulating either finite or fluid renditions of self as a coherent narrative is problematic for *any* nominalisation of identity.

Donna Haraway, in her much cited 'Cyborg Manifesto' highlights difficulties with the unitary nominalisations of 'female', 'woman' and 'feminist' that may equally apply to 'gay' and 'queer'.

> There is nothing about being 'female' that naturally binds women. There is not even such a state as 'being' female, itself a highly complex category constructed in contested sexual scientific discourses and other social practices... And who counts as 'us' in my own rhetoric? Which identities are available to ground such a potent political myth called 'us', and what could motivate enlistment in this collectivity? Painful fragmentation among feminists (not to mention among women) along every possible fault line has made the concept of *woman* elusive, an excuse for the matrix of women's dominations of each other. For me – and for many who share a similar historical location in white, professional middle-class, female, radical, North American, mid-adult bodies – the sources of a crisis in political identity are legion... But there has also been a growing recognition of another response through coalition – affinity, not identity.
> (Haraway, 1991, p. 155)

Haraway's argument for a politics of affinity rather than clearly defined identity is a powerful one. Gamson holds that fixed identity categories serve social control and are at the root of oppression. He argues that liberation may be found in their deconstruction:

> ...academic 'constructionist' thinking, holds that sexual identities are historical and social products, not natural or intrapsychic ones. It is socially-produced binaries (gay/straight, man/woman) that are

the basis of oppression; fluid, unstable experiences of self become fixed primarily in the service of social control. Disrupting those categories, refusing rather than embracing ethnic minority status, is the key to liberation. In this *deconstructionist politic,* clear collective categories are an obstacle to resistance and change.

(Gamson, 1995, p. 391)

Gamson and Haraway have held these positions, like other queer theorists for over 20 years. However, in popular discourses a fondness for identity categories persists.

Larry Gross highlights the disjuncture between gay and lesbian studies and the post-structuralism of queer theory, and further, emphasises the problematic disconnection between theory and political strategising:

...there is a great distance between seeing through the false consciousness of heteronormativity and dismantling the social system that embodies it. A glance at the morning newspaper or the evening news broadcast these days will likely remind us that we are in the midst of a cultural and political struggle over the rights of 'gay people' in the United States to be treated as full citizens. For many, queer theory's rejection of gay (or lesbian, bisexual, transgendered) identity seems utopian in the context of this still far from resolved fight for equality in a country that stubbornly understands politics in minority bloc/civil rights terms.

(Gross, 2005, p. 517)

The pragmatic difficulties of organising around a fluid collective identity category have resonance for digital storytellers who are brought together in a unified workshop context despite disparate understandings of identity and divergent political motivations. An organising principle evident in social movement theory (discussed further in Chapter 4) holds that, in order to achieve social change, a marginalised group must organise around common goals and utilise cohesive lobbying strategies. However, frictions within queer communities lobbying for equal rights are numerous. They have been well documented during the AIDS crisis of the 1980s (Gould, 2001, 2009) and are evident in current campaigns for same-sex marriage equality in numerous Western countries. Casual observation of the campaigns of 'Australian Marriage Equality' and a politically-oriented queer yahoo list 'AusQueer' yields numerous examples of debates for and against the conflation of love

56 Digital Identity and Everyday Activism

with nuclear family structures, monogamy and property rights. Alternative models (including polyamorous relationships and unconventional family structures) have been abandoned for numerous reasons, often summarised as 'too complicated', 'unwinnable' or 'too challenging for conservatives'.

Meanwhile the mother of a transsexual child, a participant in the *What's Your Story?* initiative, is all too familiar with debates over nominalisation of gender:

> There are many arguments constantly going on within our support group and I get so frustrated – it is supposed to be a place of solace and comfort and we are arguing about 'correct terminologies and political correctness'. The medicos have labelled our children as having Gender Identity Disorder (or GID) – imagine having to refer to yourself as that? Advocates from our support group including some within a legal realm who say our children are 'living with the predicament of transsexualism'. Mainstream media will say our children are 'transgender' kids. I just say we have a daughter. The rest is no one's concern. We gave up worrying about how other people feel about the situation a long time ago.
>
> (email interview, Molly)

While there is potential in a workshop context for conflict over understandings of identity, in my case studies this did not eventuate. Instead they offered evidence of people actually valuing divergent perspectives in pursuit of a common goal – producing a diverse DVD compilation of digital stories. In these microcosmic illustrations of the conundrums that take place on a larger social scale, ideological differences are sometimes reconciled through finding other less divisive similarities – like common technical frustrations and shared fears about recording an imperfect voiceover. As everyday rather than organised activists, participants frequently have quite specific individual goals for their stories and are less likely to come into conflict about overarching campaign strategies. If anything, they unify with the slightly amorphous aim of complicating an audiences' stereotypical assumptions about GLBTQIS people.

The constitutive aspect of self-representation throws up another problem for performances of identity and social change. The way a group represents itself contributes to the formation of new norms. By defining who is 'in', some are left 'out' creating a problem for those who are newly defined as 'other'. Butler argues that an individual's iterative performance of normative gender also shapes social expectations of the same.

> Gender is the repeated stylization of the body, a set of repeated acts within a highly rigid regulatory frame that congeal over time to produce the appearance of substance, of a natural sort of being.
>
> (Butler, 1990, p. 33)

Butler articulates a common concern that runs something like this: if we perform in order to achieve social acceptance (and in turn understand ourselves as part of the world), and these individual performances accumulate over time to constitute a collective code of conduct that we then endeavour to comply with, how can the cycle ever be broken? Butler offers analysis and deconstruction of the codes:

> A political genealogy of gender ontologies, if it is successful, will deconstruct the substantive appearance of gender into its constitutive acts and locate and account for those acts within the compulsory frames set by the various forces that police the social appearance of gender.
>
> (Butler, 1990, p. 33)

The question remains whether revealing 'that the very notion of the subject... admits of possibilities that have been forcibly foreclosed...' (Butler, 1990, p. 33) is an adequate compromise for people who are living on the edge of gender normativity and social judgement.

In *Blue for Boys? Pink for Girls?*[1] (Figure 3.3) Molly and Brendan (pseudonyms chosen by the storytellers) describe their journey as parents: from the birth of their baby boy and the gradual growth of her female identity. This story speaks explicitly of the social codes that determine gender identity. The story starts with the sound of a heart beating and the image of blue and pink pencils hovering over a noughts and crosses (also known as tic-tac-toe) grid. Some of the squares are already filled in with gender symbols, rendered in the appropriate colour, blue for boys and pink for girls. The narration follows over a pregnant belly painted with a question mark:

> 'Congratulations! Do you know what you're having? Are you hoping for a boy or a girl?' they ask. And nine months later you were born: a beautiful baby boy. And so it was, before you even had the chance to fill your lungs with that all important first breath, you were branded...

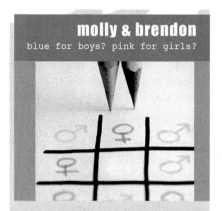

molly & brendon
blue for boys? pink for girls?

We have a daughter who was born our son… or so we thought. As soon as she was able to talk, she told us otherwise. This has taken our family on a journey filled with some significant challenges yet wonderful insights. When my husband and I sat down to write this story, I had visions of the opening scene from 'The Lion King': when the monkey holds the baby for all in the animal kingdom to see as the mother and father look on with pride, love and adoration. This is how proud I am of our daughter and what she has taught us.

Our reason for telling this story was to raise awareness of the predicament of transsexualism (often referred to as "transgender") in children, whilst honouring our brave and unique little girl. However, we were also concerned about how she would feel about the story as an adult. Plus, the process involved for adolescents requiring sex affirmation treatment (i.e. hormone blockers) in this country necessitates legal approval. At risk of exposing our daughter's identity and taking away her right to privacy we decided to conceal pictures and any possible connection to her.

Our child's lawyer gave us additional advice and we adjusted the story a little more in order to protect her in the future. This became a technical and creative challenge in our storytelling process that in a way hampered us from truly celebrating our daughter, free from shame and secrecy… However I think we succeeded in still encapsulating her joyful essence!

Figure 3.3 Blue for Boys? Pink for Girls?

These words 'you were branded' are emphasised with text on screen as the voice over continues:

> After a brief glance at your genitalia someone in that room ticked a box. Everyone gets one: an 'm' or an 'f'. The 'm' in your box was because you were born with a penis. This was the beginning of an untruth that was forced upon you.

The story continues with photographs of a baby becoming a young child. The images are deliberately blurred and I discuss choices that were made to maintain the privacy of the child later in Chapter 5. Initially the description is one of a 'normal' toddlerhood, until:

> We saw you move through the boys' toys that surrounded you, instead reaching for the girls' toys. And then you spoke, at the ripe old age of two... You wanted dresses and fairies and all things beautiful. You wanted pink... NOT the blue! You asked us why God gave you a penis and when he would turn you into a girl and make things right. We heard you pray, asking the angels to turn you into a girl... but we kept on telling you that you were a boy. We were wrong, we just didn't understand.

Blue for Boys? Pink for Girls? concludes with:

> Thank you, our beautiful nine year old daughter, for showing us and others what it means to really be true to yourself. We love you very much... So how do we know what sex we are? Not from a tick in a box or any body part... Just close your eyes, you'll know it... because you'll feel it.

The story highlights some of the central tensions between essentialist and socially constructed notions of identity. The child's parents and the world around her tell her what it means to be a boy and yet she is more attracted to social manifestations of femininity – dresses, girls' toys and beautiful things. If, for arguments sake, these distinct categories and all their accompanying window dressing didn't exist, would the child experience any 'gender dysphoria'? Would she want to be a girl if, for example, it was socially acceptable to be neither gender? 'Gender queer' is a nominalisation gaining in popular currency as an attempt to describe a category, neither male nor female, which manifests an idiosyncratic blend of conventionally gendered characteristics. 'What if' questions like the latter are virtually impossible to answer because contemporary Western societies demand that boxes must be ticked and school must be attended. Paramount social importance is placed upon the child understanding which toilet door she must enter.

Despite an implicit recognition of socially constructed aspects of gender, the narrator also refers to inner truth as a guiding principle, the light that illuminates a path out of confusion. In a later interview Molly reinforced this: 'The reality is we have learned that we never did have a boy – she has always been a girl. It is who she is.' This is a paradigm often referred to in transgender literature as being trapped in the wrong body.

For storytellers, nominalisations of gender, sexuality and more importantly identity serve as a descriptive and crucial means of sharing personal stories with a broader public. The fact that these nominalisations also play a constitutive role in shaping social roles is problematic, particularly for storytellers whose stated aim is to deconstruct or disrupt normative categories that entrap them.

Disrupting categories

Storytellers frequently find creative means of manipulating both the form and content of their stories to disrupt normative social categories. Some of them do this consciously; others undertake disruption as an unconscious articulation of their everyday disruptive performances of self. One of the forum discussions on the *Rainbow Family Tree* website invited people to discuss identity categories: 'GLBTTQIA... Gay, Lesbian, Transgender, Transsexual, Queer, Intersex, Ally or Other... Which letter are you? Want to add another?'. Fanny responded with the following humorous and insightful post:

> I claim T as my letter but it's not either of the Ts on offer... btw – I don't do T altho I have contemplated it at times. (that's a joke) The term transensual femme was coined around 2002 by a group of (mostly) dykes who found themselves often on the outside of the lesbian community being neither butch enough nor lipstick enough (or overlipsticked) to be recognised. Furthermore there seemed to be a theme running that most of the women were attracted to or very close friends with trans men (although there was a massive outrage about the notion that we may be defined by this) and were struggling with new identity issues ie: if now attracted to men, were we heterosexual, bisexual, something else? What did that mean about

our status in the lesbian community and how to use some of the new privileges of being in a 'straight' couple plus what if our partners were stealth? How to continue to navigate the queer community?

(Fanny, Rainbow Family Tree post, 2009)

There is playfulness in Fanny's self-identification (the 'T' joke refers to testosterone and is pitched at people 'in the know' mostly within the trans community) that does not belie the many serious political conversations in which Fanny has clearly been involved. Inventing her own customised label, one that is both precise and obscure, serves Fanny's individual needs. It also represents a collective disruption of existing categories (dykes, lesbian, bisexual, heterosexual) and a political commitment to investigating the constitutive elements of identity. Is identity based upon who we are attracted to, who we have sex with, how much lipstick we wear? Fanny's comment alludes to the power implicit in social representations, particularly the privileges attached to appearing straight. In further conversation she explained that, if your partner is stealth (i.e. not publicly identifying as trans) then proclaiming a queer or even 'transensual femme' identity outs them by implication and violates their privacy. Nevertheless, among her group of '(mostly) dykes' the thought of supressing any identity (let alone joining the ranks of heterosexual privilege that they had spent years railing against) was problematic. This highlights a common tension in relationships between trans and cis-gendered queer identified people – whose identity is more significant (or vulnerable) in joint social representations of their coupledom?

Another participant in this forum discussion, Sean, offers further strategies for disrupting fixed identity categories:

Hey there GLBTTIQ and friends!!! Well, I came out as Bi when I was 15yrs, then realised I identified as Trans when I was 23yrs and now identify as Male, but also Queer/Gay and Pan/Bi depending who I'm talking with (some people really don't understand Pansexual or even Bisexual for that matter). I suppose I also consider myself Intersexed, but not in the technical sense.:) Does that answer the question?

(Sean, Rainbow Family Tree post, 2009)

Sean acknowledges that he adapts his self-representation for his audience and that his identity has shifted throughout his lifetime, suggesting an understanding of the ongoing performative nature of being rather than a belief in a fixed and finite self.

In an interview with Fanny in which we spoke about her two digital stories *Bye Bye Baby* (made in the *What's Your Story?* workshops) and *Pixilola's Winter Walk* (made at home, for fun) she reveals another strategy for disrupting social stereotypes of identity categories. *Bye Bye Baby* works through her grief about several lost opportunities to have a child.

> ...there's nothing in my story that talks about sexuality or my gender identity at all. I think that that's really important because [on the website and DVD] you've got all these little different pieces [stories] that are maybe vaguely related by theme, or a cohort or whatever. But what happens is, when you present all of it together, you get a map of community, and a diminishing of otherness, because with each story, there's somebody else out there who connects in with the community. So there's another woman out there who's had an abortion. There's another woman out there who's been adopted, etcetera.
>
> (Fanny, interview, 2011)

Fanny refers here to the power of divergent stories in representing both amorphous collective identities (in this case, queer) and more precise identities (lesbian, gay, etc.). She points to the diverse themes within these stories as a means of diminishing difference between a marginalised community and a mass audience. This argument resonates with the humanist principle that, despite superficial differences, we share essential human commonalities and experiences. As various queer theorists have pointed out (Gamson, 1995; Gross, 2005; Seidman, 1994) the humanist argument has some merit in GLBTQIS political battles for civil rights; an approach detractors critique as assimilationist.

Pixilola's Winter Walk also bears no direct reference to sexuality. The short hand held video follows Fanny's dog on an average morning walk. Its very ordinariness and familiarity is underlined by her video's descriptor: 'Pixilola is my family...she makes me laugh and be good'. The only human voice in the piece is Fanny issuing instructions: 'Pixilola, wait for Mum!'. This apparent inanity is also subversive in that Fanny represents 'family' as a social unit of woman and dog. This might be a less significant claim outside the *Rainbow Family Tree* site that offers it context. However, in that space (and viewed alongside her companion story that articulates a poignant loss of traditional motherhood), Fanny claims terrain for herself and her family on her own terms.

Crafting 'authenticity'

So far in this chapter I have established that digital storytelling provides an opportunity to script a preferred version of self and, as encapsulated performances, digital stories are constitutive of identity. While queer people may be skilled at concealing aspects of identity (Gross, 2007) many are nevertheless concerned with maintaining personal integrity, often expressed as 'being authentic' or 'being true to myself'. Some speak about having 'congruence' between how they think of themselves 'on the inside' and what they present to the rest of the world. Others are more concerned that various aspects of self, presented at different times and places to different people, are perceived by the world to be 'coherent'. While dictionary definitions of coherence refer to 'consistency' and 'the quality of forming a unified whole', congruence is defined as 'agreement or harmony; compatibility'. Taken together it could be argued that congruence (harmony between inner and outer understandings and representations of identity) and coherence (consistency between representations over time, place and audience) might add up to authenticity. Authenticity is defined as 'truth', 'veracity' and 'reliability', (New Oxford American Dictionary, 3rd edition, 2010).

Notions of authenticity, congruence and coherence are central to self-representation in digital stories but they are also deeply problematic for reasons I detail shortly. In this section I look at how individual performances of identity attempt to reconcile discrepancies or inconsistencies, perceived both personally (something I link to congruence) and socially (something I link to coherence). I argue that, rather than striving for authenticity, storytellers might pursue congruence (something I develop further as agency and ownership in Chapter 5) in creating and distributing their representations of identity.

Performance and self-representation

Much of our sense of social wellbeing and capacity to survive in a family or community is bound up in constantly reproducing a cogent and plausible rendition of self. Giddens puts it like this:

> The existential question of self-identity is bound up with the fragile nature of the biography which the individual 'supplies' about herself. A person's identity is not to be found in behaviour, nor – important though this is – in the reactions of others, but in the capacity *to keep a particular narrative going*. The individual's biography, if she is to maintain regular interaction with others in the day-to-day world,

cannot be wholly fictive. It must continually integrate events which occur in the external world, and sort them into the ongoing 'story' about the self.

(Giddens, 1991, p. 54)

As Giddens points out, philosophical and pragmatic questions of identity are intertwined and while the former may never be settled, the latter manifest in social behaviour. Anthropologists, social scientists and psychologists are arguably less interested in ontological questions and more oriented to empirical epistemologies of being. Many distinguish between 'inner' and 'outer' aspects of identity, as argued by Goffman in the late 1950s.

Broadly speaking, Goffman suggests we might understand ourselves as actors engaged in a variety of face-to-face social performances. Our 'public' lives are performed on stage (where we attempt to manage the impressions we give off, representing ourselves at our best) while our 'private' lives take place backstage (where we can relax and be our 'true selves'). However, even in private we perform for an audience, albeit a more intimate circle of friends and family members who know us well. Our performances are contingent on the complicity of others in a mutually agreed upon 'definition of the situation' (i.e. we all agree we're in the same play). The goal is to maintain coherence in both the performance and the play, in order to avoid being embarrassed or causing embarrassment. When a performance fails in some way (e.g. an elegant woman stumbles in her high heels) it is likely to be ignored or glossed over by fellow cast members in order to save face. Goffman calls this the 'bond of reciprocal dependence' (Goffman, 1959, p. 82). Performers who refuse to follow a social script (e.g. of gender normativity) may threaten the integrity of other cast members' performances and may therefore be shunned or ostracised.

Performances are interactive and can be tweaked according to the responses of fellow performers and the audience. When an actor finds herself in a different social context she will attempt to respond to this context, using the props and various items of 'expressive equipment' available (including clothes, voice, mannerisms, age, body size, gender, class and race) to deliver a coherent performance (that may nevertheless be inconsistent with other performances delivered in other contexts). To some extent Goffman's performance analogy bridges the question of structure versus agency arguing that a performer has a degree of autonomy and control over their performance that is nevertheless influenced by the social context in which it is delivered. The 'script' that is central in Goffman's performance analogy is partly improvised and partly determined by the 'given definition of the situation' (Goffman, 1959, p. 83).

However, while congruence may be something that an individual can determine, coherence and authenticity is predicated upon judgements made by an audience. As most media scholars since Stuart Hall (Hall, 1980) would agree, what an audience makes of a text is not something that is wholly controllable by its producer. Digital storytellers cannot control how an audience reacts to their story or the judgements that are made about their representation of identity. Goffman also differentiates between the expression of a performance and the impression that is 'given off' (Goffman, 1959, p. 2), a distinction that rests with the audience's ability to discern gaps between verbal performance and non-verbal cues. For example a shy person may attempt verbal confidence and yet their more intrinsic (bodily) mannerisms, posture and eye contact may be interpreted as anxiety or perhaps aloofness. Where there is a discrepancy between verbal and non-verbal the performance falters and an audience is likely to give credence to the non-verbal as a more authentic representation of the performer's backstage 'truth'.

Similarly in a digital story moments that 'feel contrived' or don't 'ring true' are frequently not ascribed the same value by an audience as moments that are narrated with a wobbly voice, making emotion audible. Digital stories as a genre are distinguished from more professional texts by the rawness of editing style and unsophisticated production values that, in turn, contribute to their apparent authenticity. Clearly the question of form, quite distinct from content, is significant and relies upon digital storytellers either accidentally striking the right balance between narrative naivety and textual coherence or a skilful contrivance of same. Most digital storytellers, by definition, are not skilled media producers and are heavily reliant on workshop facilitation for advice on narrative devices. I consider the acquisition of narrative sophistication and use of rhetorical modes further in Chapter 4. Here I consider problems emerging from self-awareness and self-expression when it comes to articulating a coherent identity.

Narrative coherence

Composing a brief story that summarises rich lived experience and complex identity is much more difficult than maintaining a coherent embodied performance for a finite period of time. The author must consider her life and identity from an omniscient point of view before making carefully oriented and wilful representations (Ahmed,

2006)). Myerhoff, who undertook ethnographic work with the elderly Jewish attendees of a Venice community centre, calls this personal meaning-making 're-membering'. She describes this as beyond mere recall, rather the process of imbuing people, places and events with significance in retrospect – adding them as 'members' to a 'tidy, edited tale' (Myerhoff, 1982). Myerhoff argues that the meaning-making effort reflected in the coherent 'tidy tale' is inspiring to a majority of audience members who are themselves invested in a search for personal significance.

> When it is done properly, presentationally, its effect on the listener is profound, and the latter is more than a mere passive receiver or validator. The listener is changed... Anyone in our times struggling toward wholeness, self-knowledge based on examined experience, and clarity about the worth of the enterprise exerts a great attraction on those searching for clarity.
>
> (Myerhoff, 1982, p. 111)

While Myerhoff skips over what constitutes a 'proper' story and is referring largely to oral accounts, her analysis is pertinent to digital storytellers whose distillations are quite literally 'edited tales'.

One of the rhetorical promises of digital storytelling practice is that mastery of the tools enables future creative production – once they've made one story, participants (theoretically) have gained the technical capacity to make many more. In workshops it is not uncommon for participants to report 'feeling overwhelmed' by all the choices they need to make – which story to tell; how to represent self and simultaneously win over an ambivalent audience; which photographs to use; which words and music might best accompany them, and so on. As a facilitator I have, on occasion, argued that it is okay to make one story stand in for many, as there is always the possibility of making others. However in most cases this is not actually the case; storytellers often don't go on to make second and third stories for a variety of reasons. Additionally, even if three or four stories are gathered together in a common viewing space online or on DVD, there is no guarantee that an audience will choose to explore an entire collection.

Regardless of whether one is undertaking the creation of one story or many, or sharing one anecdote or a life philosophy, a process of distillation is invariably undertaken. Facilitators who are guided by the traditional tenets of digital storytelling practice (outlined in Lambert's 'Digital Storytelling Cookbook', 2002) may also encourage honing a story in pursuit of a narrative arc that features an identifiable beginning, middle and end. Lambert's second point of 'seven essential elements' explicitly encourages participants to define the 'point' or 'dramatic question' of their story in narrative terms that position the storyteller as the protagonist who encounters obstacles in search of a goal. This focus on conventional dramatic structure is in line with what Hyvärinen et al. refer to as the 'coherence paradigm'. They argue that some common elements prevail in both scholarly and cultural usage:

> (i) good and competent narratives always proceed in a linear, chronological way, from a beginning and middle to an end, which also constitutes a thematic closure; (ii) the function of narrative and storytelling is primarily to create coherence in regard to experience, which is understood as being rather formless (which may be understood as a merit or disadvantage of narrative); (iii) persons live better and in a more ethical way, if they have a coherent life-story and coherent narrative identity (or, in contrast, narrative is understood as being detrimental because it creates such coherence).
> (Hyvärinen et al., 2010, p. 2)

Hyvärinen et al (among others) contest the moral desirability and primacy of coherence. Like Giddens, linguist and narratologist Charlotte Linde maintains 'in order to exist in the social world with a comfortable sense of being a good, socially proper, and stable person, an individual needs to have a coherent, acceptable and constantly revised life story' (Linde, 1993, p. 3). Coherence is problematic for anyone with a non-linear or fragmented experience of reality, including trauma survivors, displaced people, Alzheimer's patients, people with mental illnesses and many creative thinkers, writers and artists.

Nevertheless the social imperatives that underpin the pursuit of a coherent narration of identity are also supported in many popular psychology manuals (Tregoning, 2006). Many social service providers and counselling services are influenced by popular discourses that ascribe to the transformational power of storytelling where 'stories are seen to be catalysts for healing change, ways of overcoming physical disease, spiritual emptiness, personal disintegration, and loss of meaning' (McLaughlin, 1996, p. 87). On the other hand, opposing scholars argue that narrative imposes 'very specific and culturally determined patterns of meaning on lives that could be understood quite differently' (McLaughlin, 1996, p. 96). This is a particular concern in facilitated digital storytelling practice, especially in initiatives that have objectives located in personal or social transformation.

Critics of narrative coherence take aim at 'a built in tendency to flatten and homogenise the very experience it seeks to tell about' (Freeman, 2010). McLaughlin sees summaries that are 'too simple' or 'too complete' in conflict with the messy and elusive reality of real life, particularly a life lived in a fragmentary postmodern environment. The contributors to 'Beyond Narrative Coherence' (Hyvärinen et al., 2010) offer an assortment of examples in which people have not been well served by the prevailing social attachment to coherent narratives; instances in which legitimization of certain narratives have further marginalised and constricted others. They challenge the coherence paradigm from a number of perspectives:

> *theoretically* (positioning it historically; indicating its problems), *methodologically* (in showing its often problematic consequences, finding out new methods with which to approach broken narratives) and *ethically* (by showing how the coherence paradigm privileges middle-class conventionality and marginalises the experiences of artistically creative as well as politically traumatised people).
>
> (Hyvärinen et al., 2010, p. 2)

The following example from my own case studies illustrates some difficulties at the intersection of narrative coherence in theory and practice.

Brian (Figure 3.4) is a gentle, spectacled, middle-aged HIV positive gay man. Over some years he has grown what he fondly refers to as his 'alter ego' and 'bosom-buddy', Brenda, and has performed in several stage shows and short films. When Brian first attended a digital storytelling workshop, hosted by the AIDS Council of SA, he was experiencing writer's block. Consequently he worked hard to develop the concept of not being able to write/speak as a digital story theme. He said in the past he had found it difficult to talk openly about being positive and could only do so by 'wearing a mask' (perhaps referring to performances as Brenda). Brian was dumbfounded by the task of crafting a singular definitive script but over time. As he realised his problem was too many stories, rather than none, he shifted away from his first idea. He started working on another three, separate though interrelated, stories. The first recounts a street bashing in which he was confronted both by a stranger's homophobia and his own fear of 'contaminating' friends and strangers with his blood. The second covers the history

Figure 3.4 Brian as Brenda

of falling in love with, marrying, and finally grieving his HIV-positive lover, Darren. The final story describes the experience of living with HIV drug regimes, and fear of illness and aging. I spent an afternoon with Brian at his home, talking through his scripts and taking photographs of him beside his meditation pond. We went through some of the existing photos he was thinking of using and I took additional photos of artwork and an array of medications. We discussed the concept of linking the three aspects of his story by talking about HIV from three different perspectives – that of his alter ego drag persona Brenda; that of a carer of somebody with HIV (Darren); and that of a 'patient' or person living with HIV. His draft script was very long (nearly 1000 words instead of the recommended 250 or so) and we worked through several drafts together via email.

At one stage we experimented with 'speaking back' to HIV as if it were a person living outside of Brian.

> This is a story about me and HIV. When I first met HIV I had to work out how I was going to treat her... She has something to say about just about every aspect of my life... she can be a bit of a bully but I'm not her victim (bitch?).

This narrative strategy of 'externalising' the problem seemed useful for several reasons; because it helped hold together the different strands of the story and because it resonated with a theme that Brian spoke of regularly, that 'HIV is just a disease, not something I am defined by'. It is also one of the tenets of Narrative Therapy that proclaims 'the person is not the problem, the problem is the problem'. Strategies that encourage a client to externalise a problem help them consider what impact said problem (behaviour, idea, etc.) has on their life (White & Epston, 1990). While Brian eventually shifted from the personification of HIV as 'she' to the more neutral objectification 'it', the three speaking positions remained and determined the structure of the final story. The end story, *Bloody Brenda!*, runs a little longer than many, at 5 minutes and is somewhat episodic, without a traditional beginning, middle and end. However, bookends spell out the storyteller's intent: 'talking about HIV in different ways' and 'helping other people to understand'.

In a later interview Brian responded to questions about whether he ever modifies his behaviour to make others feel comfortable with 'not at all, honesty is the best policy'. At first glance this might seem at odds with the fact that Brian celebrates (at least) two quite distinct personas, Brian and Brenda. Clearly his behaviour is quite different when on stage or out with friends as Brenda, compared with Brian hosting a quiz night or coordinating FEAST Festival volunteers or Brian studiously endeavouring to master Movie Maker. The final words of his story help shed light:

> I used to feel like I had to be in disguise to tell my story. I was afraid of people's reactions, the repercussions and the verbal abuse. I no longer have to hide. I live with HIV. It doesn't run my life. I do what I do. I am what I am and what I am needs no excuses.
> (extract from Bloody Brenda!)

According to conventional social norms Brian's presentation of self, both in everyday life and in his digital story, might be deemed incoherent or inconsistent. However within the safe framework of family and friends in the gay community, this is not the case. First, challenges to gender norms are not unusual among these intimate publics. However, when stepping outside these safe places onto a public street, the challenge posed by a drag queen (as a violation of Goffman's 'definition of the situation') is punishable by violence. Second, Brian's friends know and love Brenda and accept that Brian finds congruence within himself by inhabiting both personas. When asked what he thinks his identity says about those around him, Brian responds simply with 'they are all proud of me'. While clearly Brian hasn't always been 'HIV+, out and proud' he has arrived at congruence and negotiated coherence to the extent that he can proclaim 'I am what I am and what I am needs no excuses'. His story is not structured as a linear journey but nevertheless represents personal growth, strength and wellbeing. Analysis of the social context gives the narrative extended meaning, supporting the argument that coherence lies in the eye of the beholder.

Partial opacity and inadequate communication

Some ideas and states of being are difficult to define. Some stories are more difficult to craft because of the inadequacy of self-awareness and language itself. Sometimes the attempt to name feeling and articulate stories somewhat modifies the original experience. Naming something erases the complexities that weren't named; defining something places parameters around something that was formerly imprecise. Both past and future possibilities are foreclosed.

The process of narrating self is one that Judith Butler deconstructs in detail in 'Giving an Account of Oneself' (Butler, 2005) where she argues the philosophical impossibility of standing outside of ourselves in order to offer an objective and verifiable rendition of selfhood.

This means that my narrative begins in media res, when many things have already taken place to make me and my story in language possible. And it means that my story always arrives late. I am always recuperating, reconstructing, even as I produce myself differently in the very act of telling. My account of myself is partial, haunted by that for which I have no definitive story. I cannot explain exactly why I have emerged in this way, and my efforts at narrative reconstruction are always undergoing revision. There is that in me and of me for which I can give no account.

(Butler, 2001, p. 27)

Butler extends the idea of 'partial opacity' to debate whether we can be held morally accountable for our actions if we do not have complete transparent self-awareness. She lists multiple 'vexations' to giving an account of oneself and includes among them not just the inadequacies of language and memory or the impossibility of an objective omniscient point of view but the fact that the 'structure of address' also influences the account as do the 'norms that facilitate my telling about myself but that I do not author and that render me substitutable at the very moment that I seek to establish the history of my singularity' (Butler, 2005, p. 39). For some storytellers an accurate reproduction of past events blurred by memory is just as difficult as finding a suitable storytelling voice.

A storyteller involved in the *What's Your Story?* initiative offers a practical illustration of some of these difficulties in her story, *Notice One*. When I first spoke to Kirsten about the digital storytelling workshops she said she didn't really want to make a story about sexuality, she wanted to explore mental illness. We talked on the phone for a while as I tried to establish how safe she felt about sharing a potentially vulnerable story in public and whether she had appropriate support networks on standby should she find the whole experience very stressful. Over the next week or so she sent me some examples of stories she'd made previously on Movie Maker and it became apparent that, as an artist, she was accustomed to exploring mental states and had been doing so for some years. She worked quite independently in the group but enjoyed opportunities to mentor less experienced participants, and on several occasions offered both technical and creative solutions to frustrated facilitators. Her story *Notice One* is a fast paced montage of art works (both well-known and personal) and photographs with occasional text superimposed.

Animals. TV. Paintings on the wall. I hurled furniture. Attacked the teacher. Depressed. And Violent. I was four. My refuge was art. Books. Watching my mother paint. Life skills were faint. And I didn't feel. Safe. Out of control. For the next. 35 years. Self sabotage. Self medication. Nothing was clear. My sexuality. One in a list. Of unknowns. No identity. Isolated and toxic. Unable to keep. Faking. Relaxed only when. Alone. Learning love and trust. Now. Mirroring my siblings. Colour still. Significant. Still my theory. For living.

(transcript of *Notice One* superimposed text)

Kirsten elects to use slow pans across fragments of images and this movement constantly and unexpectedly changes direction. The images themselves feature dark, anxiety-ridden colours and facial expressions. Superimposed texts are fleeting and form incomplete sentences. These combine with discordant music to create a mood of unease. Of the collection made for the *What's Your Story?* DVD it is the only story without voiceover and the most experimental in form.

During preparation of the facilitator's guide that would accompany the DVD in classroom and training environments, the steering committee were troubled by how to contextualise this story. Prevailing concerns were articulated in statements like 'if I don't understand it, how will others?' and 'what clear message can we offer about mental health?'. After substantial discussion the guide writers were able to add peripheral notes about research that linked experiences of homophobia and lack of social acceptance with depression, suicide and self-harm. They asked provocative questions about 'feeling unsafe' and strategies that might potentially help to 'create a safe space for someone' (SHine SA, 2010). While the story lacks traditional narrative coherence this is, in fact, part of its message and the facilitator's guide offers the story this context. The experience of watching the video creates, for some audiences, feelings of anxiety and discomfort that might help them to understand the experience of mental illness. This distinction between storyteller process and audience impact is significant. As Citron points out, in the case of traumatic experiences presented in experimental or traditional narrative genres, form and content may be at odds with intended impact:

> In representing the incest trauma, experimental and narrative film strategies have very different meanings and functions for the author than they do for the viewer. For the filmmaker, narrative can integrate experiences for which memory has not always functioned adequately. Narrative renders the incomprehensible understandable. Narrative offers the much needed illusions of coherency and cause

and effect where there were none. Narrative puts the author at ease. For the audience, however, narrative reduces a complex, confusing, over determined tidal wave of experiences and half-found awareness into something that is linear, understandable. It cleans up the trauma, makes it tidy, and makes it, at the structural level, familiar. Narrative makes it seem safe. This is a lie. Everything that makes narrative honest for the author is precisely what makes it false for the audience. Pieces not wholeness, discontinuity not fluidity, is a more authentic language for the expression of trauma and its aftermath.

(Citron, 1999, p. 50)

While Citron argues on the one hand that an experimental form is better suited to recreating the experience of trauma, on the other hand it is possible to argue that a film has failed to communicate if an audience doesn't understand and is alienated. This is a question I will take up further in Chapter 5 when I discuss storytellers' efforts to maintain personal integrity while communicating effectively with an audience; efforts to speak across difference. However, here I offer this example as an opportunity to illustrate first how difficult it is to create and breathe life into coherent narratives when the content they represent is fragmented, and second how partially coherent narratives may nevertheless serve as tools to build congruence in the storyteller's life.

In an interview reflecting back on the experience of making the story, Kirsten states that initially she was making the story for herself and for a general audience who might identify with it. As she got further into the creative process she started hoping that she might be able to share it with her family, in particular her mother, as a means of talking more about her childhood. This ambition was achieved and the story successfully prompted conversations between Kirsten, her mum and her siblings about subjects that had never before been touched upon. Kirsten describes some of the other influences of the story and her general feelings about identity:

> I have many scars from years of self-harm and have only recently worn short sleeves in public. Telling my story has made this easier, though I am often still self-conscious. Sometimes I worry about looking 'butch' but I usually get around that by telling myself I look androgynous, which I feel more comfortable with, probably because that's how I feel. I am shy meeting new people unless I am in my studio, which is a huge part of my identity.
>
> (Kirsten, email correspondence, 2012)

Kirsten attributes the experience of making and sharing the story as a step forward in 'liking herself'. It seems that this process, quite separately to the influence the story may have on any audience, has helped affirm identity.

The communication quandaries that underlie synchronicity between content and form (i.e. how is it possible to talk simply about complicated things? how is it possible to find a form that communicates effectively with divergent audiences?) are also evident in language itself. Goffman's analysis of impressions 'given' and 'given off' draws attention to discrepancies between verbal and non-verbal communication, with any misalignment being interpreted as inauthentic or lacking coherence. There is an implication that, if we can make words (or, one might extrapolate, digital story texts) align accurately with our embodied performances, then we can maintain control over the impressions we give off. It is only a less than skilled bodily performance (or an inaccurate, inconsistent story) that might betray us. Just as a 'natural performance' communicates perfect alignment and a seamless transition between inner and outer selves so a digital story could be judged to be both coherent and authentic only if it could be collectively regarded as a perfectly accurate summary of self. This might already seem a tall order but the fact that a digital story is brief (3 minutes long) and finite (unable to be easily modified) and potentially available to all audiences across all time frames, makes the task well-nigh impossible. However if the representation were only tasked with an expectation of being a singular (among many) somewhat flawed effort at self-expression (something like a child's drawing) then accusations or fears of inauthenticity (and conversely hopes and expectations of authenticity) would be made redundant.

Interestingly there is a precedent for this acceptance of imperfect or inadequate communication in the study of language. Scholars of linguistics and affect argue that a moment of elision occurs in the actual translation of inner emotion into words or, as Reddy calls them, 'emotives'. For example, Reddy argues that 'emotives are influenced directly by and alter what they "refer" to' (Reddy, 1997). In other words the actual naming of 'anger' leaves behind some of the complexity of what was previously an inarticulate muddle of emotions. This naming, in turn, shapes the experience of anger.

> A statement about how one feels is always a failure to one degree or another... Emotives constitute a kind of pledge that alters, a kind of getting-through of something nonverbal into the verbal domain

that could never be called an equivalence or a representation... This is true whether one's 'intention' is to speak the 'truth' about one's feelings or not. This problematic link between emotive and emotion, this dilemma, is our activity as a person.

(Reddy, 1997, p. 332)

Regardless of intention to accurately reflect self or life philosophy in a digital story, these representations can only ever be qualified and, through their incompleteness, partially inaccurate. Like Reddy, Sartwell asks 'what, in our everyday experience and in our everyday world, escapes linguistic articulation: at a rough estimate, almost everything' (Sartwell, 2000, p. 5). If there is a fundamental failure inherent in language whereby complex emotional states are irrevocably simplified in their iteration it can be argued that the same reduction occurs in the iteration of identity in a digital story.

Transgression, complexity and fluidity

So far I have outlined numerous difficulties with distilling complexity into a narrative with any degree of representative accuracy. A life journey, squashed into approximately 3 minutes, can only ever capture the journey so far. Temporality is problematic in digital stories not just because of their brevity but because they crystallise a moment of lived experience. They are fundamentally static entities. Storytellers who have journeyed across mutually exclusive poles of identity, firmly staked out on a normative social terrain (including transitions across gender norms, transitions from able-bodied to disabled, from party-animal to poor health and so on), must reflect upon contrasts between current and previous articulations of self as well as considering which versions of the story intimate audiences might be familiar with. There is a tendency to emphasise the most recent incarnation as the final and either omit previous incarnations or diminish their significance as merely a means to an end. This is evident in transgender narratives that comply with a 'trapped in the wrong body' discourse. Author and transgender rights activist, Roz Kaveney, notes:

> Far too often, individual transgender autobiographies, particularly transsexual ones, come across as conversion narratives in which one used, for example, to be a heterosexual transvestite, or a drag hustler, or a radical queen, or a butch, but has transcended this forever and moved into a radically different state... 'I once was lost, who now am found/Was bound, who now am free'. Even a butterfly, whose tissues have more or less gone into meltdown, has some somatic features in

common with the caterpillar and chrysalis it once was; we talk as if we are changed, changed utterly.

(Kaveney, 1999, p. 149)

This elision of previous identities is not necessarily conscious or motivated by convenience. In some cases there is an understandable desire to forget a painful period in favour of celebrating a happier time. Many trans storytellers ascribe to popular notions of gendered inner truth and this is a logical response to a lack of social acceptance for people who identify as permanently or temporarily between categories – neither male nor female but gender queer. Butler points out that the very process of seeking medical and psychiatric approval for gender transition shapes a normative gender discourse of binary oppositions.

...it is for the most part the gender essentialist position that must be voiced for transsexual surgery to take place, and...someone who comes in with a sense of gender as changeable will have a more difficult time convincing psychiatrists and doctors to perform the surgery. In San Francisco female-to-male candidates actually practice the narrative of gender essentialism that they are required to perform before they go in to see the doctors...

(Butler, 2006, p. 191)

Green highlights the fact that declaring a trans-identity (especially in a public space as an activist) is at odds with the normative goals of medical and psychological treatment for transsexual people:

We are supposed to pretend we never spent 15, 20, 30, 40 or more years in female bodies, pretend that the vestigial female parts some of us never lose were never there. In short, in order to be a good – or successful – transsexual person, one is not supposed to be a transsexual person at all. This puts a massive burden of secrecy on the transsexual individual: the most intimate and human aspects of our lives are constantly at risk of disclosure.

(Green, 2006, p. 501)

From this point of view any narration of childhood biological origins by a trans person is permanently and radically revelatory.

The narration of *I am Sarah*[2] (Figure 3.5) appears on one hand to ascribe to gender essentialism while, on the other hand, complicating social discourses of visibility, beauty and transformation. Interestingly

Succinctly...
As a wordsmith I take pride in being able to fully express myself in numerous ways, genres and linguistic styles. While I can do this, often with relative ease, some things cannot be stated adequately or precisely by words alone, and in certain circumstances, occasionally, words are not the solution to expressing oneself effectively, but the inhibitor.

Given just a couple of minutes to make an impact and say everything I want to express was, to say the least, challenging! Lucky for me that I am also, by nature, a visual writer. I need to have images in my head before I can describe them. Best of all was the choice to employ a cartoon – it was a means to have fun and get a message across.

However, as a technical Luddite (despite the fact I use computers in my work every day) the very thought of making a short film was daunting... yet so exciting. I'm a very private woman, so saying anything about myself was never going to be easy. Therefore, I compromised – focusing instead on who I am, and the journey so many women like me have experienced.

The cartoon is simplistic as is the message; it is about identifying and being identified for who we are – ourselves; no facades, no illusions or social stereotypes; no pretence. I am me, proud, strong, happy and content, but most of all – free.

Figure 3.5   I am Sarah

Sarah uses the transformation of caterpillar to butterfly (referred to by Kaveney above as a quintessential symbol of metamorphosis) to illustrate her story. *I am Sarah* is told almost entirely with hand drawn images of a slightly cartoonish pair of caterpillars, one brown and plain, and the other attractive and with long eyelashes. The narration starts with: 'I was different; not how other people wanted me to be... my body alien to my inner self', and becomes increasingly poetic and slightly abstract. As the caterpillars become chrysalises we hear: 'fear cannot deny truth any longer, nor hold sway... all that was wrong has finally become right'. Finally we see first one beautiful butterfly, then a flock, accompanied by: 'Into such a diverse world I am not unique... different perhaps, depending upon your perspective... but I know who I am.' Much of Sarah's story comments implicitly on gender norms as measured by physical representations of beauty. However, by using symbolic images of caterpillars and butterflies she maintains her privacy (by not using before and after shots or images that might identify place, family or friends) and avoids affirming the very gender stereotypes she wishes to deconstruct. To the untrained eye, butterflies and caterpillars are without gender or social roles. The issue of visibility and invisibility (raised by Green above) is also apparent in the subtext of Sarah's story. She describes herself as a private person and in a perfect world she would choose to 'blend in'. She also recognises this impulse in other M2F (male to female) friends.

> The majority of girls that I see, while they may not be as reclusive... as socially isolated as me, by choice, um... they tend to want to be invisible. Now, as I am, I can't be invisible, unfortunately. Not without, um [makes noise], a road closure, or a scaffold, and a building team, reconstruction papers, and certificates, whatever. I joke about it.
>
> (interview with Sarah, 2010)

Towards the end of the story Sarah breaks with the visual style she has established by showing herself in a head and shoulders photograph, dressed and beautifully made up, half smiling against a neutral background. The narration states: 'I am Sarah, not part of a clique'. Sarah reflects upon the inclusion of this photograph:

> I changed my mind on that about 10 times I think... 'cause I'm not photogenic. I never have been. The camera does not like me. I always look about 500 years older... The idea was to get people to see that

I'm not comfortable with being upfront and in your face, and exploring my entire life history in open, you know? But what putting that photo at the end does, is it shows that people can get past that. And I hope that with people who want to transition, or people who are in transition and struggling, I'm hoping that that final frame takes them by surprise, and they go, 'Oh, that's what you look like!' That final image just validates the message, and says, 'Look, here I am. Um, I'd rather not be here. But here I am. So if I can do it, why can't you?'

(interview with Sarah, 2010)

Sarah's decision to maintain a sense of privacy through poetic abstraction while taking a stand in support of other trans people treads a fine line typical of the everyday activist. While a superficial reading of her story may support an essentialist interpretation of transition from one gender to another her representation of self is nevertheless clearly transsexual, bearing traces of her origins. She acknowledges she stands out and proceeds regardless. A second transgender story, made during the same *What's Your Story?* workshops has some striking points of resonance with Sarah's story though the two storytellers were not close friends and worked quite independently of one another in the workshops.

Karen made *Sisterhood* (Figure 3.6) as a tribute to her sister, the only family member who stood by her throughout the early days of her male-to-female gender transition. Karen recalled that at age seven she became aware that something was wrong in her otherwise unremarkable conservative family life in the UK during the early 1960s.

I wanted to be a little girl, just like my sister. To play a role and hide my truth, both for my safety and their ease... seemed easier. This strategy clearly didn't work. Constantly flowing beneath the surface was a stream of unhappiness, confusion, silent yearning, pain, suffering and unfulfillment.

(excerpt from Karen's story, 2009)

Later Karen describes her struggle to conform to the 'social role[s] that were expected of me', being a good husband and dad. When her 'uninvited dilemma' became overwhelming and she spoke 'out loud' she lost all of her 'nearest and dearest' except her sister. Once again the story reveals an understanding of gender identity as inner truth rather than socially constructed. Like Sarah, she uses words like 'yearning', 'silence' and 'hiding'. Like Sarah, Karen also speaks of her discomfort

karen
sisterhood

My story crystallised into a tribute to the only member of my immediate nuclear family who was prepared to accept me... my younger sister. On the basis of our shared sibling relationship she was able to accept my uninvited lifelong transgendered dilemma, and my humanity... unconditionally. I wanted to make a heartfelt, public declaration of gratitude and to try to explain how much her unconditional love, support and encouragement meant to me.

This project did bring its challenges by forcing me to confront my grief and loss at the total rejection from my children, partner and parents. It also demanded revisiting childhood memories both good and bad...

Despite the challenges, I have gained a sister estranged to me for almost 40 years and a sisterly bond I've always yearned for that will last a lifetime. Importantly, I've also gained a level of self acceptance / self confidence never before experienced.

Finally I can say I'm at peace, congruent and true to myself – comfortable in the skin I'm in.

"To be Loved, Accepted and Belong are the most basic cries of our heart. To be befriended in life is the blessing which enables their realisation."

Figure 3.6   Sisterhood

with socially constructed and 'assigned' gender roles that she feels are imposed.

While the identity exploration that is undertaken in constructing a digital story occasionally includes a critical examination of socially constructed versus biologically determined conceptions of identity most storytellers are more engaged with celebrating the here and now. Despite overt discussions during workshops that encourage consideration of divergent audiences and the perpetuity of stories that are circulated in online spaces there is rarely substantial reflection upon how creating a story might memorialise an isolated and finite rendition of self.

We live at a time when everyone from celebrities to politicians to Facebook users are frequently maligned for presenting inconsistent opinions, beliefs or articulations of self. Anticipating that a story will remain congruent despite ongoing evolving identity is perhaps naïve, yet it is a common expectation. We are accustomed to hearing expressions like 'It's just so unlike her!' or may even have been directly accused of 'changing our tune' or 'going through a phase'. Everyday rites of passage include becoming a mother, discovering (or abandoning) a religion, leaving a bad relationship (or falling in love)... and simply 'growing up'. For storytellers narrating a journey of 'coming out' (discovering a truth about sexual identity or transitioning in gender), a digital story has capacity to make simple sense of what is often a long and difficult process of personal development, thereby making its subject recognisable to an audience. Many digital stories use narrative constructions that conform to social values; values that regard personal growth as movement towards normative incarnations of gender and sexuality, that privilege wealth, education and health over their alternatives. On the other hand, an accurate rendition of fluid identity would need to acknowledge the possibility of further development beyond current identity and include the possibility of reverting back to a prior incarnation (e.g. the homosexual falls in love with a person of the opposite gender; the trans person embraces their biological gender identity). Definitive statements of self tend to foreclose other possible future incarnations and may prove disruptive to future personal journeying. Perhaps trans identity highlights the instability and inconsistency of all identity? Kaveney puts it like this:

> ...we are prone to vary across time. Often, to describe oneself is simply to describe a particular moment, to say who we were in a particular year. It is a matter of prudence not to burn bridges that we may, as individuals, find ourselves in need of sooner or later.
>
> (Kaveney, 1999, p. 149)

Identity: Nominalisation, Authenticity and Incoherence 83

While Kaveney is speaking specifically about trans narratives she might well be talking about *any* story of personal growth. Karen's story, *Sisterhood*, has an epilogue that illuminates the problematic issue of fluid, evolving identity and the difficulty of foreshadowing further change in a permanent digital artefact. In an interview with Karen over a year later she revealed that 'Karen's days are numbered'. For a number of complex reasons, Karen decided to become male again. One might imagine that the substantial nature of the gender transition she narrates in her digital story, in particular the alienation she experiences from her wife and children, might be difficult to retract or stand by. However Karen is pragmatic about the story. While she frequently used words like 'success' and 'failure' to describe the latest stage of her journey she was also keen to state that any new incarnation of identity would reflect aspects of all previous selves.

> I believe that it's a little bit like a history record... it comes from the perspective of the writer... you ask different people about that history and they'll see it differently but it was true to the writer... Also, that story didn't finish at that point, in fact that was the beginning of a journey in many ways... But it doesn't diminish the truth of that story and the experience at that time...
>
> (Karen, interview, 2011)

Here Karen offers her personal insight into the unexpected paths that all our lives take. She also highlights the arbitrary nature of choosing any one point as the beginning, middle or end of a digital story. Although articulating this journey in a permanent digital document that can be found by audiences for years to come is a step beyond dealing with people day-by-day and face-to-face, it was a step Karen was happy to make because she believed the benefits outweighed the risks. She felt that it was more important to publicly and profoundly thank her sister and further, that sharing her story might be affirming for other trans people. Karen doesn't regret making the story and doesn't feel she has burnt bridges with family members. She is happy to stand by the truths she has declared. FTM (female to male) author and actor, Max Wolf Valerio writes:

> I celebrate the human capacity and right to change, rediscover, reinvent and continuously experience revelation; to re-evaluate and to renounce any aspect of myself that is no longer authentic; to live beyond my own fears and preconceived notions as well as those of the people around me. Without a doubt, anything can be revealed

at any moment. Without a doubt, anything usually is... I claim the right to change my mind.

(Valerio, 2003)

The acceptance of mutability that Valerio demands of society is a radical and yet somewhat self-evident one. Nobody expects new parents to maintain their pre-children 'party-animal' identity. Love points out

> in part it is because of the visibility and the supposed immutability of gender that such changes encounter such widespread resistance... While such subjective flux tends to be stigmatised in transsexuals as either mental illness or lack of political commitment, Valerio presents it as a crucial aspect of human subjectivity.
>
> (Love, 2004, p. 99)

Some of the generalised moral panic that surrounds young people's use of social media, pivots upon the way future incarnations of identity (and employment prospects) may be jeopardised by publicly acknowledging socially maligned aspects of self (e.g. drunken party photos). Perhaps this discourse would acquire greater complexity if it incorporated some of the pragmatism and awareness of identity in flux raised by Love, Valerio and Karen.

At the time of interview, Karen felt that she 'couldn't see the wood for the trees', but she nevertheless thought it possible that at some point in the future she might update her story, perhaps as a new digital story, or as a *Rainbow Family Tree* blog entry or other online post. This capacity to complicate and re-iterate identity is a possibility afforded by developments in digital media including self-publishing via blogging platforms, linking different representations of self across different platforms, and the life streaming capabilities of social media. These possibilities were not available in the early years of the digital storytelling movement and they represent new opportunities for storytellers. I discuss them further in the conclusion to this book.

This chapter has explored identity at several levels. First, I canvassed tensions in theoretical and popular understandings of identity, particularly the nominalisation of queer identities. For everyday activists, eager to challenge stereotypes, naming sexuality or gender in any fixed fashion is both politically and personally problematic. I propose that artful and humorous disruptions and deconstructions of identity, alongside rich and diverse descriptions, to some extent counter the constitutive effects of nominalisation. I offer examples of storytellers enacting their own categories – like 'transensual femme'. They also disrupt stereotypes by telling stories of queer identity that are not so different – like grieving an abortion or forming a family unit around 'mum and dog'.

In the second section, I scrutinised theoretical notions of embodied, performed and articulated self-representation alongside description of the complicated ways storytellers narrate identity with words and images. I considered some of the difficulties of striving for narrative coherence and problematise social expectations of authenticity. There are some positive and therapeutic aspects to condensing complexity to a 'tidy, edited tale' (Myerhoff, 1982), illustrated here by a storyteller in the *Positive Stories* initiative:

> The issues haven't gone away but if I need to tell that story again it's there, nicely wrapped in a box, but organised, explored and honest.
>
> (Frank, email correspondence, 2012)

However, for other people, the evolving and fluid nature of identity (epitomised by trans storytellers) makes it difficult to lock down a crystallised articulation. Social convergence amplifies the problems with rendering an 'authentic' persistent and searchable identity. For these reason, I argue for construction of congruent rather than coherent identity – a strategy broadly applicable to any construction of postmodern identity. In so far as all identity is opaque, fluid, evolving and impossible to accurately summarise, all identity is, in fact 'queer'. In the context of this research, I described queer digital storytellers, who are aware of both the possibilities and limitations of the digital story form, making informed decisions about their content, thereby demonstrating agency over the process and ownership of the end product.

4
Case Studies in Voice

This chapter considers digital storytelling from a *meso* perspective – or middle distance. First, I describe the considerations of facilitators, organisations and web curators as they conceive digital storytelling initiatives and distribution strategies – in particular the facilitation of voice in my three case studies. The fact that digital storytelling is principally organised around non-expert media-makers signals the explicit involvement of experts as mentors throughout creative production and distribution processes. Mediating influences are inevitable and they occur at numerous intersections: the translation of organisational objectives into practical outcomes; the enfolding of individual identities into collectives (e.g. 'GLBTQIS' storytellers); and the compilation of personal anecdotes into edited media documents and web archives. What influences do these mediators of voice have upon self-expression?

Second, I describe the considerations of storytellers in using their own voice and in bringing their voices together as a form of political and cultural activism. In this second section I discuss some of the rhetorical strategies storytellers use to modulate their voices as they negotiate speaking on behalf of (often their children) or back to (often families who have rejected them) both intimate audiences and large social institutions. How do storytellers orchestrate voice; consciously and unconsciously using their voices and the voices of others to communicate a persuasive narrative; how do they speak across differences? Throughout this chapter I equate voice with agency in order to reflect its common usage in digital storytelling practice and community arts initiatives, as in the ubiquitous 'finding a voice' or 'having your say'. I analyse the influence of emotive language in constituting new social norms. Finally, I describe examples of stories used explicitly as tools for everyday activism and consider their use in social movements.

Mediating voice in theory and practice

Rather than the more widely used and all-encompassing 'mediation', in this book I use subcategories 'facilitation' and 'orchestration'. In the case of digital storytelling workshop practice, institutions, steering committees, workshop co-ordinators, editors and web-curators/moderators actively coax, shape and translate voice. This facilitation process has profound impact upon every stage of the communication process. While it is often portrayed as being neutral I argue that this is, in fact, impossible. Even detached facilitation has an influence. In the case of individual storytellers their orchestration of the voices of friends, family and society at large involves active reflection about how they represent other people and reflection upon their intentions to influence audiences. The practical and theoretical issues arising from purposeful facilitation and orchestration of individual and collective voices at both personal and institutional levels can be summarised as the mediation of voice.

The question of creative control is a particularly perplexing one – in the case of digital stories it would be easy to assume that bestowing final cut and copyright upon a storyteller would assure ownership and agency over their stories but this negates the complex process by which identity and story construction (and eventually distribution) is mediated. As I have argued in the previous chapter, the prevailing notion of autobiographic 'authenticity' in digital storytelling is deeply problematic and I stand aside many scholars who have offered similar critiques (Hertzberg Kaare & Lundby, 2008; Taub-Pervizpour, 2009; Thumim, 2008). Similarly, scholars in other fields of practice engage in analysis of power, embedded in and realised through, storytelling. The work of narrative therapists offers empirical insight into therapeutic practices that revolve around 'de-centred listening', 'loitering', and exploration of 'rich stories' (White & Epston, 1990). In brief, these practices attempt to counter the expert counsellor-receptive client relationship that underpins many therapeutic encounters, by positioning people as expert on their own problems; problems that are external to people rather than defining of them. Penn and Sheinberg write:

> For the therapists to resist declarative language and to stay in a questioning and speculative mode...acts as a counterweight to the inherent properties of language that represent reality as though it were independent of our construction of it...Maintaining

this position also protects the therapists from assuming a hierarchical posture and reconfigures the idea of the therapist as an expert.

(Penn & Sheinberg, 1991, p. 32)

Digital storytelling facilitation can replicate this style of communication by regularly affirming the primacy of the storyteller's voice. The technical skills of facilitators are acknowledged but not predominant; they are harnessed in service of story production directed by participants. Additionally, when facilitators value the expertise of the storyteller, space is opened up in all interactions for mutual learning; not just technical but social and cultural. This is an occurrence of 'speaking and listening across difference'.

Facilitators may also draw attention to the context of story production and distribution and the influences that shape construction of preferred identities, including friends and family members and the subjective nature of memory itself. Myerhoff, who is perhaps best known for the contribution she made to ethnographic practice in the form of an Academy Award winning documentary 'Number Our Days', challenged the anthropological conventions of the day by acknowledging her own relationship to her community of interest and her role in facilitating their storytelling. Myerhoff reflects upon the process of arriving at 'collective self-definitions' including 're-membering' stories in which attention is called to the:

> ...reaggregation of members, the figures who belong to one's life story, one's own prior selves, as well as significant others who are part of the story...The focused unification provided by re-membering is requisite to sense and ordering. A life is given a shape that extends back in the past and forward into the future...Completeness is sacrificed for moral and aesthetic purposes. Here history may approach art and ritual.
>
> (Myerhoff, 1982, p. 111)

Extending the normally tight time frames for digital storytelling production allows storytellers to undertake 're-membering' conversations with friends, family and other storytellers. This 'loitering' (White & Epston, 1990) affords in depth scrutiny of story tropes and, in some cases, also results in re-framing of stories that affirm personal convictions, survival strategies and preferred identity narratives.

Case Studies in Voice 89

While personal empowerment is not necessarily the principal motivation of activist storytellers (an important distinction from people engaging in therapy), endorsements from collaborators and peers during the pre-production and production phase nevertheless inform decisions to undertake wider distribution of finished stories. Myerhoff argues that sharing stories offers transformational potential by creating situations or 'definitional ceremonies' in which 'outsiders' can 'witness' lived experience and preferred identities.

> Socially marginal people, disdained, ignored groups, individuals with what Erving Goffman calls 'spoiled identities,' regularly seek opportunities to appear before others in the light of their own internally provided interpretation.
>
> (Myerhoff, 1982, p. 105)

Aspects of Myerhoff's ethnographic process, sometimes resulting in visual testimonies/products, resonate strongly with digital storytelling practice. A traditional digital storytelling workshop often culminates with a 'ceremonial' screening for invited guests, an event that affirms the strength and moral fortitude required of storytellers. These affirmations are especially valuable for activist storytellers who may later share their stories with less sympathetic audiences.

Myerhoff observes that definitional ceremonies require nuanced mediation and that, in some cases, the stories she helped gather and present resulted in a 'third voice'; a collaboration in which she actively facilitated the discovery of communal values and beliefs. In the book version of 'Number Our Days' (arguably a 'definitional document' in itself) Myerhoff includes verbatim passages from interviews with elders, and acknowledges they are 'heavily edited and selected'. Her friend and collaborator Marc Kaminsky critiques this process by comparing Myerhoff's 'third voice' with Bakhtin's 'double voiced discourse':

> Myerhoff's formulation emphasises the fusion of the two voices into an abstracted third voice in which their distinct semantic intentions are erased. In Bakhtin, who is ever conscious of the power relations among speaking voices that enter into contact, the boundary marking the separation between different semantic intentions is never obliterated in double-voiced discourse. The liquidation of this difference, in Bakhtin, marks the destruction of the dialogic context and its passage into monologism. Although Myerhoff's third voice

moves into the discursive terrain that Bakhtin recognises as double-voiced, her formulation evades the whole problem of the relationship between her discourse and 'somebody else's discourse,' thus rendering it wildly inappropriate to ask the question that the caterpillar poses to Alice, concerning the meaning of words: the question of who shall be master.

(Kaminsky, 1992, pp. 129–130)

The reoccurring question of who is controlling 'master' of the final digital story text can be further extrapolated to online distribution contexts. Just as face-to-face and online workshops are facilitated, the web spaces in which the digital story products are distributed are, to a greater or lesser degree, curated. This moderation may be explicit (e.g. several administrators are tasked with approving new members, content and comments) or implicit.

Website navigability and design influence participation just as face-to-face workshop facilitation does. Clay Shirky, popular culture commentator and author, argues that Web 2.0 technology enables new forms of group formation and self-expression for 'everybody' (Shirky, 2009). However, he has been critiqued for eliding the obstacles to participation and over-simplifying the 'rules' for mass engagement. He proposes that a successful web community requires a clearly articulated 'promise' (why join the group?), accessible 'tools' (facilitating participation), and a 'bargain' that constitutes the rules of engagement (or what you can expect and what is expected of you). While Shirky acknowledges some difficulties, he fails to address the detail of how his 'promise, tool, bargain' trifecta could be articulated by a disparate community of users. As with face-to-face workshops, an empowered individual (or small group) generally defines the terms of engagement on behalf of a divergent collective. The choice of 'tools' and 'bargain' clearly influence participation – for example a space that functions primarily as a story archive may invite feedback in the form of 'comments' whereas other spaces may accommodate personalised member pages, blogs and facilitate interaction between community members. Arguably, the greater the degree of interactivity and flexibility of design, the greater the likelihood that a storyteller will be able to shape a context for their preferred identity narratives that reflect their semantic intentions, both present and future. In the following description of my three case studies, I offer reflection and analysis of the facilitation of voice through various means (including web design and workshops formats) in both on and offline contexts.

Facilitating voice: Working with groups

What's Your Story?

History and context

SHine SA is a sexual health and education network located in Adelaide, South Australia. The organisation has multiple locations spanning the city and outlying suburbs and they offer state subsidised health services including consultations with doctors and counsellors and a sexual health hotline. They also undertake community and workforce education by running workshops and training for a variety of groups (from young people to teachers and professional organisations). They participate in many health-focussed public events and maintain a library. Occasionally, when there is a perceived gap in resources and additional funding can be sourced, they produce resources themselves. *What's Your Story?* is an example of a community engagement initiative that also resulted in production of an educational resource.

It can be argued that sexual health education in Australia is more progressive than its American equivalent. However, during various periods of history, there has been substantial opposition articulated by groups associated with the US-based Christian right (Peppard, 2008). In 1999, the Australian federal government adopted a national framework entitled 'Talking Sexual Health' that emphasised 'the social constructions of gender and power which affect young people's ability to negotiate sexual encounters, and highlighted the need to address diversity, including sexual diversity' (Peppard, 2008, p. 501). The policy document highlighted the importance of including sexual diversity in sex education and was supported by Australian research that showed same-sex attracted and questioning young people experience a significant level of harassment at school (Hillier et al., 1998). In line with this framework SHine SA developed a programme entitled 'Sexual Health and Relationships Education', more commonly known by the acronym 'SHARE'. The programme was piloted in a handful of schools in 2003 and almost immediately faced a tumult of opposition typical of many culture wars between the Christian right[1] and progressive stakeholders. The programme was inclusive of but not exclusively focussed on (as some of the opponents claimed) same-sex attracted people and discussed a variety of sexual health practices including birth control and abstinence. Community debates were amplified by news coverage and debates in parliament and featured much of the rhetoric of moral panic, including accusations that the project was being used to 'recruit' for the gay and lesbian cause and that the education department was trying to 'steal your children's innocence' (Peppard, 2008). While the SHARE programme eventually proceeded with some modifications (including a reduction of the number of scenarios that featured same-sex relationships) SHine SA had been affected by the publicity and were eager to avoid any further tumult. The SHine SA project manager mentioned this history briefly when we first started to discuss the prospect of a digital storytelling initiative and in some regards it influenced the way the initiative took shape and was eventually marketed to the community.

I met with the SHine SA project manager several times to discuss how a digital storytelling initiative might serve SHine's needs and those of the GLBTQIS community. Digital storytelling frames the storyteller as expert and this was appealing to SHine SA, as was the potential to include many diverse perspectives from the GLBTQIS community. Similarly appealing was the balance between community engagement as a process and a marketable DVD as an end product. In late 2008, management approved a budget of AU$30,000, allocated from a government grant. The brief outlined production of a DVD compilation of digital stories for use in a variety of training and educational settings, ranging from senior and primary schools to training police recruits. The aim was that a diverse collection of stories would help raise awareness and acceptance of gender and sexual diversity in the wider community. A steering committee was established to support the project but the details of the initiative (including budget, schedule, technical requirements, sub-contracting of facilitators, post-production of DVD and communication with prospective participants) were left to me as primary facilitator.

Recruitment of participants

Defining what exactly 'diverse storytellers' look or sound like is difficult, especially without nominalising them in a fashion they may find inappropriate. A recruitment flyer was circulated via email to a variety of queer networks and social service providers, including BFriend (a support service for newly identifying GLBTQIS people offered by Uniting Care Wesley) and Second Story (a government run youth health service). The steering committee also sought out individuals they felt might be interested and/or had interesting stories to share. Some people were quite specifically recruited because they represented a marginalised or rarely heard voice (e.g. the accepting parents of a young transsexual child; an out lesbian church minister; disabled and queer, indigenous and queer). Identity descriptors were discussed at length and at one point it was suggested that an 'A' for 'Allies' be added to the already lengthy GLBTQIS acronym, to accommodate children, parents and friends. Some people were hesitant about participating when first approached; often declaring 'I've been pretty lucky!' (i.e. they hadn't experienced overt prejudice) or 'I haven't really got any stories that other people would be interested in'. Further discussion with the Steering Committee shifted the emphasis from stories of discrimination to stories of acceptance that, despite their positive focus, might reveal concomitant themes of rejection and bigotry. In later interviews, participants spoke of a range of motivations including highlighting social injustice on behalf of themselves and others. Several people used their stories as activist tools with which to lobby parliamentarians on issues ranging from access to fertility services through to gay marriage. Others sought affirmation and acceptance of their preferred and often complex identities from more intimate audiences including friends and family members.

Design of workshop process – Face-to-face and online

In planning the SHine SA initiative, optimal modes for engaging marginalised participants (particularly those living in social or geographic isolation and those with significant work and/or family commitments) were discussed. As a researcher I also tabled my interest in developing a sustainable digital storytelling practice, although this was not necessarily an issue for SHine SA. I hoped that, beyond the auspices of this particular initiative, storytellers would be able to use the skills they had learned to make their own digital stories, using computers and free software that they had access to either at work or home.

Two workshops were offered to over 18 participants, over an extended time frame and with both face-to-face and online options. The first workshop followed the conventional route of organising hardware, facilitators and storytellers into a physical location but was modified by spreading the three 'contact' days out over five weeks. In the interim periods, a Yahoo Group was established to facilitate group communication, which included technical queries, updates on drafts of scripts and eventually anecdotes about private screenings with friends and family members. During the face-to-face sessions, participants workshopped their scripts and learnt to use editing software that they had access to on their own home computers. Four manuals were written to guide participants, the first being an overview of digital storytelling with the others focusing on the software that would be used – iMovie or Movie Maker (for editing), Audacity (for editing of multiple sound tracks) and

PhotoPlus (for manipulating still images). Some time and resources were spent on the selection of appropriate free and user-friendly software and numerous workarounds were necessitated by software limitations. For example, both iMovie and Movie Maker offer limited capacity for multiple soundtracks so storytellers who wished to include music and/or sound effects as well as their voiceover needed to mix their synched sound design in Audacity before re-importing it into their primary edit software. As a result stories needed to be meticulously planned and storytellers had to privilege either music or voiceover when synchronising images (either to a beat or a pertinent narrative point). After music and voiceover had been merged any variations to the flow of images required parallel adjustments to sound via secondary software. Additionally the commitment to offering the workshop in a cross-platform format (i.e. both Mac and PC) proved complicated as dual demonstrations were necessitated and facilitators were often expert on one platform only. On these technical complications, Daniel Meadows (primary facilitator in the development of the 'Capture Wales' initiative) acknowledges that all their efforts to offer a cross-platform workshop were abandoned early in the piece and a decision was made to simplify the technical challenges by offering instruction only in Final Cut Pro. This decision comes with its own limitations as Final Cut Pro has (until recently) been marketed as sophisticated professional software with a price tag of approximately AU$1800. Participants who had mastered skills on this software would either need to buy it or substantially adapt their skills to undertake further storytelling at home.

The second workshop was conducted primarily online via a customised Ning website (and became known as *Rainbow Family Tree*), with two informal face-to-face workshop opportunities in which some storytellers recorded their voiceovers and added finishing flourishes to their edits. While the intention was that storytellers from the first workshop would mentor participants in the online workshop this support was largely informal and involved sharing their digital stories and brief anecdotes about their digital storytelling experiences in the online space. In one case, support was offered in a more hands-on fashion when a previous and current participant (who were also already friends) got together to work on a story.

Despite taking on the role of primary facilitator, I had no experience designing or facilitating an online workshop. While I referred occasionally to examples of webinars and had participated in various forms of online education I had not come across any specific examples that were focused on bringing digital storytelling to life in a fun and interesting way. My expertise was in gently guiding participants, both reluctant and enthusiastic, through the group dynamics, personal vulnerabilities and structured technical learning of digital storytelling. While it seems a little naïve in retrospect I could see no reason that the key components of digital storytelling facilitation could not be replicated or adapted for online participation. I called on the expertise of a local web design company for advice on appropriate platforms and I describe this process in more detail shortly in a section that canvasses the *Rainbow Family Tree* case study.

Having arrived at a shortlist of potential participants, I spoke at length with each of them by phone, gauging their technical expertise (and noting their hardware/software configurations) and storytelling confidence. I encouraged them to ask questions either by posting online or calling me on the phone. I broke down the online workshop into 10 sessions that would be posted twice weekly over a 5 week period:

- *Week One – Session One*
- Intro to Digital Storytelling – overview and some examples
- Who am I? Why am I here? Name games... and a few sentences about your story
- *Week One – Session Two*
- Write down and share 250 words about your story
- Find 10–15 photos or images to 'bring it to life'
- Together these elements form your draft script
- *Week Two – Session Three*
- How to Edit – introductory concepts
- Setting up your project, Software tutorials
- *Week Two – Session Four*
- Recording a 'guide track' voiceover
- *Week Three – Session Five*
- How to Edit 2 – Creative choices for sound and picture
- *Week Three – Session Six*
- Finding music/sound FX/images on-line
- *Week Four – Session Seven*
- Photo editing (PhotoPlus or photoshop.com)
- Sound editing (Audacity)
- *Week Four – Session Eight*
- Pulling it together
- *Week Five – Session Nine*
- Fine tuning and tech checks

96 *Digital Identity and Everyday Activism*

- Week Five – *Session Ten*
- Export and Upload

The tone of each session was informal and I encouraged people to join as many interest groups as they liked. Some people started sharing during the first activity – 'the name game' – swapping stories about what they liked and disliked about their name and how they had acquired it. This first activity encouraged reflection upon identity and self-representation while also providing an opportunity to engage in storytelling with workshop peers. Other people were reluctant to participate and I called these individuals by phone to see how they felt about their participation. Some people indicated that they were happy to follow along with activities without getting actively involved; others were just too busy. Some people expressed frustration with their own technical ineptitude; others were confused by site navigation.

By the time the group had arrived at week three or four it became apparent that we needed a face-to-face session for general consolidation and in order to support those who were having difficulty recording their voiceovers at home. I invited the storytellers to my home on a weekend and while some recorded narration others sat around the lounge room sharing afternoon tea, taking turns to offer updates on the experience so far. Many months later, a storyteller asked why I had called this session and the final one that followed it 'rescue sessions'. She said she had loved meeting the people she'd been chatting with online and saw these face-to-face sessions as a bonus rather than a failure to complete her story independently. She was one of the most advanced in the group but nevertheless valued the opportunity to hear the stories surrounding the actual digital stories – including the difficulties finding appropriate images; the complicated negotiations with loved ones; and the (apparently) universal experience of hating the sound of your own voice.

The final face-to-face session followed the last online activity. I booked editors, a suite of computers and a room at the Media Resource Centre (a centrally located equipment and service provider for entry level filmmakers) and in the course of the day most of the stories were finished off to the point where they needed only minimal post-production (finessing sound edits and titles in most cases). The production stage of the initiative was completed with the launch of the DVD and website at a theatrical screening of the 18 digital stories. I discuss this phase of the initiative – distribution – further in Chapter 5. While SHine SA auspiced the entire initiative they chose not to be associated with the website on an ongoing basis (citing the lack of organisational control over content) and elected to brand the DVD and educational resource as *What's Your Story?*[2] to distinguish it from the evolving *Rainbow Family Tree* community.

Positive Stories

History and context

In April 2010 I was invited by FEAST (the annual GLBTQIS cultural festival in Adelaide) and the AIDS Council of SA (ACSA) to facilitate a digital storytelling initiative that would explore experiences of living with HIV. Financial support was provided in the form of a grant from SA Health. It was initially conceived as a community theatre piece in which newly diagnosed (less than 10 years) HIV positive people would be invited to create and perform stories of seroconversion and living with HIV. While it was hoped that the creative process would allow participants space for cathartic reflection and therapeutic sharing, there was also an imperative to deliver a product that would be a vehicle for educative health messages aiming to increase social awareness and acceptance of living with HIV. Due in part to a lack of interest from prospective participants the project languished and the steering committee acknowledged that it might be problematic for some people to share their stories in such a public fashion. The initiative was re-conceptualised as a digital storytelling project in which participants could choose to conceal their identity. Sharing the stories with a wide audience was important, so online distribution that also extended the life span of the project (beyond that of a theatre project) as well as a physical screening was planned. The focus upon recent diagnosis, risk behaviour and consequences was retained. This criteria aimed to engage with a younger community who were slipping through the cracks of other educational outreach work. However, recruitment proved difficult.

Recruitment of participants

Difficulties were partly due to the parameters of the initiative being quite particular (i.e. 'recently diagnosed'). Many prospective participants said they felt uncomfortable about sharing personal stories about their health status, especially seroconversion. Ideally the group would have been diverse, with a mix of sexualities, genders, CALD (culturally and linguistically diverse) backgrounds and technical/creative capacities, however those that eventually came forth (following a more generalised call-out) were older educated white people who were already in possession of a degree of cultural capital and agency. They were mostly long-term survivors who had come to terms with their diagnosis and felt sufficiently safe enough in their social surroundings to now share their stories more publicly. Nevertheless, each storyteller had specific aspects of their lives that they did not wish to discuss and throughout pre-production and production they were encouraged to define the terms of what they wished to share, taking into consideration not only their own needs but the wishes of their friends and family.

Design of workshop process

The framing of the initiative as 'educative', 'engaging' and 'authentic' proved problematic as it became apparent that these objectives were potentially irreconcilable. If storytellers were encouraged to tell whatever stories were most important to them what would happen, hypothetically, should somebody tell an up-beat story about how 'bug-hunting' and positive diagnosis was the best thing that ever happened to them? While I was aware that this prospective scenario was a provocative one to pose to the steering committee I felt it was important that they recognise the primacy of the storyteller's voice and their right to tell whatever story they chose. Like the SHine SA initiative, copyright of each digital story product was retained by the storyteller, although there was an expectation that they would license ACSA the right to screen their story online and potentially in a DVD compilation.

After an extended recruitment period (and a loosening of the original parameters) a modified workshop process was designed to accommodate the needs of a small group of storytellers – three men and one woman. Rather than the traditional format of 3 consecutive days and hands-on editing tuition this initiative stretched out over an 18-month period. This expanded production period allowed the stories to unfold through several incarnations and afforded flexibility to participants who were not always able to attend every workshop, whether through ill health, geographic isolation or other logistic complications. The connections forged between storytellers and the five story facilitators/editors also enabled a collaborative creative process whereby the storytellers chose how engaged they wished to be in technical aspects of production. This took place in a variety of forms – all participants wrote and recorded their voiceovers, did rough storyboards, and sourced imagery, while some were also very involved in music and sound effects design. While everybody had exposure to Movie Maker and most experimented with the software only one storyteller undertook a rough edit. Some of the later editing took place during face-to-face sessions in which the storytellers instructed the editors on what they wanted where. By this stage established relationships had formed between particular storytellers and editors who were each editing several projects using Final Cut Pro installed on their personal laptops. At the end of each session the editors would leave with a to-do list that they completed at home and brought back to the next session to screen for the storyteller. This process was carefully monitored and evaluated and I took care that both editors and storytellers were very clear that the storytellers' voice and choices took precedence. However in several cases (*Greg's Sermon* and *Bloody Brenda!*) the editor was highly instrumental in the crafting of the story.

Greg's Sermon (Figure 4.1), its earliest incarnation and by Greg's own admission, was a somewhat cynical vent aimed at young men who claimed they 'didn't know' about HIV and thought that the disease 'was just for old men'. An idea was floated between Greg and the editor, Andy – perhaps the tirade could be set to music, thereby softening the bitter edge and potentially making it more appealing to its target audience of young gay men? With this in mind Greg recorded a voice over that was dramatic and a little arch in tone, something Greg, as a community radio presenter, felt quite comfortable performing. Andy arrived at the next session with an audio only cut – the voice overset to a dance beat with a reoccurring chorus/motif of 'Love Yourself!'. The group, and

Figure 4.1   Greg's Sermon

Greg in particular, were enthusiastic and eager to see what the editor had in mind next. Greg and the editor disappeared into another room for most of the afternoon with some costumes, a small light and a digital video recorder. Afterwards Greg confessed he wasn't sure how it was all going to come together but that he completely trusted Andy 'to come up with a work of genius!'. When the editor returned to the next session with a highly stylised video clip for the 'Love Yourself!' sermon, it received unilateral positive feedback. It was apparent from the edited footage, which featured Greg as a dancing DJ and a bank manager intercut with various explicit images (both personal and generic), that Greg had been highly involved in the performance of the production.

Bloody Brenda! (described earlier – Figure 3.4) also featured an unconventional digital storytelling production pathway, enabled by the extended workshop process and the substantial creative involvement of facilitators. Brian was thwarted by a series of minor and major illnesses that prevented his attendance at several scheduled workshops and I described the co-creative scripting and pre-production of Brian's story earlier. During production Brian was confronted with the problem of how to realise an event – a violent street bashing – for which he had no photographs. Andy (the aforementioned facilitator and editor) offered to help him video a re-enactment. As the original occasion involved numerous friends, fancy dress and drag, a car, a taxi, passers-by, and took place at night, this re-enactment proved to be quite a substantial logistic task. Unlike a professional film shoot, Andy and Brian co-ordinated the whole event with only the most cursory of shot-lists, no call sheets, no catering and no official permission to shoot at the location. The re-enactment proved empowering in an unexpected fashion. Brian cast several of the people who had been at the original attack and the energy and enthusiasm everybody put into re-living the event somehow dissipated the pain and shock that had been lingering ever since. The co-creative production process enabled Brian to orchestrate and include the voices of his friends and peers in his story.

Many storytellers speak about the process of digital storytelling as being 'cathartic' and yet, when questioned about how they think this happens, they find it difficult to pin down a particular phase of the process. Some speak about digging through photo albums and remembering past events in a different light. Others speak about being surprised and energised by witnessing an audience's reaction to their story. Brian regretted not being able to be more involved in the edit of his story and admitted there were probably some things he might have done differently had he been more involved in editing. However re-enactment of the traumatic event helped reinscribe the encounter with new memories. The end product gave Brian and his friends a voice that addressed and countered the violence in a way that was not possible in the first instance.

The *Positive Stories* initiative concluded in November 2011 with a screening of the stories, launch of the DVD compilation and community forum at the FEAST Festival in Adelaide. I consider aspects of this screening in Chapter 5. I also wrote about the initiative in an article published by HIV Australia in 2012 (Vivienne, 2012).

Rainbow Family Tree

Context

I previously described the history of the *Rainbow Family Tree* web space as an interface for the online phase of the SHine SA digital storytelling workshop and I will return to further discussions of the web community as a means of understanding storytellers' engagement with networked publics in the following chapter. This section focuses explicitly on the particulars of orchestrating voice in online spaces, using the first year of the *Rainbow Family Tree* website as a case study. How do online production and distribution spaces and processes orchestrate storytellers' voices?

Everything, from the design aesthetics and architecture of a website through to the task-based activities that constitute an online workshop, influences user engagement. While the degree of intervention intrinsic in a face-to-face production process may be diminished in an online equivalent (simply because, in the absence of a more experienced editor, the storyteller is most likely to be the primary editor of their story), this may also mean that storytellers seek technical support from friends and family members who are unfamiliar with nuanced ethical considerations and practices that privilege the storyteller's voice. Additionally, strategies designed to engage users in a web space, and the architecture of the platform itself, may inadvertently flatten complex self-expression. Further, even web spaces that aim for communal collaboration and ownership must in some way seek consensus from divergent users, potentially eliding the voices of lurkers and quiet people. With myriad identities and political agendas, how can the *Rainbow Family Tree* web space remain centred around the preferred (and divergent) identity stories of the participants rather than those deemed 'worthy' or 'empowering' by a workshop facilitator, site moderator or auspicing institution? Are grassroots, communally moderated online environments conducive to complex narrative representations and activist distribution strategies? What are the favourable circumstances in which purpose built web communities flourish?

Since the site's inception as an interface for the SHine SA online digital storytelling workshop in mid-2009, it has become a repository for additional digital stories, some created by community members at home and others created in the *Positive Stories* initiative. At the time of writing (late 2012) the *Rainbow Family Tree* online community (www.rainbowfamilytree.com) has 156 members made up of queer digital storytellers, their friends and family members and it currently hosts 33 digital stories. A series of decisions were made in how this online digital storytelling space would be constituted during two substantial transitions: the first from a Yahoo group to the Ning platform and the second, from an online workshop space to an open access community and video archive.

Site architecture

After some reflection and discussion with storytellers and facilitators, it seemed the core elements of a digital storytelling web space might include a forum (that would be utilised as a workshop space); a blog (that would include reflections on storytellers' experiences); a 'how to' archive of links and workshop manuals; and a screening area (in which members and visitors could view digital stories). I visualised these components as an interactive tree with emblematic portals that linked to secondary spaces – the forum as a cubby house; the blog as a collection of letter boxes; the resources nestled in the roots; and the leaves representing a burgeoning collection of stories. I consulted with Freerange Future, a small web design company in Adelaide and, given the very small budget available, I came to the realisation that designing such a web space from scratch was not feasible. I was encouraged to investigate the possibilities of a white label social network. There were various alternatives available for different subscription fees, with a variety of utilities. Some offered capacity to embed video, facilitate online chats, host groups and blogs; some offered a high degree of customisation but required greater skills than were in my possession. After some experiments with several platforms, I settled on ning.com and commissioned Freerange Future to create a very simple 'welcome' header and animated central feature that represented the central components of the *Rainbow Family Tree*. The header read: 'A haven for Queer Digital Storytellers and their friends and families... view, create, share... and do your bit to "change the world" '. During this initial design stage I drew on insights

Case Studies in Voice 103

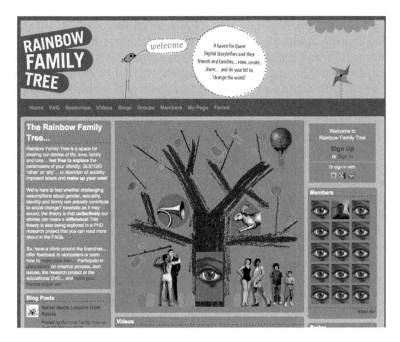

Figure 4.2 Rainbow Family Tree home page

gleaned from interactions I had observed in the Yahoo forum (during the first phase of the SHine SA workshop) and my previous experiences in cross platform (here used to connote multimodal platforms like broadcast, DVD and online) delivery of traditional film content. I also asked for advice and feedback from the digital storytellers who had been involved in the first phase, although their offerings for the most part were linked to quite specific difficulties they had already experienced rather than being directly pertinent to the expanded web design (Figure 4.2).

Once the Ning website had been established, comments and criticisms were more constructive. Some users found the differences and similarities between discrete blog and forum spaces confusing and this was no doubt exacerbated by the workshop context. Individual members author the 'blog' spaces on the site and I used it to give an overview of activities for each workshop session, updated on Tuesday and Friday mornings. The 'forum' was divided into numerous different subject headings and accommodated engagement from multiple users, represented as a thread. It was intended to be the space where people could actually participate in activities. However the fact that both the blog and the forum space were visually similar, presented overlapping information, and allowed participants to post responses in a similar format, left many participants anxious about where they were 'supposed' to be. At this stage there was also a 'chat' function enabled for people who were actually online at a pre-nominated time to ask questions and receive quick responses. Only one participant used this function and it was quickly shut down to curtail further confusion. Another function offered the potential to join 'groups' to facilitate discussions that may not be pertinent to the wider site membership (and only visible to those who had been approved as members). The benefit of this space from a facilitator's point of view was that message 'broadcasts' could be targeted to specific users without spamming all users. However, getting all relevant members to actually join the respective groups proved problematic and I often needed to undertake additional follow ups individually, in many cases by phone.

Overall the somewhat chaotic structure of the site, in combination with the technical challenges already posed by undertaking digital storytelling on new software at home, left many storytellers feeling a little overwhelmed. Four facilitators and myself offered hours of support and advice and all but one participant (who was relying on the part time involvement of a social worker and a computer in a public space) successfully created a story. It was nevertheless apparent that momentum during the workshop and sustainability of the web-space as a digital storytelling community was highly dependent on leadership and facilitation. This is an issue I will take up again in Chapter 7 as part of a discussion of the feasibility of self-sustaining digitally mediated communities.

Site access and membership

Early discussions with stakeholders (storytellers from the first and second phase workshops, workshop facilitators and SHine SA steering committee members) canvassed whether the site should be open to the general public or accessible only to invited members. While most of the first-phase storytellers were keen to circulate their stories widely there was nevertheless a degree of uncertainty as to how the online workshop would function. There was a concern that participants might be cautious about opening up in forum discussions if there were possible lurkers present. It was decided that the site would be closed to the general public during the initial workshop phase and opened when all the final videos were uploaded and launched at the physical screening. One of the advantages of the Ning platform was that it also allowed each storyteller the opportunity to determine their own privacy settings, not only for their video but for their profile page and all blog posts. Customised moderation also allows each member to determine who can post comments ('anyone', 'just my friends' or 'just me') and whether comments are automatically published or held for approval. Despite (or because of) this array of possibilities most participants remained with default settings that allowed all content to be visible and open to comments by anyone. The site also allows members to invite friends (by importing a database of contacts or specifying individual email addresses) and several participants did this right from the outset. This had an unforeseen consequence – the site (and the workshop process) immediately became accessible to these friends rather than just the storytellers and facilitators that had been discussed. Fortunately none of the participants appeared terribly concerned and in fact one participant informed me that she was unnerved by the fact that she knew some of her fellow storytellers in a professional context (as clients or participants in her own workshops/groups) and this made her slightly self-aware – much more so than the prospect of strangers being witness to the workshop process. This awareness of being observed by both familiar and unknown audiences foreshadowed many of the issues of public self-representation that also emerged later during production and distribution.

Visitors to the site can watch stories and read other people's posts but they must register as a member themselves to actively participate. Registration is free and relatively straight forward, taking approximately 5 minutes to complete. Like many other websites, one must supply an email address and password and interpret and retype randomly generated reCAPTCHA words. There is also the option to sign in using a previously established Google identity. Following this is a series of three optional questions:

> What would you most like to change about the world?
> What can you do to make it happen?
> When you're not busy changing the world, what do you do for fun?

Lack of response to these questions and nonsensical names and email addresses remain the biggest indicator of spam.

Online distribution

As online digital literacy increases, storytellers' decisions regarding distribution change. While few workshop participants regard themselves as net savvy in the first instance, they nevertheless take the terms and conditions of potential web distribution platforms very seriously. Offered the opportunity to set up profiles and share their videos on *Rainbow Family Tree*, Vimeo, Facebook or YouTube, most elect to use the former two platforms because they offer a range of privacy settings controlling who can view, share, comment or download content and the option to elect various creative commons licenses. While many storytellers were attracted by the lure of larger audiences on YouTube, few were willing to sign up to terms and conditions that require licensing content to YouTube for potential re-use by unknown third parties. Most storytellers avoid even the smallest possibility of anyone (including commercial media) using their words or images for homophobic purposes. While some storytellers were vaguely concerned that the re-purposing of their content was a technical possibility regardless of which distribution platform they chose, a pseudonymous or bounded approach to the textual production of this content allowed them to feel reassured. Addressing a lowest common denominator in the text of their stories enables those storytellers who undertake wide distribution to post links with an accompanying call to action – 'please share this' – in the hope that the stories will be circulated virally.

As well as the technical parameters of any given platform, the perceived safety of a space also figured. The *Rainbow Family Tree*, for example, is curated around stories of queer identity for community members and visitors who are presumed to be sympathetic. Few storytellers share their stories on their personal Facebook profiles because, while they understand the concept of selective sharing to specific friends lists, not many people were confident about setting these up and several mentioned that they 'didn't trust Facebook to change it all again'. Regardless, many were happy to support their fellow storytellers by sharing their stories via the Facebook 'like' button that appears under stories on the *Rainbow Family Tree* site. Some were also happy to share their own story as a link on the Facebook groups or pages associated with particular interest or lobby groups they follow. This appears to be a workaround that enables sharing with like-minded strangers rather than a flatly undifferentiated list of Facebook 'friends' with potentially incompatible political beliefs and social values.

Moderation/curation and community ownership

One of the pragmatic research goals of the *Rainbow Family Tree* web space was to gain better understanding of the feasibility of a self-sustaining online digital storytelling community. To a large extent this took place by engaging directly with the opportunities and obstacles experienced firstly in a digitally mediated workshop and secondly in a less goal-oriented and deadline-defined web community. After the launch of the *What's Your Story?* DVD compilation and unveiling of the *Rainbow Family Tree* web space there was an initial peak in interest and activity, reflected by requests for new memberships and comments on the digital stories. I was very keen to see storytellers and members continue to be actively engaged in the space and frequently (both formally and informally, individually and collectively) asked 'Where to next for *Rainbow Family Tree*?'. Very few people responded to these queries. However, there was generalised enthusiasm for staying involved and doing 'whatever I can'.

In March 2011 some discussions were summarised and posted on the site (Figure 4.3). Following this post, in April 2011, a group of nine storytellers and two facilitators gathered together to discuss what they'd like to see happen with *Rainbow Family Tree*. I organised the get-together via the website, email and phone calls and described it as part focus group, part social catch up. In the evening in question, we all sat in a circle, drinks and snacks in hand, and everyone looked to me to facilitate

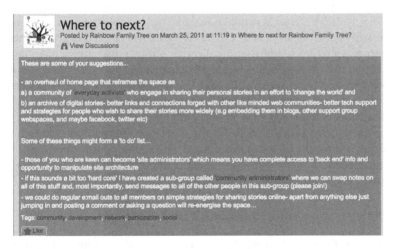

Figure 4.3 *Rainbow Family Tree* community engagement

discussion. I thanked people for coming and offered a short overview of what I hoped we might cover during the evening. I flagged that I was seeking particular feedback on communal ownership and responsibility; simplification of the architecture of the site; and the pros/cons of hosting videos on third-party sites like Facebook, Vimeo and YouTube. Finally, I put forth several questions to get the ball rolling: What purpose does the RFT site serve and how can we use it better? In the ensuing discussion several useful and tangible 'actions' were suggested but at the end of the evening I was left with the disturbing feeling that it was still all up to me and, no matter how hard I tried to stand back and listen, the kind of speaking I was inviting had already been shaped by participants' previous experience of me and the web space. While people were eager to participate (as they had demonstrated by coming along) they were reluctant to undertake any action without specific direction and several referred to *Rainbow Family Tree* as 'my project'.

My field notes of the time explore whether people are more willing to invest time and energy when there are personal gains and a clear goal. In times of crisis or when there is a specific issue that needs action (e.g. blatant discrimination or a law that is perceived as unfair) people appear to be more motivated to act. In 1965, sociologist and political scientist Mancur Olson challenged prevailing philosophy by arguing that: '[U]nless the number of individuals in a group is quite small, or unless there is coercion or some other special device to make individuals act in their common interest, rational, self-interested individuals will not act to achieve their common or group interests' (Olson, 1965, p. 2). This later became known as 'the book of zero contribution'. Perhaps better awareness of established theories derived from observation of social movements and collective online engagement may have assisted me in overcoming some of the barriers to orchestrating group participation in the website. Despite this my online experiences affirmed insights I had gained in face-to-face workshop contexts – group participation is dependent on many variables, not the least of which is enthusiastic and sustained leadership. This is at odds with the somewhat utopian prospect of spontaneous and sustainable grassroots collective engagement. I reflect further on these issues of facilitating and curating collaborative group spaces in Chapter 7.

Orchestrating voice: Speaking across difference

Many of the digital storytellers in my case studies speak of a duty to communicate with others who share their trials and triumphs. Others undertake speaking across difference – sharing personal insights in a persuasive fashion with people who they perceive 'don't get it'. Storytellers summarise these efforts, sometimes with self-deprecating humour, as efforts to 'change the world'. They strive to enlighten their audiences, whether family or foe, and reduce the differences of opinion, beliefs and values that divide them. They recognise they may also benefit from hearing alternate points of view – 'listening across difference'. Understanding the beliefs of opponents is a more difficult task. Shifts in opinion between storytellers and their audiences as well as facilitators/organisations and storytellers are, arguably, a core element in social change. Iris Marion Young, with insights grounded in political philosophy, refers to various ways in which speaking and listening across difference forges shifts in opinion among interlocutors:

> (1) confronting different perspectives teaches me the partiality of my own; (2) knowing that I am involved in problem solving these differences transforms self-interest into appeals for justice; (3) expressing and challenging differently situated knowledge adds to the social knowledge of all participants.
>
> (Young, 1997, pp. 68–69)

When they decide to participate in a digital storytelling workshop, storytellers generally form some kind of an affiliation either with publicly stated workshop criteria or collectively defined activist goals. Their engagement charts a growing awareness that their personal voice is worthy of taking up public space and that they are appropriate representatives. Listening to other storytellers within a workshop simultaneously broadens individual and collective social knowledge. Facilitators must also listen across difference, first to acknowledge the content and substance of stories and second, to offer constructive suggestions as to how these analyses might be shaped into a persuasive personal story.

The gift of the voice: Rhetorical devices and tonal qualities

Speaking to multiple imagined audiences simultaneously requires a modulation of voice and consideration of rhetorical styles that many storytellers have not previously considered. Vocal nuances and speech styles are not always apparent to people until they are pointed out or heard on a recording. Most digital storytellers don't like the way they sound and need to be reassured and persuaded of the value of their individual voice rather than a more generic authoritative voice or subtitles.

Lambert highlights the 'gift of the voice' as point four of his seven components of digital storytelling:

> The Gift of your Voice – natural inflections and speech idiosyncrasies help tell the story – don't hide them and try not to sound like you're reading
>
> (Lambert, 2002)

Lambert advocates for the storyteller's uncoached voice as a tool for communicating a unique story but the task undertaken by activist-oriented storytellers is closer to the art of rhetoric or persuasive speaking. While rhetorical speech styles are often critiqued for their false extravagance, I use the term to refer to consideration of how best to speak across acknowledged differences between storyteller and audience. Iris Marion Young points out that this form of communication has always been 'partly seduction':

> Socrates faults the rhetorician for aiming to please the audience rather than telling them hard truths. But Plato shows in Socrates' person that there is an important erotic dimension in communication that aims to reach understanding; that persuasion is partly seduction. One function of rhetoric is to get and keep attention. The most elegant and truthful arguments may fail to evoke assent if they are boring. Humor, word-play, images, and figures of speech embody and color the arguments, making the discussion pull on thought through desire.
>
> (Young, 1997, p. 71)

While many storytellers use humour and word-play deliberately, some forms of discourse are less conscious and simply reflect patterns of everyday speech. Soep and Chavez (2010), writing about their involvement in youth media production, use Bakhtinian ideas of 'reported speech' and 'double voiced discourse' as tools in their analysis of how marginalised youth voices speak back to power.

> Reported speech includes direct quotations, sometimes attributed and sometimes not, as well as paraphrases, and citations of speech that an actual person has said, as well as occasions when an interlocutor conjures speech that is fully imaginary – presented as if it had been said before, or might be said, by someone else (Tannen, 1989). A person might report someone else's speech as a way to align with

a voice of authority, or to mock another speaker, or to dramatise a scene, or to convey a sense of empirical reliability, to name just a handful of pragmatic implications of reported speech. Perhaps, most interestingly, Bakhtin identified a form of reported speech called 'double-voiced discourse,' in which another person's words enter a speaker's utterance in a concealed form.

(Soep, 2006, p. 202)

Reported speech can also be used to include the perspective of a third party in the story, in other words 'speaking for'. In the following example I analyse one of my own digital stories, in which I utilise reported speech and double voiced discourse as a means of articulating a subjective experience of subtle familial homophobia. Interestingly these are linguistic devices I used unconsciously at the time and I am unsure whether greater critical awareness would have been useful to the creative process. In workshops, storytellers have reported that they find 'overly intellectual' analyses of storytelling quite confusing. Screening examples of stories that use an array of narrative devices is often more inspirational.

In my role as facilitator of the *What's Your Story?* workshops I screened *Dear Sister*,[3] as an illustration of the impact digital stories can have on friends and family. Originally, I had hoped that my story would help my sister and I talk to our kids about our polar opposite perspectives on spirituality and sexuality. The story describes several conversations I overheard between our kids (about God's creation of the earth and gay marriage) and unfolds into the perplexing problem of how the kids would talk about my plans to have a second donor-conceived child, without some kind of guidance from their parents. The story addresses my sister directly. However, in writing it, I became aware that I also wished to address other audiences. These included my family members (who are implicitly involved in any discussions between my sister and I) and members of our wider overlapping social communities (who may also speak to my child about our family structure and my sexual preferences). Themes of silence versus voice and visibility versus invisibility resonate throughout the piece.

The story is narrated as if it were a letter to my sister. In the following excerpt I have represented voiceover with italics:

image of handwritten text: 'Dear'... with the name that follows scribbled out so as to be illegible

> Dear Sister... We've been through a lot together even though we don't always see eye to eye. Now there's some things I need to say to you...
>
> photo of my sister and I, both pregnant, with her face blurred so as to be unidentifiable
>
> montage of still photos – a close up of a child's hands holding two model farmyard chickens, one brown, one white
>
> You know back when the chooks were chickens? One day I heard your son and my daughter playing: 'Yours is the girl, and mine's the boy and they're married OK?' he says. 'Did you know two girls can get married too?' says she.
>
> the chickens move up and down in a series of images, as if they are arguing
>
> 'No they can't' 'Yes they can' 'No they can't'. Hmm, I thought. Interesting. But I didn't say anything.
>
> fade to black. kids drawing of Noah's Ark with rainbow
>
> Another conversation. On Christmas day, your son says 'Rosie did you know, some people ACTUALLY believe that God made the world by accident?'. I didn't say anything.

Reporting the speech of my daughter and nephew enlivens the story with (the illusion of) children's voices and evokes the feeling of helplessness I experienced as I witnessed their play, innocent reflections of our divergent family values. In this story, my response to the conversations I overhear is silence. Later there is a direct reference to the consequences of my sister's decision not to speak to her kids (silence) about 'rainbow families' or, more specifically, our family structure, as: 'making me and my pink parents community silent and invisible'. I describe a text message I received from my sister that thanked me for being respectful of our different beliefs. This description is illustrated with a photo of my mobile phone screen displaying the message 'love u DESPITE who u r' as I narrate: 'you said you love me and accept me despite everything'. There is a wobble in my voice as I recall receiving the message. Tone of voice and reported speech in both visual and spoken form effectively speak back to the silence that I felt had been imposed upon me in family discourse. However, within the text of the story, by recounting anecdotes from my perspective rather than inviting my sister to contribute her point of view directly, I am also denying her voice; making her silent.

The text makes an explicit point: invisible equals powerless or even wrong. Rendering my sister and her child as blurry images so as to obscure their identities ironically (and unintentionally) inverts the marginalising power of heterosexism and homophobia by diminishing their prominence in the family photos. Later in the story double-voiced discourse is used to offer a social critique of gay marriage. I use photoshopped headlines from imaginary newspapers to stand in for many other real headlines. They read: 'Gay parents – risking the kids?' and 'Same-sex marriage: Evil unleashed'. These headlines 'serve...two speakers at the same time and express...simultaneously two different intentions: the direct intention of the character who is speaking, and the refracted intention of the author' (Bakhtin, 1982, p. 324). The author's intention is revealed in a not so subtle manner when I superimpose a smashed egg over the headlines, along with the sound effect of squealing car brakes and collision. The story ends with a final visual representation of voice. A self-portrait is defaced with child-like scribble over my mouth and accompanied by narration: 'It's not really a problem the kids should have to sort out between themselves. Can't we find a way to talk to them about it?'.

While *Dear Sister* was made with the primary intention of stimulating a conversation among family members, other similar stories, some made during the *What's Your Story* initiative and others in response to public events, have their sights more squarely set on mass social change of the fourth and fifth varieties referred to in the introduction.

Same-sex parenting recognition

In Australia in 2012, legal recognition of same-sex family units and non-biological parents is split between federal and state jurisdictions. Access to IVF (in vitro fertilisation), ART (assisted reproductive technologies), fostering and adoption are determined state by state. In the last 5 years (between approximately 2007 and 2012) Parliaments in three states (Victoria, Queensland and South Australia) have all conducted inquiries into current inequities and the Federal Senate also undertook a major review in 2008. During the same period there have been numerous challenges to precedents in the Family Law Court (a Federal jurisdiction). In some instances Federal and State laws conflict, manifesting in confusing situations. For example Centrelink (Federal social security administrators) currently recognises same-sex relationships and evaluates the income of both parents when determining what support payments can be made, while those same parents may not be recognised on a child's birth certificate and therefore have limited capacity to make legal or medical decisions on the child's behalf. The following examples provide two illustrations of digital stories made to lobby for law-reform on same-sex parenting.

Molly, a lesbian mother of toddler twins, made *Where did we come from?* (Figure 4.4). Addressed specifically to her children and with accompanying nursery rhyme ('Twinkle, Twinkle, Little Star') soundtrack, she sees the story as a discussion starter for future childcare workers and teachers. She also screened and sent the story to various members of parliament in Queensland who were considering a bill to recognise non-biological same-sex parents. Her story starts and finishes with the name of the campaign – *Love makes a family: Vote to recognise our families in '09* – that also offers it context. In addressing divergent audiences with the same story, Molly struggled with tone – both the tone of the story and the tenor of her voice – and was concerned that both might be too 'saccharine' to achieve her political goals. Her vocal presentation is reminiscent of reading-to-toddlers but she also includes several examples of reported speech: 'Some people say that "to be a mummy you have to grow a baby in your tummy"... we don't think that's true.' She goes on to list things that do 'make a mummy' and also offers images of a range of family structures – one mummy, a mummy and a daddy and a step-mum, two daddies, a grandma, and so on. She finishes with: 'Families can look different on the outside. On the inside all families are made of love'. In addressing multiple audiences Molly makes a space for her family among them. Her children have acquired a story of belonging with which they have become so familiar that at one stage they were requesting nightly re-tellings. Their teachers and childcare workers are offered a language (e.g. 'two mummies', 'Uncle Harry', 'IVF') they can use to relate to the family, demonstrating acceptance. Politicians and policymakers are offered insight into the daily-lived reality of same-sex family life rather than a theoretical possibility. While the law reform she hoped for was eventually achieved, Molly speaks of what is perhaps a more significant realisation:

> One thing I learnt was that even though, for political purposes, we like to present ourselves as 'just like any other families', it is really clear how deeply radical queer families are. It is no wonder conservative people get so concerned about us. We are reshaping society. Our children are learning about embracing difference...
>
> (Molly, storyteller statement, 2009)

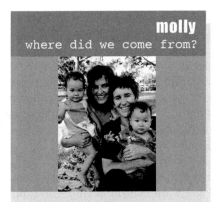

I tried to make this story on several levels. Firstly, it is simply a story for my children. I want their family story to be a taken-for-granted part of their identity – no secrets, no surprises, just who we are – something I could imagine them taking to kindergarten, to explain their family story to other kids. I like the fact that concepts like IVF, sperm donors and diverse families are part of my children's conceptual vocabulary now. Lucienne and Joseph, who are now two, love this story and request it several times a day, as well as getting me to recite the words when they are falling asleep at night!

I also wanted to make something I could send to Queensland members of parliament. At the moment (2009) Queensland politicians are debating whether to recognise non-biological parents. I hoped that something as simple as a child's story might be powerful enough to get them to see that we are a family, regardless of the legislation.

Making the story was a lot of fun. One thing I learnt was that even though, for political purposes, we like to present ourselves as 'just like any other families', it is really clear how deeply radical queer families are. It is no wonder conservative people get so concerned about us. We are reshaping society. Our children are learning about embracing difference and we adults are forming unconventional childrearing networks. Of course, they are only unconventional when viewed through Western eyes – other cultures have long traditions of care shared among many adults and older children.

Figure 4.4   Where did we come from?

116 *Digital Identity and Everyday Activism*

Speaking across difference enables Molly to consolidate connections with both familiar and unknown publics. While it is difficult to gauge the breadth of audience response it is interesting to note that, on the *Rainbow Family Tree* website where it has received 188 views, many of the comments and affirmations are from parents, several articulating their intent to share the story with their own children. This is an audience that Molly did not perhaps anticipate and it seems that the story's child-friendly tone has in fact met an unfilled demand, expanding its potential audience rather than limiting it.

Like Molly, Bronwen made her story, *Rowan's Family Tree* (Figure 4.5), for both personal and political reasons. She had already made *Welcome to the World, Pip!* as an affirmation of hopes and dreams for her soon to be born child. A year later, when it was announced that there would be a Senate Committee considering public submissions for the same-sex parenting inquiry in South Australia, Bronwen and her wife, Melina, were invited to contribute. Bronwen explains what she was trying to achieve:

Figure 4.5   Rowan's Family Tree

To explain in a visual/clear, perhaps surprising or new way, how our family IS a family, with or without validation from the 'state'. To express the love and connectedness that people within our family feel, despite the fact that the 'normal' or 'straight' family relationships are not quite there. To show the love offered to our child through being a part of this family.

(Bronwen, interview, 2011)

The story features a drawing of a family tree animated on a white board, with origami birds representing every new member populating the branches. Again, reported speech is used to include other people in the family structure and the story. For example, a discussion about what Melina's adult children wish be known as is described: 'No, we're not siblings' they said. 'Half-siblings?' we asked. 'No, that's just not true.' 'Step-siblings then?' 'Yes. That's ok...'. The earlier part of the story is accompanied by a voice-over with the familiar cadences of a well-known children's story, read aloud, not unlike that in *Where did we come from?* Later, as the narration opens out to explore how society defines their family, this child-friendly tone is maintained but with a noticeable edge. The narrator tells how, according to social services, Bronwen is 'stepmother' to Melina's adult children, who she has known for only a few years, yet, Melina, as a co-parent involved in the daily care of their son, has no biological relationship to him and therefore no legal one. The story ends with an explanation of what Bronwen and Melina think constitutes a family – 'relationships and love' – followed by a montage of happy snaps of Rowan with a diverse array of family members, both biological and non. A recorder sets the mood with a children's nursery rhyme and beautiful birdcalls bookend the piece, representing the voices of the paper-crane family in unity.

I asked Bronwen, via email, whether she thought anything had changed between her and friends and family, or her and the world, and she responded thoughtfully and at length. She saw shifts in their personal family dynamics in that 'it solidified what we are doing in creating a family, and gave me some ideas for different ways of talking about and presenting who we are – together.' She felt that it was also useful for friends and family members with kids who used it as a tool for discussing different kinds of families: 'I know my sister in law did that with her daughter when we posted it.' Bronwen was less sure about whether it influenced anyone on the Senate Committee. She was unhappy about the fact that some technical difficulties during the screening made it impossible to play on the big screen and that she had to default to her back up alternative, being a laptop with tiny speakers. She also considered that the story's significance was probably subsumed by the fact that it was only part of a bigger conversation she and Melina were having with the committee (that included access to IVF). She added that the committee were overwhelmed with submissions. Interestingly she considered that the medium of the digital story itself possibly made it less easy to quote from (than written submissions) and therefore assumed it was less likely to be referenced in the final report.

Social movements, framing processes

Casual observation of news and political commentary as well as closer observation of interest based e-lists and blogs reveals a generalised international groundswell, at least in Western democracies, debating same-sex relationships, family structures and GLBTQIS identities. Does this public interest constitute a social movement? Goodwin and Jasper define a social movement as 'a collective, organised, sustained, and non-institutional challenge to authorities, power holders, or cultural beliefs and practices' (Goodwin & Jasper, 2003, p. 3). Queer everyday activists act primarily as individuals, coalescing as a collective only on specific occasions. On the other hand, there is little doubt that their activism is sustained as it takes place in ongoing daily life as an enactment of identity. There is also no questioning the challenge they pose to widespread gendered and heteronormative cultural beliefs, as well as specific discriminatory institutions and policies. Perhaps it is possible to understand the collective actions of these everyday activists as a cultural movement or a liminal social movement? How can framing processes derived from social movement theory be applied to analyses of queer digital storytelling?

Social movement theory has evolved considerably since the early 1960s, a period when theorists generally understood mobs as dangerous and uncontrollable. Several years later, theoretical shifts were dominated by economic rationalism, resource mobilisation, political process theory, frame analysis, collective identity and emotion or affect theory (Goodwin & Jasper, 2003). It is these last three paradigms that are of most pertinence in understanding queer digital storytelling as everyday activism. How are storytellers influenced by the way issues are 'framed' by organisers? How do individual storytellers respond to the creation of a normative collective queer identity? How do they respond to emotive calls for participation and how do they use emotives in their own stories?

Social movement scholars generally acknowledge Goffman (1974) as the originator of frame analysis but adapt his generalised social theory significantly. Movements sometimes condense aspects of the 'world out there' offering interpretive simplifications that are intended to mobilise supporters and demobilise antagonists. However, these interpretive frames are not merely aggregations of individual attitudes but outcomes of negotiated shared meanings (Benford & Snow, 2000; Gamson, 1992). In the above examples, *Where did we come from?* and *Rowan's Family Tree*, the storytellers acknowledge that they are treading a line between assimilationist arguments for social inclusion and law reform (as in 'our families are just like everyone else's') and acknowledging differences that include diverse structures (e.g. two dads, two mums, step-siblings and four sets of grandparents) and beliefs (like 'embracing difference'). A similar schism divides lobbyists on both sides of the gay marriage debate with assimilationist overtones apparent in the chant 'equal love, equal rights, marriage is a civil right!' versus the disruptive and less popular critique from queer people against gay marriage, a focus that celebrates queer idiosyncrasies and otherness.

Many storytellers respond to some kind of catalytic event in their personal lives or social worlds as a call to arms and an opportunity to enact 'speaking across difference'. This may also be regarded as a step towards formal engagement in a social movement. These events or opportunities may take the form of discord between daily-lived reality and an authoritative social order, either codified in law or in entrenched social values. In the case of same-sex relationships, Australian responses to social discord have been characterised by a range of cultural activism, including online petitions, rallies, marches, mass 'weddings', kiss-ins and voicing beliefs and values to a political representative. Responses to familial discord are more subtle and difficult to characterise but represent a deep-seated desire to bring out into the open moot issues that have been avoided or completely disregarded. In analysis of the following stories, thematically linked by content pertinent to the current gay marriage debate in Australia, I consider expressions of voice that affirm individual identity and align with collective identities in part constructed by a wider GLBTQIS social movement.

The gay marriage debate

Where did we come from? and *Rowan's Family Tree* were responses to government reviews into the legal and social standing of same-sex relationships and families. In the period since they were made (2009 and 2011 respectively) gay marriage has become a hot social issue on an international stage. In Australia, federal laws accord same-sex couples the same legal rights as de facto heterosexual couples, while some states allow civil unions (currently Tasmania, ACT, Victoria and New South Wales). Civil unions do not afford the same practical legal benefits of marriage and some courts internationally have found that 'civil union schemes do not meet the test of equal treatment of all citizens' (Australian civil unions, 2012, p. 2). Additionally, activists argue that not allowing same-sex couples to marry implies those long-term monogamous same-sex relationships and their entire incumbent social and moral belief systems (arguably aligned with conventional heterosexual marriage features like conjoined property, shared parenting, etc.) are less valuable to society.

Melina was involved in the online phase of *What's Your Story?* during which she made *La La Land* (Figure 4.6). It describes the celebration of an unconventional marriage of cultures (Jewish and Christian), and people (lesbians), for which family and friends travelled from far and wide. Bronwen's grandparents, however, didn't respond to their wedding invitation. The story explores voice and silence, along with 'speaking across difference' in several interesting ways. Melina opens the piece with a montage of dog poo, compost and hair in the sink drain. Her narration explains that singing 'la la la la la' makes all 'yuckiness go away'. The 'la la las' were recorded by other workshop participants and there is an evident gleeful delight in the overlapping voices, united by Melina's direction. The 'la la' idea next appears on screen as a superimposed text when the grandparents ignore the wedding invitation. As Melina explains 'it's really hard to accuse someone of doing something when what they've actually done is NOT doing something...'. Melina and Bronwen decide to confront their fear and fly to Brisbane to seek the grandparents' blessing. A title card appears 'Fear is no reason to not do something' over which other text scrolls briefly 'Homophobia itself is a kind of fear'. In bringing the two experiences of fear together, Melina forms an alignment between *us* and *them*, emphasising common humanity and speaking across difference. When Bronwen's grandfather refuses to see Melina and Bronwen, and grandmother refuses to speak to Melina at all, Melina remains relatively unperturbed. The story comes to a close with Melina's description of the family meal that night in which she 'committed an unforgiveable faux pas by referring to the elephant in the room: "I think your grandmother was quite civil to us today." There was silence'. She zooms in on the image of people gathered round a dining table (constructed from

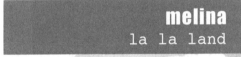

The storyboard for La La Land was originally a lot longer. It started as a direct personal message that challenged one person's worldview and position of power. Instead, it became a more universal story that speaks of the hurt and confusion that is perpetuated by the silencing and covering up of the deviance and diversity that exists in every family. Thank goodness we are not all clones of one another.

Making the story was a lot more fun than I expected it to be. I was so happy to have an excuse to do something creative, and I totally surprised myself by meeting the deadline. It was challenging to have sole creative power to determine all aspects of the story, and I worked hard to put it together just right. The humour developed as I gained confidence with using the different software and equipment. I have been bitten big-time by the bug – I'm now much more curious and aware about the work that goes into producing a visual story, and I keep thinking of more ideas for other digital stories.

Figure 4.6   La La Land

blocks of 2D colour with cut out photos pasted on her and Bronwen's faces) and superimposes speech bubbles of 'la la la la la'. As a final round of 'la la las' play on the soundtrack she concludes with voiceover 'It was really rather weird', a line that invariably causes viewers to giggle. I asked how she arrived at a humorous tone for her story and she said:

> Shoving stuff down people's throats is usually pretty painful for them...and just being who I am is the best way I think...I've had lots of fights in my life and I don't enjoy conflict at all...[Humour is]...not even.. a conscious conflict avoidance strategy...it's just OK, I can pick my battle, I'm going to fight it in this way, just be myself, try and be a good person, try and do what I think is the right thing and not hide and not be invisible anymore...

Melina reflects further on the use of her 'la la la' theme by pointing out that she too uses wilful ignorance as a strategy when she ignores the tension in the room and blithely names the unacceptable. She sees this as a strategy that is preferable to directly pointing out or naming homophobia.

On another level, analysis of the social context in which this story was created offers further insight into mediating voice. Melina proclaims 'really quite a strong commitment to speaking on my own behalf and not speaking on other people's behalf as much as possible'. Out of this arose several discussions with Bronwen about whether the story, as a description of something that had happened with Bronwen's family, was in fact Melina's story to tell. At one point, while Bronwen was also developing a story around the same encounter, Melina abandoned her version of the story entirely. When, due to other commitments, it became apparent that Bronwen would be unable to be involved in the workshop, Melina took up the reins again but was quite conscious of telling the story from her point of view rather than attempting to represent Bronwen or anyone else in the family. Despite this, 'la la la' serves as a form of reported speech in that it articulates an imagined, perhaps subconscious, response from the grandparents in the first instance and then from the family around the dinner table. *La La Land* was made in response to a familial crisis rather than a social crisis. However, it implicitly contributes to the social debate around gay marriage. The following examples do so in a more explicit fashion.

Regular rallies are held in Australia to lobby for 'Equal Love' – a loose coalition of organisations and interest groups campaigning for reform of federal definitions of marriage. Rallies and marches are often scheduled on other symbolic days of the calendar, for example public 'kiss-ins' held on Valentine's Day. IDAHO day is the 'International Day Against Homophobia' and in 2011, capital cities across Australia hosted rallies. In Adelaide vociferous protestors from a group who identify themselves as 'Street Church Adelaide' also attended the event, resulting in police intervention and mainstream news coverage. Several digital stories were made as a result of the interactions between pro and anti-gay marriage groups on the day.

Gay Rights Rally – Adelaide, 2011 (Figure 4.7) is a 4 minute sequence of stills and video of the rally accompanied by a popular song by 'One Republic' titled 'Marchin' On'. It was originally uploaded to YouTube

Figure 4.7 Gay Rights Rally – Adelaide 2011 screen shot

by a non-*Rainbow Family Tree* member and subsequently re-posted on *Rainbow Family Tree*. Unlike a conventional digital story there is no voiceover. However, the photographs are intimate and feature a group of young people who are presumably the storyteller's friends. The images are more personal than journalistic and the manner in which they are assembled, with accompanying uplifting and unifying soundtrack, follows a linear timeline from the mass gay-wedding ceremony and speeches, to the intervention of the Street Church, the march, and the ensuing rally on the steps of Parliament House. Close ups feature Street Church banners with excerpts from biblical tracts like: 'As wax melts before the fires so the wicked perish at the presence of God' and 'Warning Fornicators, Liars, God Haters, Drunks, Thieves, Adulterers, Homosexuals: Judgement'. Other photographs show heated conversations between opponents standing face-to-face and attempts from young gay marriage supporters to veil the Street Church banners with their own 'Equal Love' flags. It was widely circulated via Facebook and email links in the days following the protest, and received over 3,000 views on YouTube and 172 on *Rainbow Family Tree*. *Gay Rights Rally – Adelaide, 2011* is more typical of user-generated content on YouTube than conventional, laboriously devised, digital stories but is nevertheless produced by a non-professional media maker about his own community. The timely fashion in which it was made tapped into an already interested audience and amplified possibilities for viral circulation. The event itself and the numerous people who were affected by it represent what social movement theory refers to as 'political opportunity'. Developing an awareness of the potential these brief moments provide for amplified voice is a useful strategy and skill for everyday activists.

Melina also made a digital story in response to the rally, one that was put together more quickly than her previous, *La La Land*. *My Idaho 2011* is even more personal than *Gay Rights Rally* as it describes Melina's response to the rally and uses photographs of her wife and baby. The photos evoke moments described in superimposed rolling text – laksas, a tray of homemade biscuits and the child playing with wooden cut out letters that spell 'family'. Melina sings 'If I had a hammer' over the images and the text reads:

> We all have our own coping strategies... I found, when I got home, that singing helped. A lot! They have not damaged my perception of myself. I am not a fornicator. I am not a sinful, degraded person. I am not evil. I did not 'subject my child' to this unpleasant situation... It is 8:00pm, post the IDAHO rally. My wife came home

and baked biscuits. Now she's in bed already with a nasty headache. We had to buy laksas afterwards, to settle our stomachs... and tea (for me) hot chocolate (for her) after the baby woke up... If a peaceful rally like ours today can be so subverted by a homophobic so-called Christian agenda, then clearly the need to commemorate IDAHO is not yet over. Bring it on, good folks, good people of the world, you people of faith, you people of love, you people of God. We remain firm in our belief that we are a family.

Interestingly, there are no images of the rally itself and Melina doesn't describe what actually happened, relying instead on common knowledge of the event and the context that was offered by *Rainbow Family Tree* where it was uploaded. I asked Melina to describe the experience of making it:

> I made 'My Idaho 2011' when I couldn't sleep. I was so worked up about the rally, that for once I had a reason not to even try to sleep... I felt that through making 'My Idaho 2011' and owning it as my personal experience which was representative of an experience as one of a crowd, gave me some power back. I was buzzing with power by the time I uploaded it, and hoped that it would be taken on, appreciated and related to by others. The perceived audience was of people in my position; not a didactic reaching out to those oppressors.
>
> (Melina, interview via email, 2011)

Like *Gay Rights Rally*, Melina's story addresses an imagined intimate public of friends and strangers 'like me'. While these stories have limited potential for social change in that they don't speak across difference or to 'those oppressors', the storytellers involved in my case studies, regularly report subtle but profound shifts in self-understanding and changes in beliefs among friends and family. These occur both as a consequence of the story-making process and circulation of the story products.

I also made a digital story on the subject of same-sex marriage called *Marriage is So Gay!* It grew out of an assignment my nine year old daughter, Rosie, was doing on 'Rights and Responsibilities' at school. She drafted a short speech on 'why gay people should have the right to get married'. It was fairly exasperated in tone and I was more than a little concerned about what response she might receive were she to read it aloud at school but I helped her rehearse and I videoed a couple of her practice read-throughs at home. She was quite keen to 'upload it to YouTube'.

During this same time frame the IDAHO rally was publicised and 'Equal Love' promoted the mass gay wedding in Victoria Square. My girlfriend and I decided to take the kids and, partly to affirm our relationship and partly to reassure my daughter, we decided to participate in the mass wedding. As might be anticipated, the 'ceremony' was more political than personal but nonetheless quite moving. It was described in news coverage as a 'mock wedding' (a choice of words that has interesting symbolic and emotive connotations I will discuss later). A lesbian Uniting Church minister spoke about love and read from a children's book featuring two ducks who decided that, despite opposition from their community, they needed to be together. Some singing followed. Soon after, the group of about 10–20 Street Church people arrived, wielding loud speakers and 6-foot high banners The mood of the gay crowd was a curious mix of defiance and jubilance and at that stage I wasn't particularly concerned about how Rosie or my three-year-old son would cope. As we marched from the square down to Parliament House we slowed a little, hampered by the kids and pram. We fell behind the main contingent almost literally into the arms of our opponents. By the time we arrived at Parliament House everything was getting a little heated and the police had arrived. At one point the pram (now unoccupied by son but laden with bags, jacket and camera) was tipped over and my daughter started crying. The moment was captured for posterity by news cameras rolling nearby.

During the following week I composed a script and collated some images and an excerpt of the news footage. It features one of the Street Christians on microphone 'You must repent of your sin! You will die and you will go to hell!' and, later, my daughter crying. The news clip finishes with the impassioned, wobbly voiced minister: 'We're sick of being bullied. We're sick of... we're sick of people who are part of our community committing suicide because they can't see any hope!'. My voiceover continues:

> My daughter wrote her speech 2 weeks ago. Since then she's learnt what it feels like to be the target of hatred. I *wish* she didn't have to experience that. Homophobia, in its many forms, affects everyone, gay or straight. In a way though, I'm glad that it's made visible something that's sometimes hard to see. We need to make acceptance visible too. For kids like my daughter it's simple... a community that accepts same-sex marriage is more likely to accept her... and her family.

The story finishes with another short clip from Rosie as she finishes writing the original speech (prior to the rally) at the kitchen bench.

Sonja: So what do you think the class response will be? Rosie: Well, I don't know... if I'm gonna do it to the class and the school, then I'm hoping there's gonna be a lot of cheering in all of it... fingers crossed, even from Christian people...

Making the story yielded many unexpected insights for me as a researcher and as a mother. I had, up until that point, been lucky enough to avoid all but the most mundane and subtle homophobia. Much of my everyday activism had been about making those subdued but profound influences visible to a wider audience. I had never felt physically threatened or fearful as I did at the rally. I have, to this day, never felt so protective of my children. My concerns extended beyond the influence of the *actual event* to the possible effects of circulating a digital story *about the event*. These concerns, combined with the conversations that took place on the *Rainbow Family Tree* forums after the rally inform my analysis of listening and the difficulties of speaking across difference. I also spoke to several people (including the aforementioned lesbian minister) who had attempted to engage in rational discussion with their 'opponents' without any great success. While the circumstances on the day didn't lend themselves to calm exchange, it seems neither side of the debate were well equipped to listen across difference. Further, in re-watching the digital stories that were catalysed by the encounter I followed some links back to YouTube videos and posts by the Street Christians. They were full of descriptions of the 'violent homosexuals' just as the pro-gay videos made use of descriptions of 'violent Christians'. The use of emotive language and emotionally inflected voices in digital stories, and news reportage both aural and visual, is something I consider further in the next section.

Emotive language and social norms

Why is emotion and empathy in particular considered to be such a useful rhetorical tool for digital storytelling? A significant body of literature, across sociology, anthropology, psychology and linguistics, acknowledges the role that sharing personal vulnerabilities and anecdotes plays in establishing connections between interlocutors. Reddy's concept of 'emotives' addresses the fact that language not only fails to translate preverbal emotions but also significantly transforms, in a recursive manner, the experience of the emotion itself. Gould develops Reddy's arguments about emotives in language to explore the role of emotional language in gay and lesbian politics throughout recent history.

> Emotions justify and explain lesbian and gay political actions (e.g., 'our rage made us turn to civil disobedience'); are blamed for and credited with lesbians' and gay men's political stands vis-a-vis dominant society (e.g., 'our shame makes us too accommodating in the political realm'); are invoked to advocate one strategy over another (e.g., 'if we're proud, we'll act responsibly and take care of our own'); are evoked to condemn and discourage those who engage in a politics of respectability as well as those who disregard such politics (e.g., 'gay men who condemn promiscuity are self-hating'; 'promiscuous gay men are self-hating'); are linked to specific political acts (e.g., 'our leaders should feel ashamed about grovelling for crumbs'); are credited with political successes (e.g., 'our calm, reasonable tone made them respond to our demands').
>
> (Gould, 2001, pp. 141)

Analysis of language in social discourse often reveals intentions or agendas not explicitly stated or even intended by a speaker. The use of 'mock wedding' in describing the political theatre of mass same-sex weddings is particularly enlightening in the context of civil unions that are often presented as an alternative. 'Mock' in this instance is presumably used to mean 'pretend' but it also carries connotations of ridicule and derision. Civil unions, while purporting to carry the same legal privileges as marriage, are also regarded by many as a poor imitation of the state-sanctioned norm. One of the most compelling through lines apparent in both sides of the debate focuses not on legal rights but on the emotional and cultural expression of love and the social celebration that follows a publicly affirmed union. It seems both detractors and supporters agree that endorsing same-sex marriage would reflect a social acceptance of same-sex relationships, deemed either 'immoral' or 'normal'. Gould analyses public discourse within the gay and lesbian community as it evolved throughout the AIDS crisis of the early 1980s, bringing to light the connections between emotions, emotives and social movement strategies. She argues that the great prevalence of emotional discourse in GLBTQIS politics reflects a fundamental ambivalence about identity:

> ...indicating both an instability in how lesbians and gay men feel about themselves in the context of a hostile society as well as

conscious and less than fully conscious attempts to affect those feeling states and thereby influence gay and lesbian politics. It seems clear that this highly emotional language of politics – in its focus on the relationship of gay and lesbian selves to society – is centrally engaged with lesbian and gay ambivalence, with all of its instabilities...

(Gould, 2001, pp. 141–142)

The conflicted feelings, discomfort and intense desire to resolve ambivalence that Gould describes map well onto the anxiety many storytellers speak about as they plan their stories and anticipate negotiations with friends and family members. I discuss this networked identity work further in the next chapter.

Like nominalisation (discussed earlier), the recursive and constitutive influence of naming a bundle of mixed emotions and identities, either in a digital story or in descriptions of social movements and political strategies, is something both positive and negative for GLBTQIS individuals as they position themselves in a wider heteronormative community. On the one hand, these 'making visible' and 'finding a voice' processes can be affirming; on the other hand, they potentially foreclose other alternatives. Negotiations around publicness and privacy are often described as oscillating between pride and shame – the same ambivalence Gould locates in socially maligned GLBTQIS identities. Like Gould, Scheff (1994, 2000) argues the significance of pride and shame, not just within queer communities but as part of a generalised theory of collective action. While pride often arises from positive connections with family and community, shame results from disconnection – both emotions are explicitly and implicitly social.

Goodwin adds to the argument that emotions not only have capacity to engage people in social movements, they also shape the way those movements evolve and influence their outcomes. They have a similar influence on identity formation:

> Identities matter to people, and sometimes facilitate collective action, partly because of the strong feelings associated with membership in specific groups. Group identity is typically defined in opposition to one or more out-groups – 'others' who are generally the target of negative feelings, including hatred. Scholars who study identity formation, accordingly, need to be explicit about the emotions as well as the beliefs that contingently attach to specific identities.
>
> (Goodwin & Jasper, 2003, pp. 79–80)

There seems to be a complex interplay between emotion and identity on one hand and the naming of emotion and identity on the other. In a fascinating examination of the impact of widely circulated statistics on gay teen suicide (i.e. it is often stated without citation, that suicide attempts are four times more likely among gay youth than their heterosexual peers) Waidzunas presents 'some ironic consequences including the fostering of gay youth identification with suicide as a potential correlate of their identity and the potential antigay redeployment of decontextualised numbers' (Waidzunas, 2011, p. 2). He draws on the work of Hacking (2004) on 'looping effects' in which expert identification and nominalisation of a previously amorphous category (often summarised by statistics) determine a set of characteristics and behaviours as a new norm. Waidzunas argues that, prior to the first publication of gay youth suicide statistics in a US Department of Health and Human Services Report in 1989, many American young people may have experienced themselves as 'oppressed', 'experiencing angst' or 'LGBT' but would not have understood these tentatively linked experiences as being necessarily correlated. Perhaps even more surprisingly, and drawing on work published by psychologist, Savin-Williams (2005) Waidzunas suggests that many young people, for a variety of reasons (including a more accepting social environment, and more positive images of queer people in the media) eschew specific 'gay' or 'lesbian' identity labels. Those that embrace them do so as a result of social stressors (including pressure from parents). Savin Williams therefore argues that 'the correlation is a product of gay-identifying youth expressing their identity through the enactment of a suffering suicidal script brought on in part by the circulation of suicide statistics' (Waidzunas, 2011, p. 17).

This chapter has canvassed the multitudinous challenges implicit in mediating voice – both the facilitation of voice by institutions and facilitators, and the orchestration of voices by storytellers who represent many people in their individual tales and simultaneously stand together as representatives of a social group. However, unlike a social movement unified by common goals and strategies, everyday activism, carried forth by real people living everyday lives, has capacity to articulate, or voice, nuanced and discordant complexity. It follows that digital stories about everyday life, made by real people, also reflect greater complexity than summative categories imposed by statisticians, psychologists, social scientists or the mass media. Nevertheless, in the move from individual nuanced experience expressed by a single voice to a collective expression of voices, a certain smoothing out of differences and elision of complications is inevitable. This synthesis of one to many or many to one, whether through facilitation or orchestration, is mediation of voice and, while it carries an inevitable influence in both face-to-face and online environments, this influence is not intrinsically negative. Rather, both institutions and individuals, should acknowledge this influence and attempt to make it apparent to storytellers or speakers, thereby affording them ownership and agency over their participation.

Can individual and complex stories gain traction on a broad social scale? Perhaps individual stories, grouped together and offered to a mass audience, offer diversity that counters stereotypes. These questions go to the core of digital storytelling as everyday activism and yet, arguably, they are the wrong questions. Answering them can only ever evoke a partial picture of social change. By focusing exclusively on stories and their public impact, an opportunity to evaluate the equally profound listening and speaking across difference that happens across networked publics is missed. Acquisition of sophisticated Intimate Citizenship 3.0 is a 'by-product' of the story-making process. Analysis of storytellers as 'a part of' and 'apart from' their various networked and imagined publics is the subject of the following chapter.

5
The Private in Networked Publics

As storytellers decide what images, sounds and words they use to tell their stories they negotiate new and old meanings with friends and family members, the first stage of networked identity work. As they decide what line to tread between publicness (socially acceptable revelations) and the privacy that protects them from stigmatisation, they consider safety and risk for themselves, as well as their intimate publics.

This chapter starts at a *macro* level by examining what opportunities digital storytelling offers for participation in the public sphere. I consider how storytellers constitute themselves as 'a part of', or 'apart from' imagined publics. I canvas various understandings of the public sphere, particularly Berlant's 'intimate publics', and describe storytellers' capacities to imagine and internalise the responses of unknown publics. Rather than delineate face-to-face and online communication, I consider communication with publics that are *always already networked*, mediated by social and digital connections. I reflect upon the difficulties and opportunities that arise from social convergence and context collapse and the specific mechanisms storytellers use to curate their digital identities

I group examples around three approaches to constructing a text of self – visible, bounded and pseudonymous – and three modes of content sharing – targeted, ad hoc and proxy. Storytellers' understandings of privacy and publicness change shape as they undertake digital distribution of their stories. The *agency* they wield in creating these self-representations and the *ownership* they demonstrate as they share them, constitutes a new form of digitally enabled citizenship. I contend that the iterative labour of this networked identity work constitutes Intimate Citizenship 3.0. This in turn has a formative influence on the evolving expressions of non-normative identities.

Publics and audiences

How do storytellers, traditionally situated as audiences themselves, think about audiences for their creative products? What expectations do they have of democratic communication and civic participation in the public sphere? This section considers the differences between 'publics' and 'audiences' through discussion of theoretical and vernacular understandings.

Sonia Livingstone contends that publics and audiences, and indeed 'private' and 'public' can no longer be understood as discrete categories or binary oppositions (Livingstone, 2005). However, from the perspective of my research participants, there is a distinction and, in order to reflect that understanding, I use publics rather than audiences. While they tend to conceive of audiences as consumers of digital stories (or 'the people I'm making my story for') publics are understood mostly in the sense of 'general public'. Within this amorphous category lies a wealth of meanings, constituted by shifting alliances with publics that storytellers are apart from or a part of, reflecting their complex relationship to and membership within groups they imagine viewing their stories.

Critiques of the Habermasian model of the public sphere highlight the exclusion of women, the working classes and a host of minority groups who lack the cultural capital to participate (Warner, 2005; Wolfe, 1997; Young, 1997). Fraser proposes that the elimination of social inequality (rather than the 'bracketing' conceived by Habermas) might be achieved by the social inclusion of multiple publics, both 'strong' and 'weak'. Debates or public discourse must also encompass the traditionally excluded issues and concerns of the private domain (Fraser, 1990). This best of all possible public spheres would 'facilitate a debate tolerant of diverse discursive modes, leading to a compromise among a range of interested rather than disinterested publics (plural)' (Livingstone, 2005, p. 30). Meanwhile, Young proposes storytelling (among other communicative modes) as a means of reaching understanding among divergent publics (Young, 1997).

This revised model of a public sphere is pertinent to queer activist-oriented digital storytellers – a 'weak' public drawing on stories that originate in the private domain in order to address social inequities.

Livingstone surveys definitions of publics and audiences with democratic discussion as her frame, and locates them in various historical and epistemological contexts. She considers how technology has transformed 'rational-critical' debate into something less distinctly 'political' and more inclusive of a variety of cultural discourses (a point that resonates with both Young and Fraser, above). Livingstone dismisses simplistic depictions of 'audience' as an undifferentiated mass of consumers who are easily manipulated by media. She argues instead for a definition grounded in preliminary and intimate audience of friends and family, within the home. She reasons that political sensibilities can unfold from lounge room discussions of current events into public participation. In this framing of social participation, self-understanding in relation to the world is refined at home (like Goffman's 'back stage') before being presented in public.

This resonates with digital storytellers who rehearse with friends, family and workshop story circles before they create and broadcast their tales. Livingstone proposes that the intermediary space between audience and public may be conceived as 'civic' and represents a kind of 'private in the public'.

> The resources, the competences, the motivations which lead people to participate in public draw – in a manner little understood – on the lived experiences and activities, the conditions and constraints, the identities and relationships of people in their status as private individuals.
>
> (Livingstone, 2005, p. 28)

Livingstone points out that 'civic' illuminates the conditions of participation while also expanding the boundaries for what may be meaningfully regarded as participation. Like Jenkins' definition of participatory culture, Livingstone argues that modern people wish to feel like active citizens whose contributions to culture matter. Although they use 'civic' to different ends, Livingstone's conception of an audience at home fits with what Papacharissi calls 'the private sphere' – a space in which to grow 'digitally enabled citizenship':

> The emerging model of the digitally enabled citizen is liquid and reflexive to contemporary civic realities, but also removed from civic habits of the past. Most civic behaviours originate in private environments, and may be broadcast publicly to multiple and select audiences of the citizen's choosing and at the citizen's whim. The emerging political conscience is not collective, but privatised – both by virtue of its connection to consumer culture and in terms of the private spaces it occupies. The contemporary citizen adopts a personally devised definition of the political, and becomes politically

emancipated in private, rather than public, spaces, thus developing a new civic vernacular.

(Papacharissi, 2010, p. 19)

Various forms of social change may also be catalysed in these safe 'civic' spaces before being projected and amplified in public. In the next section, I discuss these imagined publics in more detail.

Imagined publics and social convergence

Digital storytelling requires negotiations between divergent real and imagined social worlds. While some stories are quite explicitly targeted at a known person, others are pitched to macro publics. They also implicitly include the very intimate, domestic publics of a storytellers known networks. Further, there is the internalised imaginary public that storytellers consider themselves to be a part of or apart from.

Molly, the lesbian mum who made *Where did we come from?*, addresses her children, part of a familiar public of which she is both apart from (i.e. she is not her children) and a part of (they are a family together). She speaks on behalf of an intimate, familiar public she is *a part of* (her family and other families like hers) when she addresses an imagined public of parliamentarians that she is *apart from*. She imagines the story being received by fellow parents at work or childcare and considers whether they know her as lesbian and/or parent, and whether they will be sympathetic or antipathetic. When she shares her story on social media platforms like Facebook, Molly addresses a mixture of unknown, intimate and familiar publics – inherently 'imagined' virtual publics.

Warner describes an alternative 'counter-public' in which marginalised people may constitute themselves as a smaller public, differentiated from and in opposition to the world at large. In a similar vein, Berlant proposes the concept of an 'intimate public', which she characterises as sharing 'a worldview and emotional knowledge that have derived from a broadly common historical experience' (Berlant, 2008, p. viii). My research participants address publics that share attributes of both intimate and counter-publics; these publics intersect and shift as storyteller's relationships to and with them evolve.

Further, these publics are all *imagined*. While storytellers certainly undertake face-to-face negotiations with real people, they can never really know their response to the story they are creating; they must *imagine* their response. Boyd describes networked publics as 'simultaneously (1) the space constructed through networked technologies and (2) the imagined community that emerges as a result of the intersection of people, technology, and practice' (boyd, 2008a). She acknowledges that, while networked publics share many of the qualities of other publics, their technologically mediated nature imbricate communication issues arising from 'invisible audiences, collapsed contexts and the blurring of public and private' (ibid.).

Not all everyday activists opt to make digital stories or engage in online distribution of their stories. However, most engage in a daily negotiation of identity both online and face-to-face. Rather than 'imagined publics' (a frame that does not necessarily encompass the persistent, searchable and converged qualities of networked communication) I prefer the functionality of 'networked publics', inclusive of imagined publics

In this research, as represented in Chapter 1, Figure 1.1, I refer to *familiar, intimate, counter* and *unknown publics* converged as an imagined public in the following ways. 'Familiar' constitutes an inner circle of nearest and dearest, whether biological family or chosen supporters. However, also included in this category are antipathetic family members. 'Intimate' publics overlap in that they are culturally aligned with the storyteller, having some affinity with the storyteller's experience. 'Counter' publics typically represent a less well-known or familiar circle that are nevertheless empathetic to the storytellers cause. 'Unknown' publics are strangers, their affinities are imagined by the storyteller and may be either sympathetic or antipathetic.

In the following section I consider the simultaneously online and offline networked identity work that digital storytellers undertake with various publics in order to share their stories.

Networked identity work

During the course of my research I have come to think of the labour undertaken (1) in the co-creation of digitally mediated identity to (2) speak across differences among imagined publics, as networked identity work[1] that in turn underpins Intimate Citizenship 3.0. Regardless of whether their labour is conscious or unconscious, storytellers shape their stories (and their identities) in anticipation of the responses they imagine from a variety of people.

These negotiations begin with an invitation or call to participation when they first receive an email or a phone call asking them to become involved in a digital storytelling workshop. Early in the workshop process, concerns about 'not having a story that anyone will want to hear' unfold into questions like 'Which story shall I tell... and who knows which story about me?' as well as 'What will people (or a particular person) think?' and 'How do I speak for my community?'. Storytellers find and refine an individual narrative voice with feedback, criticism and affirmation from a collective. Bakhtin, with his focus upon the interactive dynamics of speech (and I argue storytelling) puts it like this:

> As we know, the role of the others for whom the utterance is constructed is extremely great. [...] From the very beginning, the speaker expects a response from them, an active responsive understanding. The entire utterance is constructed, as it were, in anticipation of encountering this response.
> (Bakhtin, 1986, p. 94)

Regardless of whether they receive an actual response, stories are constructed in the knowledge that they will provoke a reaction of some kind, and with consideration of persuasive modes of speech. When they are asked 'who did you make your story for?' participants frequently name multiple publics or 'me, my family, people like me... and people who don't get people like me'. Rather than simply affirm their identities among like-minded people, they commonly articulate a wish to impact upon unknown, imagined, even antipathetic publics as well. Gubrium and Holstein argue that analysis of these expectations are revealing:

> While experiences may be thought as mainly personal and subjective, expectations are always social, local and conventional. The analysis of expectations focuses on the dialectics of recognizing, following and deviating from scripts.
> (Gubrium & Holstein, 2009, p. 456)

Following Gubrium and Holstein, I distinguish between the narratives that storytellers weave, and the hopes and ambitions that are woven into them. The former reveals shifts in social dynamics and understandings of identity that are not necessarily apparent in the stories themselves. Goffman uses frame analysis to 'isolate some of the basic frameworks of understanding available in our society for making sense out of events and to analyse the special vulnerabilities to which these frames of reference are subject' (Goffman, 1974, p. 10). In the context of networked identity work, Goffman's 'frame' could apply to (1) the framing anecdote in which a story is articulated or (2) the social context in which the storyteller and their interlocutors are positioned or (3) the

138 *Digital Identity and Everyday Activism*

interpretative paradigm that frames analysis. In the following I consider both the expectations of storytellers and the meaning they make of their networked identity work.

When I first invited Max[2] (a pseudonym) to be part of the *What's Your Story?* initiative, he was 17 years old and openly gay in both his high school and home contexts. 'I'm popular because I'm good at sport' he joked when we spoke on the phone. Max wanted to make a story to thank his family for their love and support. He also wanted to address his peers in an effort to explain how it hurt when they use the derisive 'that's so gay!'. In the process of negotiating with his family about including particular photos in his story, Max recollects his grandfather telling him: 'I don't mind you being gay but I don't want you to shout from the rooftops about it'. His family denied Max permission to use images of themselves in his story and he didn't want to blur them out of the photos, because he thought that implied shame. He was so upset by the unexpected reaction of several family members that he withdrew from the workshop. Ironically it was his peers that offered him support in the ensuing personal crisis. In his debriefing session with myself and other *Rainbow Family Tree* group members Max was able to put an optimistic spin on the whole experience: he hoped that one day he might make a digital story about his accepting group of school buddies.

Many storytellers uncover discordance among their networks about socially sanctioned representations of self (and, by implication, representations of the network itself). Digital stories that are destined for the public domain require consent from all individuals who appear in the story, occasionally exposing skeletons in the closet. Conversely, accounts of interactions in public spaces also expose social and institutional disjuncture and prejudice – as in the hypothetical examples of hospital staff refusing access/consultation with non-biological parents or unmarried same sex partners. As is evident in Figure 6.1, publics overlap and intersect both face-to-face and online, presenting an overwhelming array of prospective negotiations.

The undisputed risks and discomforts of making and sharing digital stories sit alongside other unforeseen benefits. Sometimes they offer impetus for ongoing conversations about issues that have previously been ignored. When petty prejudices, dealt by individuals or institutions, are exposed on a larger scale, discussion takes place openly and small shifts in attitude ensue. According to my participants, these conversations can be simultaneously therapeutic and catalytic of social change. Whether perceived or not, in some cases change is verifiable, as in the example of a conservative minister crossing the parliamentary floor to support a conscience vote for same-sex marriage. The labour of networked identity work is Intimate Citizenship 3.0. – building bridges between publics as they negotiate more flexible, parameters to social norms and congruent new identities.

Building bridges: Tributes, affirmations and provocations

Digital stories often emphasise humanistic points of commonality that are intended to overshadow and speak across difference. The workshop process and the story circle in particular offers opportunity to rehearse a performance (or script) in front of a preview audience that influences the development of the story. Some storytellers are encouraged to seek a more provocative stance, despite potentially alienating some audience members, but few do so without the support of the trusted fellow performers who effectively form an 'intimate public' or 'counter-public'. In organising stories by theme I noted some dominant categories – stories that sought to pay tribute (like *Sisterhood* Figure 3.6) and stories that affirmed a collective identity (like spiritual denomination in *O.M.G....Is she really?* Figure 5.2) and family structure in *Where did we come from?* Figure 4.4 and *Rowan's Family Tree*, Figure 4.5. There are also stories that aim to provoke discussion on a personal level (as is the case in *Dear Sister*) or social level (*Marriage Is So Gay!*). Many stories fall into more than one category, reflecting the diverse networked identity work that was undertaken in order to produce and distribute them. These stories build bridges between approving publics (that storytellers feel a part of) and disapproving publics (that storytellers feel apart from).

Back to Happiness (Figure 5.1) bridges two differences – one temporal, one social. The time between childhood as tomboy girl and adulthood as a confident young trans man is bridged, as is the social distance between Sean's two families, his biological one and his trans friends. Sean describes a 'happy, adventurous and confident childhood'; racing matchbox cars, dressing as a superhero, climbing trees and riding a BMX bike. The accompanying photos show what appears to be a cheeky blonde boy. The next part of the story reveals the impact of social and media messages about 'how to be a girl...not a boy' and the onset of female hormones, accompanied by images of a shy/sullen teenage girl. Sean states: 'I rarely wore dresses because they made me feel like I was in drag', and 'I lived with anxiety and depression for nearly two decades'. A change in background music and visual style heralds the next phase in the narrator's existence, including online research and meeting 'my first transgendered person'. He states: 'I realised I was the cliché of being male trapped inside a female body...but at last I found how I could finally

Figure 5.1 Back to Happiness

become happy again. I decided to transition to become male'. The rest of the story summarises the experience of 'becoming male' in a few short sentences and skips over the accompanying tumultuous changes with the gloriously understated, 'after a period of adjustment my family and friends were very supportive too'. The narrator speaks positively about having two families who can now see the 'confident and happy person I am once more'. The story is both a tribute to them and an affirmation of their support. Sean connects the two, very different, families by naming their acceptance. In linking them he also breaks down the barriers between the two groups, surreptitiously introducing them to one another so that when they physically met at his 'two year anniversary' of being male, faces were already semi-familiar.

O.M.G....Is she really? (Figure 5.2) is made by Leanne, an out lesbian Uniting Church minister. It is composed of a simple sequence of rainbow themed images (Leanne in white minister's robes and rainbow sash, rainbow flags draped over pulpits and displayed outside churches) and their antithesis, Google images of Westboro Church[3] type banners proclaiming: 'God Hates Fags', 'Turn or Burn', 'Hell is Horrible: No Warning is too strong'. Slowly these images give way to banners that read: 'God Hates Hateful Christians' and 'Jesus Loves Me, This I Know, Even Though I'm a Big Homo'. Leanne was very specific about the music she wished to accompany her piece and negotiated a small fee with the copyright holders for its use. Her voiceover is carefully timed to allow for the music to swell in volume in some parts with lyrics dominating. While her words reveal little about her personal life, they are nevertheless personally revealing and at times anger is apparent as she speaks of her frustrations with Church homophobia. Her narration speaks often of listening and storytelling:

> I'm constantly listening to stories about people struggling with their Christianity and their queerness. And I've listened to lots of stories of people rejected by the Church or their Christian families...and I get really angry about so called Christian people who kind of single us out and want to witness to us about the evils of homosexuality. (*O.M.G....Is she really?* excerpt)

Later she speaks of 'help[ing] people *hold together* their queerness and their spirituality and their faith in God' (italics added), literally evoking the bridge that crosses not only personal conflict but differences between homophobic and queer Christians. Leanne's story is one of

142 *Digital Identity and Everyday Activism*

leanne
O.M.G... Is she really?

When I was first asked to make a digital story I found the idea very exciting. It was a challenge narrowing down what to say and then thinking about the best way to present it with music and pictures. I think for me, my story is trying to put an alternative Christian viewpoint out there... there is so much hype in the media from conservative Christians about the sin of homosexuality. Often the progressive viewpoint is not heard as a balance. I wanted to communicate that some people in the church think differently now and welcome us into their communities. I really want anyone who is struggling with their sexuality and Christianity to know that there are people 'out' there who can help.

I feel a little awkward still when I see the story on the big screen but deep down I feel very proud of it. It's like I have given birth to something... and I am yet to know its impact. I feel very honoured to be part of a great resource. I hope that all the stories bring hope and new possibilities for people who feel they have no voice or place to be who they are.

Figure 5.2   O.M.G. ... *Is she really?*

provocation (for the former public) and affirmation (for the latter). Leanne's position as an out minister is unstable, somewhat risky and constantly negotiated. Her parish is relatively conservative and, while the Uniting Church is more liberal than some, it still has many staunch and vocal traditionalists within its ranks. In an interview Leanne spoke about how she treads a line between her Church congregation, the Church itself and the publics she wished to address.

> ...this community here, I'm still aware that there are people, particularly with the gay marriage issue, [that] aren't in the same place as me. So I just walk a fine line. I try to give them enough, so that they understand that this is really important... It's a different message for a different audience, I suppose... I haven't shown the digital story on a Sunday morning 'cause it's not the right audience. The fact that some members of the congregation know that the digital story is out there, is enough just to say, you know, that's me – that's the activist part of me.
>
> (Leanne, interview, 2011)

Leanne's example offers illustration of networked identity work that actively builds bridges between intimate and unknown publics, supporters and detractors in both online and face-to-face contexts.

Publicness and privacy

What constitutes private and public and how are these definitions arrived at and agreed upon? Storytellers wish to participate in the wider world while shielding themselves and their families from public attention. As Wolfe argues:

> Modern individuals require both a realm of private self-expression and intimacy buffered from the larger world of politics and a sense of belonging to a larger community that expresses obligations to all its members, even if they are strangers.
>
> (Wolfe, 1997, p. 187)

Meanwhile, understandings of 'public' and 'private' are not fixed or without context. My research participants do not necessarily equate 'being private' (understood by some as holding something back, or being 'coy' or possibly even ashamed) with 'privacy' (understood by some as safety or possibly an abstract but inviolable human right). Similarly 'being public' or 'publicness' (permitting insight) is by no means the same as 'publicity' (whereby one might actively seek exposure). 'Private' might be conceived as 'the thoughts in my head'. However, when they are shared with a lover do they automatically become public?

If the lover refers to these thoughts in front of friends or in a Facebook update is that 'too' public? Further, intensely private thoughts and experiences may, through the passage of time, be distilled into a 'life story' that is re-worked and re-presented for various public audiences. Socially acceptable levels of self-disclosure are subject to debate between lovers, friends and across a cultural landscape in which many consider the private actions of celebrities and public leaders to be 'of public interest' (Thompson, 2000).

For queer people there is a constant turning back and forth, a shuttling between Goffman's front and back stage, depending upon when it seems appropriate to reveal what to whom. Homophobic bullying in schools and other public places has been causally linked to youth depression, drug abuse, homelessness and suicide (Corboz et al., 2008; Gibson, 1989). Despite global education campaigns, HIV-positive people still report routine prejudice based on misconceptions of health and illness that are formulated into stereotypical evaluations of identity. If bigotry was only a response to physical appearance or behaviour then individuals might attempt to modify their self-presentation (and they frequently do) but when prejudice is based on family structure, health status and fundamental relationships then huge compromises must be made in order to stay under the radar or avoid unsolicited attention. Storytellers who court social attention in pursuit of social change experience something of a quandary in expressing an activist voice.

Warner describes the closet (a back stage space) as being a safe and private place that is also filled with shame; an insight that has affective resonance with many queer activist storytellers:

> ...common mythology understands the closet as an individual's lie about himself – or herself. We blame people for being closeted. But the closet is better understood as the culture's problem, not the individual's... It is produced by the heteronormative assumptions of everyday talk...
>
> (Warner, 2005, p. 52)

The forces of heteronormativity are apparent in many aspects of everyday life. For example, many official forms leave space for 'mother' and 'father', and same-sex couples holding hands in the street are still subject to comments or stares in most parts of Australia. Claire, emerging from a heterosexual marriage with three children, discovered there were many invisible social boundaries to be negotiated with her new girlfriend.

I asked: do you ever conceal parts of yourself in order to feel comfortable or safe/make others more comfortable?

> Sometimes at school with new parents I don't know, I say nothing rather than identify my family context. I don't talk openly about sexuality around my son's soccer games or team either so that he is comfortable...But no one asks either so it's kind of a 'don't ask; don't tell...none of their business situation'. But my partner does not come to soccer games with me yet...I don't kiss my partner in front of my kids usually, but I do hug her and cuddle with her in front of them, in front of my and their friends. We don't hold hands in public places like at shops with the kids beside us and that's so the kids are not subject to any harassment that 'may happen'. It's about them less than about me...I don't kiss my partner in front of our mums! But I didn't do that sort of thing with my ex-partner (who was male) either!
>
> (Claire, email correspondence, 2012)

Claire's story of managing representations of intimacy in public and private illuminate some nuances of social expectations. In her day-to-day life, she considers the expectations of a school community, strangers on the street, her children, her ex-partner, her partner and all of their mums. In making her digital story she considers these same publics because, while they may not see her story, there is a chance they will. Warner expands on the affective dimensions of the closet:

> In such a regime of sexual domination, publicness will feel like exposure, and privacy will feel like the closet. The closet may seem to be a kind of protection. Indeed, the feeling of protection is one of the hallmarks of modern privacy. But in fact the closet is riddled with fear and shame.
>
> (Warner, 2005, p. 52)

In interviews and workshops many storytellers speak explicitly about the conflict between being 'out and proud' (visible in public) and being 'safe' (maintaining privacy by concealing identity).

There are many complex intersections between privacy, secrecy, fear and shame. Molly, as the parent of a transsexual child, is painfully aware of the social regulation of public and private aspects of gender. Weighing up all the ramifications of seeking an audience for their daughter's story (publicity) and the damage perpetrated by invisibility (or 'secrecy' as opposed to privacy), Molly and Brendan had a lot to consider in constructing their digital story, *Blue for Boys? Pink for Girls?* (Figure 3.3).

At risk of exposing our daughter's identity and taking away her right to privacy we decided to conceal pictures and any possible connection to her. This became a technical and creative challenge in our storytelling process that in a way prevented us from truly celebrating our daughter, free from shame and secrecy.

The motivations of parents of transsexual children are highly scrutinised and any behaviours (like blatant political activism) that may be construed as not in 'the best interest of the child' may be penalised. Endocrinologists, psychiatrists and family court judges must approve use of the hormone blockers required to redirect a trans child's adolescent development. Any variance from what is medically, legally and socially constructed as 'normal' may have serious ramifications for the people involved. Nevertheless the child's right to determine who knows the details of their biological sex and gender identity is not always of paramount concern to authoritative figures and Molly spoke of 'accidental slips' perpetrated by teachers, lawyers and other parents. Molly describes the conversations she has had with her daughter, distinguishing privacy and secrecy:

> 'Secret' is nearly always shame-based. Like, there's always this, this dirty little secret, your little family thing... Yeah. And so when we talk about privacy, we say, 'That's meaning that it's nobody's business'.
>
> (Molly, interview, 2011)

Molly describes many quandaries. In one example she and her husband became increasingly friendly with new neighbours who were not aware of their child's genetic history. A harmless enough conversation about their two daughters' physiological development (being similar in age) came to an awkward halt on the subject of menstruation. Similarly a school camp became complicated by one of the daughter's classmates disclosing her gender variance to previously unknown camp participants from another school, causing a great deal of distress and humiliation.

The daily nuances of privacy, secrecy and publicness are already complex and yet the codified and distributed form of a digital story amplifies these complexities. The behind-the-scenes labour of networked identity work sometimes escapes scholars and Berlant and Warner employ 'queer commentary' to bridge the space between vernacular performances of identity and the abstractions apparent in some scholarly renditions of queer theory.

> Queer commentary has tried to challenge some major conditions of privacy, so that shame and the closet would be understood no longer as isolation chambers but as the architecture of common culture, so that vernacular performances would no longer stammer with the ineloquence of tacit codes, barely self-acknowledged, and so that questions of propriety and explicitness would no longer be burdened by the invisible normativity of heterosexual culture.
> (Berlant & Warner, 1995, pp. 346–347)

This illumination of privacy, shame and the closet are closely aligned with experiences described by the storytellers in my case studies. Claire speaks of the 'tacit codes' of negotiating intimacy with a girlfriend in public (not in front of the children). Molly and Brendan 'stammer with... ineloquence' in face-to-face assumptions about their child's gender. While online engagement throws up additional complexities in considerations of privacy and publicity, the capacity to regulate the content of their 'queer commentary' in digital stories also affords new opportunities.

> Amalgamating politics and feeling in a way that requires constant syncretic gestures and movements, queer commentary has tried to drive into visibility both the cultural production of sexuality and the social context of feeling.
> (Berlant & Warner, 1995, pp. 346–347)

Digital stories combine philosophical abstract issues with heartfelt descriptions of everyday life, a manifestation of the cultural engagement to which Berlant and Warner refer.

Digitally mediated identities

Digital storytelling is mediated by technology in several ways. Digital tools are used throughout production, creating a digital artefact that can be watched by many more people than a face-to-face performance. Digital devices (DVD & TV) and platforms (internet) amplify broadcast potential. It is principally alterations to modes of sharing, moving from face-to-face screenings to widespread online distribution, which alters storyteller's conceptualisation of both audiences and publics. Meyrowitz (1985) argues that the mediating effects of technology mean that we are no longer bounded by Goffman's 'definitions of situations' in which we are physically co-present, hence there is a merging of front and back regions and formerly separate social situations. Where previously being co-located in different geographic spaces allowed locker room conversations (Goffman's example) to be contained backstage, expanded social networks enabled by online communication allow that, potentially, mum and wife might 'overhear' ribald comments intended for mates. Van den Berg argues that ICTs (information and communication technology) have bearing on identity construction because they change the definition of the situation, expanding a range of possible role choices:

> ...on the one hand individuals get more freedom and flexibility to choose roles in given situations. This means they may choose more freely what they want to do (and in turn, by effect, ultimately who they are). At the same time, however, this places an ever-bigger burden of choice on these individuals. The sum total of all the roles we may play in life is enlarged, thus dramatically expanding the necessity for human beings of merging the vast amount of separate roles they play into some form of a combined self.
>
> (Van den Berg, 2008, p. 75)

For queer digital storytellers, particularly those who have experienced significant marginalisation, the expanded opportunity to play different roles, and the means to control self-representation, is simultaneously alluring, intimidating and liberating. In the following illustration, digital storytelling provides a mechanism for speaking while remaining safe from face-to-face incursions and/or public vitriol:

> Naturally face-to-face is harder. The process of doing this digi story was much like writing it down or in a book – the viewer could choose to connect to it... but not interrupt or avoid you like they could in person. It was a way to express what we needed to say (hopefully with some emotion [that] connect[s] to an audience members' compassion) and not be dependent on an outcome or a response... we didn't have to be connected to or subjected to anyone's opinion.
>
> (Molly, email interview, 2012)

Molly and Brendan are able to exploit their pseudonymity (a textual approach to publicly maintaining privacy that I will discuss in more detail shortly) to 'say what they needed to say'. They didn't wish to engage in discussion. However, they hope their story nevertheless speaks across difference, catalysing slow change that will make the world more accepting of their little girl.

Articulating a coherent identity is especially problematic for identities that transgress rigidly constructed social boundaries. However, in addressing multiple publics networked through use of technology, stigmatised people deal with previously unforeseen difficulties. Molly found that representations of her daughter's gender identity became unexpectedly complicated when she had what she calls a 'proud mummy moment' that caused her to upload some photos of her kids to her Facebook page. Later she heard from a friend of an unpleasant incident:

> There was a party... with a group of people that I went to school with... that knew me from years ago. And it was the middle of the night, and they said *'Oh, I'm friends with "Molly" on Facebook!'*. Somehow we must have come up in the conversation... *'Let me show you this'*. (They) pulled up my page, and were looking at pictures of [my daughter] going *'That's a dude. That's a dude. Oh, look what they've done to this kid!'*.
>
> (Molly, interview, 2010)

Molly immediately removed the photos and then, upon further consideration, deleted her Facebook account completely. She resented the intrusion into a space that had until then been for celebrating friendship and the ubiquitous idiosyncrasies of parenthood. She is nevertheless heavily reliant on other online networks for support:

> We have a support group that regularly sees all parents within that group communicating in a closed forum discussing ideas and challenges... which has proved to be a life saver at times for many of us.
>
> (Molly, interview, 2010)

Molly wonders what impact their digital story may have had on the exschool friends, imbued as it is with all the subtle complexities of loving and learning from a child who is simply and unapologetically 'different'. While Molly didn't feel safe enough to experiment with this strategy by sharing it on Facebook, she feels happy to present it pseudonymously on *Rainbow Family Tree* and on the *What's Your Story?* DVD, where context influences how the story is interpreted. The manner in which the story is constructed also elicits (though does not guarantee) a sympathetic interpretation. For Molly and Brendan, this degree of control over *distribution* is as significant as control over how their daughter is constructed with words and pictures in the *production* of her story. They eventually undertook similar selective representation in their approach to Facebook:

> I recently reactivated the [Facebook] account as I really find that I am needing it for networking with my business... so [I] have culled my list of friends to only people that I really do know... and [by] removing pics of my children.
>
> (Molly, email correspondence)

Where boyd (2008b) suggests we have no social script for the technologically mediated convergence of publics, digital storytellers, through networked identity work, are writing their own scripts. They challenge prevailing 'definitions of the situation' (gender norms, sexuality and wellbeing) with their digitally mediated content. Meanwhile, carefully managed production and distribution processes establish new understandings of privacy and publicness. Storytellers have potential to play different roles in different spaces (e.g. maintaining a profile for a specific online dating audience, versus a more broadly acceptable profile for Facebook) or to merge the separate roles they play. Curated exhibitions of selfhood also afford greater possibility for Intimate Citizenship 3.0.

Curated exhibitions of selfhood

Van den Berg and Meyrowitz (ibid. above) alongside many other scholars of social interaction highlight numerous differences between face-to-face and online presentations of self. Many scholars also highlight similarities (see Baym, 2010). For example Hogan points out that, just as individuals attenuate their face-to-face performance for different audiences and social situations, they may limit the digital information they make available to a 'lowest common denominator' that endeavours to befit all potential audiences online.[4] In this, digital storytellers are at something of an advantage in that they consciously consider the impact of their stories on multiple publics and the potential ramifications of their disclosures. Hogan also argues that the enduring and searchable dimensions of online identity 'artefacts' classifies them as 'representations' rather than 'performances':

> ... it is useful to distinguish between performance as ephemeral act and performance as recorded act. Once a performance has been recorded, the nature of the performance has altered. It may still be a presentation of self, and undoubtedly it continues to signify an individual. However, it no longer necessarily bounds the specific audience who were present when the performance took place. Instead, it can be taken out of a situation and replayed in a completely different context.
>
> (Hogan, 2010, p. 380)

As a result of these distinctions, Hogan proposes that online spaces, characterised by third-party mediation, are like 'curators' of a personal 'exhibition' (again, distinguishing it from physically located 'performance').

> In exhibition spaces content is submitted to a data repository; people post status updates to Facebook, upload pictures to Picasa.com or Flickr.com and post articles to a blog. This latter content may be produced and submitted with a specific audience in mind, but those who view and react to this content may be different from those for whom it was intended (if it was intended for anyone in particular to begin with).
>
> (Hogan, 2010, p. 381)

While this curation by a digital third party is pertinent to my case studies, I wish to consider the possibility of storytellers curating their own self-representations, firstly (during the production phase) through careful construction of digital story texts and secondly (during the distribution phase) through strategic sharing of content and consideration of the contexts in which their exhibitions of self are screened. In a conventional exhibition, artists (like storytellers) are unable to control who views their work or what meaning they might make of it. However, (like storytellers), they are likely to have considered the message they are attempting to communicate and with whom they are attempting to communicate. In the case of artists whose work is intensely autobiographical (like digital storytellers) there is conscious reflection of what to include (make public) and what to withhold (keep private).

Increased agency over identity management and ownership of self-representation allow digital storytellers to engage publicly with a more visible and vocal identity. I reflect upon the consequences of this agency and ownership in the conclusion of this chapter. In the second half of this chapter I consider textual approaches to story production and judicious modes of sharing as utilised by digital storytellers. Combined with their reflective insights into privacy and public participation, these practices are pertinent to a wider population engaging in identity management in an era of social media.

Otherness and outness: A typology

Curated exhibitions of selfhood are apparent in the selective representations undertaken by all storytellers and heightened in the case of storytellers who perceive themselves at risk of direct discrimination and prejudice. Most queer people are already accustomed to tweaking their self-representation in different contexts as reflected in responses like this:

> Depends on the context totally. I don't hide my sexuality, I just don't say anything either way. If I am asked about my partner I make it clear we are a gay couple and remain matter of fact about things. Then it's their problem not mine if they feel awkward as a result. I identify as Lesbian with family, friends and many work colleagues, and at my gigs, in my social activities, choirs I belong to... I would prefer to be out in most, if not all, contexts of my life just as a positive public statement in general. But I need my job. I have spoken to my boss and the CEO about these feelings of frustration and the confusion I feel at being out with colleagues but not with all the volunteers, placement students and clients. I have given them IDAHO posters and talked about IDAHO etc... but left it with them to decide if they will display them... It feels stronger to be out even though I get angry and down and frustrated about lack of full equal rights yet and homophobic comments and attitudes in society and at work, in the media, at rallies etc.
>
> (Claire, email correspondence, 2012)

Digital equivalents of being 'other' or 'out' follow a similarly complex pattern to face-to-face identity management. Lange, in a study of participants who regularly post content to YouTube, notes the multimodal fashion in which they curate their online exhibitions:

Some participants exhibited 'publicly private' behaviour, in which video makers' identities were revealed, but content was relatively private because it was not widely accessed. In contrast, 'privately public' behaviour involved sharing widely accessible content with many viewers, while limiting access to detailed information about video producers' identities.

(Lange, 2008, p. 361)

Like Lange, I have been able to discern intersections and discordances in the way people manage their digital identities – both textual (production) and social (distribution). A typology of 'otherness and outness' considers the ways people manipulate images and audio to restrict or reveal personal information in their stories (categorised as 'visible', 'bounded' or 'pseudonymous') and the processes undertaken to share their content (categorised as 'targeted', 'ad hoc' or 'proxy').[5]

Textual approaches to production

Every element of a digital story represents a directorial choice, from which story to tell, which characters to include, what images to use, how they are framed, how quickly or slowly they will be edited together, transitions and visual effects and whether to include music and sound effects. These textual decisions constitute material negotiations of privacy and publicness that are laden with richly evocative cultural significance. Creating a story requires the complicity of other central cast members, many of whom are exposed to significant social risks by association. Storytellers are encouraged to seek the permission of all family members and friends who are represented in personal photographs or identified by name. In addition to whatever risks may be associated with being public – what I describe as *visible* representation – the ideas or life experiences that underpin the story are invariably discussed and, should other cast members not agree upon central turning-points, there is likely to be discord. However, storytellers are discerning.

Rather than consider every individual cast member or every disparate group among their prospective audience, they consider what Hogan regards as two discrete groups: 'those for whom we seek to present an idealised front and those who may find this front problematic' (Hogan, 2010, p. 383). Storytellers whose 'idealised front' is contentious may edit out aspects of the story or manipulate photos to de-identify other actors – an approach I describe as *bounded* representation. Other storytellers perceive some aspect of themselves or their families as socially disparaged to the extent that they wish to maintain at least partial anonymity. These storytellers experience a great degree of social 'otherness' and, because they don't feel safe 'outing' themselves to unknown publics, they are precluded from everyday-activist opportunities in face-to-face contexts. Partly as a consequence of this marginalisation they are highly motivated to catalyse social change. While they remain aware that specific friends and family members (familiar publics) could recognise their stories they can nevertheless use *pseudonymous* representation in order to speak to an imagined unknown public.

Visibility: Growing into activism

Choosing to be identifiable in a digital story that reveals personal vulnerabilities is a marker of social capital. As Jacqui (the queer-activist-mum-blogger I introduced in Chapter 2) points out, 'putting yourself out there' for a cause generally requires the support and consensus of family and friends. Jacqui and her partner have had numerous discussions about whether their activism puts their kids unfairly at risk:

> ...it's the big-bogey man thing...in the back of your mind, if you take it to the extreme it's that some nutter out there is going to take offence and track you down and come and kill your kids...you've got way more chance of your kids getting hit by a car on the way to school...but it's 'a miniscule chance of a catastrophic thing'.
>
> (Tomlins, interview, 2011)

Here stranger danger and fear of paedophiles is linked with speaking out as a gay and lesbian parent, but this is also a widespread fear shared by heterosexual parents. After the 'Idaho 2011' March in Adelaide and prior to the next public rally there was a lively debate on a *Rainbow Family Tree* forum 'To Rally or not to Rally: that is the question'. Sophie (a parent and RFT member) started the thread:

> A big part of me does not want [my daughter] exposed to that sort of hate and violence. I can imagine it will be scary and confronting for us let alone a 6 year old... Another chunk of me wonders whether shielding her from that is the right thing to do. We are blessed to live in a supportive environment. People don't hurl abuse at us, we aren't shunned or pointed at in the streets but we know that it is not like that for all people in all places. That's part of the reason we

attend the rallies, to point that out and to fight for people who are unable to.

(Sophie, excerpt from blog post, 2011, quoted with permission)

Sophie is concerned primarily about the impact of homophobic violence on her child. She also expresses some parental angst and unresolved guilt about her role – after all, it is arguably a 'choice' to be visible as a queer family and everyday activists. Many parents choose to conceal (or not reveal) their family structure, especially when they are aware that the context of potential activism (e.g. a staunchly Catholic school) is an unreceptive one. Sophie chose to attend the rally with her wife and daughter and all went well. Further comments on the thread reveal that another member of *Rainbow Family Tree*, previously unknown to the family, helped shepherd them past the Street Christians who were again in attendance. Interestingly neither of these *Rainbow Family Tree* members has made digital stories. However, they regularly share thoughts about everyday activism on the site. This is an example of the kind of communal empowerment that can evolve from personal online story sharing.

Meanwhile Jacqui draws attention to another common fear among parents who choose the personal exposure of everyday activism as a means of lobbying for social change:

> ...as the kids get older and start to understand what's going on...we had a big piece in...'The Age' [a widely distributed Victorian newspaper] yesterday...Corin stood over my shoulder and we talked about it as I was writing it, because he's in there...& so he's in school today, don't think anybody said anything but last time they did because there was a massive picture of us. [This is a] different kind of thing to manage, does this mean Corin's gonna get teased more in the playground? That's the fear...and again I think that's a manageable thing...
>
> (Tomlins, interview, 2011)

Clearly there is sliding scale of risk associated with differing degrees of exposure. Marching in a rally (where people might recognise you but no one automatically knows your name) is different to having your name and photograph published in a newspaper. The likelihood of being abducted and murdered is different to the likelihood of being teased or bullied. Many digital storytellers undertake a journey both consciously and unconsciously, weighing risk against reward: a journey from secrecy to advocacy. As they become more visible they also become more culturally engaged. The journey Kate undertook between making her first and second story is profound, but quite typical.

I first met Kate when she was 17. She came to a digital storytelling workshop I was running for 'Pink Parents' and friends. Her dad dropped her off because she had a broken arm and couldn't drive. He brought gourmet pastries for everyone to share and I got the impression that he would like to stay and make a story himself. In the first 'getting to know you' round, Kate told how she'd written a feature article in 'Dolly' (an Australian teen monthly) magazine about her unusual family structure – three parents, being a mum and two gay dads. She eventually made this into *Kate's Story*. She describes being quite open about her family in primary school but, upon arriving at high school, she learnt quickly to share this information with only a select few friends. Much later, when I got to know her better, I realised that this selective disclosure had caused a great deal of grief – pain that she rarely speaks of. Even now, as a confident young woman, she describes feeling guilty on occasion should she choose to ignore colloquial expressions of homophobia among her peers. Kate wrote accompanying description of the production and distribution process when she uploaded her story:

> I decided to make this documentary to not only give the children of same-sex parented families a voice, but to show and express the extent to which same-sex parents and their children are not only excluded, but made to be invisible in environments such as childcare centres and primary and secondary schools. It is not only gay people who suffer discrimination; their families do as well, whether that be their parents, their children or the mother or father of their children.

Later, during the recruitment phase of the *What's Your Story?* initiative, I asked Kate if she'd like to make another story, perhaps exploring some of the responses she'd had to her first.

She ended up making *That's so Gay!* (Figure 5.3), which is similar to her first story but more explicit about the consequences of homophobic language, in particular, the popular and purportedly innocent usage of 'that's so gay!' to mean bad, wrong or stupid. In an early draft of the script she used extensive quotes from Harvey Milk and we talked about what effect she was hoping to have on an audience. I realised that she wanted to strengthen her message with words from an authority but we noticed that the story lost some of its power and warmth when she used

Figure 5.3 That's so Gay!

these quotes. With a little encouragement she worked on maintaining her first person voice. Even so the story lacks the vulnerability of her first story, where her voice is wobbly as she struggles to control emotion. As Kate gains confidence in her second story and imagines a more explicit target audience and purpose for her story, she loses the connection with the pain she originally experienced and takes on the voice of a brave spokesperson for a cause. While the first story was shared with friends and family and the limited audience of my online blog, Kate has screened the second story in a variety of conference and workshop contexts where she has been invited to speak. The second story's direct message about a popular phrase is pertinent in these contexts as it addresses homophobia in schools more explicitly than her personal story of feeling invisible in a family that is not generally recognised by society. The difference is subtle – the first story addresses absence, while the second addresses something audible and distinct. As such they represent differing activist strategies and while this was not something Kate considered in any great depth the two stories nevertheless chart a course of increasing visibility and amplified advocacy in Kate's self-representations.

Bounded representations

While many storytellers move through different approaches to self-representation at various stages of production, all storytellers effectively engage in selective representation simply by considering what to leave out or gloss over in their stories. However, in contrast to these routine and inescapable curatorial decisions, I use 'bounded' to refer to the careful and deliberate containment of identifying information that takes into consideration the 'lowest common denominator' – that is, the lowest threshold of sensitivity or negative response – among imagined audiences (Hogan, 2010). I offer four examples of bounded stories – the first made by an HIV-positive man, the second by a trans man and the third and fourth (made several years apart) made by a gay non-biological father. In these examples, storytellers limit the viewers' access to identifiable information in order to protect family members, while nevertheless affirming the significance of those family members.

During the *Positive Stories* initiative Greg (who also made *Greg's Sermon*) made *Me, Mum and Dad*. It is a reverent tribute to his parents who volunteered throughout the AIDS crisis of the mid-1980s. He originally included a montage of other family members who he thanks for being supportive. However, he was concerned that his young nieces and nephews might experience what he calls 'retribution':

> School yard kid sees his other school mate by chance in something that his Mum and Dad are looking at on YouTube. And suddenly he's marked as – his Uncle's a faggot; his Uncle's got AIDS; his Uncle....
> (Greg, interview, 2011)

After lengthy reflection, Greg decided to substitute these family album photos, endearing as they were, with images he had taken of flowers in his garden. The voiceover remains unchanged: 'I would not be here without you Mum and Dad...without my sisters, brothers...and extended families and my friends...you are my life...I am the reason I keep going...'. Greg worked with the editor to overlay complementary text ('nieces', 'nephews', etc.) that floats over the flower images. In this considered fashion Greg substitutes something encoded with significance to his family for the more conventional family snapshots. While the snapshots, as symbols of family affinity, may have been a more familiar trope, Greg seizes control over the information available to an unknown audience while maintaining the message of affirmation that he is targeting at his familial audience.

Sean, a young trans man, uses similar bounded representation of his family as a means of affirming his respect for them, in *Back to Happiness* (Figure 5.1). In his description of two families (one biological, the other his chosen trans family of friends) he uses numerous identifiable photographs of both groups. He includes snaps of a birthday celebrated with a little niece and nephew alongside snaps of friends in the trans community, resplendent in black ties and frocks. However, his father did not wish to be identified in the story and Sean debated whether or not to blur his image in the birthday party snapshot.

> That seemed to imply shame and I didn't think Dad was ashamed, more that he was simply paranoid about the internet...and at the end of the day he has the right to have control over how and where he is represented just as I do...
>
> (Sean, interview, 2010)

Sean eventually decided to discretely crop the group shot. His empowered choice in representing his families as he sees them (loving and diverse), while simultaneously respecting their rights, demonstrates listening across difference and a sophisticated understanding towards personal and collective representation.

Our Conception Story was made in 2007 as part of the small pilot digital storytelling workshop that Kate was also involved in. Josh (his chosen pseudonym) is one of the few men who are actively involved in a loosely knit community of 'pink parents' and is also a professional who has written extensively on identity and heteronormativity. Josh's consideration of visibility/invisibility is compounded by the fact that he is a single gay dad of non-biological children who, for various legal reasons, may not be publicly identified. Josh wished to find a creative means of including the children's perspectives and the warmth of their presence without using personal photos. The children did some drawings and offered suggestions for the script. Josh narrates as the drawings are piled slowly one after the other on a piece of green lawn. In the following excerpts, I have italicised words that are subtly emphasised and explored in the narration:

> ... After a while you told us we were your *parents*. You said: 'a parent is someone who makes your lunch, and puts you to bed and takes you to school. You are my parents'. You told us we were a *family*. The tricky part was coming to terms with the ways that something so simply given by you could be taken away by others... but, despite that, we live as a family.

Josh refers here not only to the capacity the legal system has to interfere with the relationships he is building with the boys but also to the way subtle judgements made by teachers, shopkeepers and other parents, in a range of everyday encounters, undermine the validity of their relationships as 'family'. After fond reference to both adults and children 'doing each other's heads in' Josh continues:

> ... You still say to us: You are the best dads ever. Even though we don't often use that word *'dad'*, we know it means *family* when you say it. We conceived of this family together. Four people together, learning, growing, loving. This is our *conception* story.

Josh questions conventional social narratives of what it means to be a 'brother' or a 'dad' (most often assumed to be biological relationships) and what constitutes an acceptable story of 'family' and 'conception'. He bridges the gap between normative nuclear structures of family and his evolving domestic clan:

> As a family of two men and two boys, it often seems that people presume it to be axiomatic that we will describe how our family came into being. Yet to us this is most often a redundant question – we know who we are and how we relate to each other. This digidoc captures the complexities of our conception story in subtle ways that render our family visible for us to see, whilst not necessarily telling all of the story that other people might like to see. As such, it celebrates

our family in a public way, whilst retaining the privacy that we wish and need.

(Josh, blog post, 2007)

Certainly it is true that Josh has chosen to withhold key narrative clues that might help an audience make sense of the story, but he felt strongly that including this information would imply acceptance of social codes he already felt coerced by – the presumption that non-biological families are not 'real' families. His refusal to clarify constitutes a challenge that is simultaneously recalcitrant and subversive.

Two years later I asked Josh if he'd like to be involved in the *What's Your Story?* online workshop. He was able to offer advice to other parents who were wrangling the question of how best to represent their children while maintaining their privacy. He was also involved in a variety of forum discussions as people swapped ideas about the themes and anecdotes they were considering developing into stories.

I had been planning on doing an updated version of our last one...now that we have three children, but...I feel like telling the story, even if it is useful for others, is actually very wearing – the day-to-day effort of dealing with being rendered invisible is enough – I am not sure if I need to rehearse it again in a digidoc. (because sometimes it feels like it just becomes a narrative which disconnects me from what it is actually like to be our family)

Josh reveals the emotional labour that goes into negotiating an unconventional identity in both everyday life and in a digital story. He also touches upon an elision that resonates with Reddy's distinction between emotion and their representatives, emotives (Reddy, 1997). Josh implies that shaping an experience into a narrative actually removes him from the lived, performative experience he is attempting to describe.

Despite his reservations, Josh did explore the parameters of family in his second story, *Our Family Matters*, this time in collaboration with his ex-partner and co-parent. The story this time includes photographs from family holidays in New York and San Francisco. Unlike most family photos they are largely taken over shoulders, with faces turned away from camera, looking out at landmarks, thereby rendering the children unidentifiable. Some photos have faces blurred. The two men speak the same script simultaneously and initially this was quite confusing because they were recorded separately and overlapped awkwardly. Significant post-production brought the voices into synch and allowed one voice to dominate at any one time with first one, then the other, slightly louder. This technical precision in some ways reflects the ongoing negotiations the two men undertake in collaborating as ex-partners and co-parents in a world that doesn't recognise their relationship to one another or the children. This is what Josh had to say about the story in the booklet that accompanied the DVD:

> In speaking together as two parents, our voices demonstrate both the strengths and harmony of our family unit, whilst also recognizing the differences within it. In so doing, the adult voices of our family do not reveal all there is to tell about our family, but rather show that as a family we gaze back at the rest of the world with strength and conviction.

The narration describes several encounters between 'family' and 'world'. In the first, a man outside Stonewall (a bar now celebrated as the site of legendary rebellion by the gay community against homophobic laws and policing in 1969) yells out 'this is the gay area, not the family area!'. In the second, a flight attendant fails to understand their family structure, assuming that they were two straight men with several children each, or perhaps 'mannies' (a colloquial masculinised version of 'nanny'). In reflecting back upon how things had changed for them in the period between the two stories the men conclude:

> Nothing much seems to have changed for us when it comes to other people in the past three years... what has changed however is our increased sense of family... At the end of the day, the five of us know who we are and what we stand for. What the rest of the world makes of us doesn't have to be our business.

The constitutive aspect of digital storytelling is apparent here. While Josh expressed concern that articulating experience as narrative functions to disconnect him from lived reality, it nevertheless consolidates and brings into being something that is otherwise invisible. One the one hand this affirms the family's experience of themselves while on the other it makes them visible as a family to a wider community. When I asked Josh who the stories were made for, he responded:

> ...for the children and for myself and ex partner. They weren't necessarily intended to serve an educative function for other people, though certainly I was cognisant of the fact there would be an

audience (and hence the framing of the narratives in a mode that could provide knowledge/information to others). I guess, to put it most succinctly, they were for 'us', but I was mindful that a 'them' would view them and hence they needed to tell our story in a way that was both special and unique to us, without them [the stories] giving too much of our story to the world. And I guess, in truth, they also make an 'us' – they make a claim about 'us' publicly, so in that sense they were always already about a viewing other who would receive us as 'us'.

(Josh, email correspondence, 2012)

In their complex use of visual and linguistic symbols, both stories illustrate the simultaneously affirming and provocative potential of digital stories. The negotiations Josh, his children and his ex-partner undertake in order to know one another and be known as 'family' offer illustration of the networked identity work central to digital storytelling. Through bounded representation Josh is able to balance the needs of his family with his needs as an everyday activist, while challenging on both theoretical and textual levels, the normative parameters of 'family'.

Pseudonymity: Being private in public

A pseudonymous approach to digital storytelling takes place when storytellers modify images, words, voices or sounds in order to conceal identities from audiences (excepting close friends and some family members who may still recognise the storyteller via the particularities of the story itself). In face-to-face encounters, storytellers who wish to maintain pseudonymity are often forced to speak via an advocate or institution (distancing themselves physically). However, digital storytelling allows them to represent themselves. In the following, I describe two examples: the first of aforementioned parents of a transsexual child, the second being an HIV = positive storyteller.

In making *Blue for Boys? Pink for Girls?* (Figure 3.3) Molly and Brendan were aware that their daughter, upon arriving at adulthood as a legally affirmed woman, might not wish to acknowledge her transsexual origins. They initially used baby photos, or over-the-shoulder or wide shots, but after advice from their family lawyer they decided to blur all images of the child. They were told of a similar American legal case in which a mother was sued by her former-spouse for exposing the child to the risk of publicly being identified as transsexual. They had also heard of family court judges criticizing parents who failed to adequately consider the child's best interest by publicly acknowledging their child's 'predicament'. Molly and Brendan wished to make a story to raise awareness of gender stereotypes and transsexualism and communicate their unconditional acceptance of their daughter:

> When my husband and I sat down to write this story, I had visions of the opening scene from 'The Lion King': when the monkey holds the baby for all in the animal kingdom to see as the mother and father look on with pride, love and adoration. This is how proud I am of our daughter and what she has taught us.
>
> (Molly, DVD booklet, 2009)

The storytellers, as a family and in conversation with a wider community (including the lawyer), worked through a series of strategies that enable them to bridge the gap between pride for their child and concern for the child's privacy both now and in the future. Molly carefully chose photos that expressed the child's joyful experiments in gender performance rather than featuring angst-ridden close ups, although her narration makes it clear that the child's exploration was not an easy ride: 'We heard you pray, asking the angels to turn you into a girl...but we kept on telling you that you were a boy. We were wrong...we just didn't understand...'. The family elected a friend to voice their carefully worded script, rather than risk the mother's voice being identified. Her insight into their journey is reflected in the tremors and cracks in her voice that, in turn, evoke audience empathy. Most importantly, throughout the process of creating their story, they swapped insights and ideas with other digital storytellers on the *Rainbow Family Tree* website, an experience that enabled them to feel supported and empowered as parents and storytellers.

In *My Secret Story* Frank shares the Catholic origins of his deeply internalised homophobia. His description of a drunken encounter with his ex resonates with many audience members; only the consequences for Frank were exceptionally dramatic – he became HIV-positive. Frank wrote a short piece to accompany the story:

> Being involved in digital story telling has been very challenging for me especially because I chose to tell one of the stories that if I could turn back time I would change. The story of how I became HIV positive and the headspace I was in at the time.

I also live in the countryside and while open about being gay, I keep my HIV status to myself. I was torn between using personal photos or representative images, being out and proud of where I am now, but not wanting to risk being labelled by a disease and ultimately a mistake. So when I somewhat de identified the film I initially felt weak yet relieved.

I could have talked about HIV and being a nurse, the challenge of sex and disclosure, the feeling of going back into the closet, but the kind caring religious little gay boy wants people to help the next generation. More positive role models, respected relationships and happy kids.

Being part of a group was vital for inspiration, persistence and sharing supportive people.

P.S Wish I'd known about P.E.P, at the time. (Post Exposure Prophylaxis)

(Frank, storyteller statement, 2011)

The revelations Frank makes, being both sexually explicit and critiquing personal and dark mental states, would be construed by most as 'private'. Conversely he uses creative and pragmatic strategies to maintain privacy so that he can share his story publicly. Photographs are obscured with a black box titled 'Me' and combinations of zooms and filters represent 'disturbed' mental states. There are no revealing 'thank-yous' in the credits and even the personal copyright attribution was omitted. Frank describes feeling a little shamed by choosing to conceal his identity but was pragmatic in pointing out that his future economic wellbeing was dependent on concealing his HIV status from his employers and local community. In any case it can be argued that, by de-identifying his story, he was able to give a detailed account of the extremely private emotional landscape (and thoughts that he didn't even acknowledge to himself at the time) that he believes contributed to his seroconversion. This description of anxiety, ambivalence and mental unrest is directly pertinent to current public health agendas and addresses with great poignancy an issue that may otherwise only be articulated as a bullet point in a HIV/AIDS policy document (Prestage et al., 2009, 2010). Greater control over self-representation, through pseudonymity, affords a voice that counters shame – and enables the expression of profoundly personal, even private, insights in public.

Modes of content sharing

Storytellers consider many factors, ranging from immediate and practical through to imagined and abstract, as they decide how and where to share their stories. These contexts include screenings at which the storytellers are present (a theatrical launch; showing the website to a friend) and many other unknown contexts physically distanced from the storyteller (screening of a compilation DVD in a workshop; online viewings by strangers). In practice, they choose strategically among three modes of distribution – targeted, ad hoc and proxy. Targeted stories are produced and distributed for clearly defined purposes and with specific audiences in mind. Ad hoc sharing tends to be more spontaneous, shaped by opportunities that arise unexpectedly in a variety of forums. Proxy sharing endeavours to maintain pseudonymity by using third parties, platforms or occasions (like the *Rainbow Family Tree* website or theatrical launches organised by auspicing agencies) to mediate distribution of stories.

Targeted sharing

Targeted sharing is intended to provoke discussions of a contentious issue – whether that is between family members, friends or representatives of parliament. Examples include the previously mentioned *Where did we come from?* and *Rowan's Family Tree* both made at least partly with members of parliament as prospective audiences and with law reform as an objective. I asked Bronwen whether she thought her targeted approach had the desired effect.

> Politically? I don't know whether it shifted any of the committee members? Our submission was quoted quite a lot in the final report of the committee – how much did the story have to do with that? It's hard to say. It's much easier to quote words than something visual, so maybe the impact of the story is more nebulous because it can't be so easily recorded – but that's not to discount that maybe it did have an impact?
>
> (Bronwen, email correspondence, 2012)

Interestingly, Bronwen highlights the technical and material limitations of the digital storytelling form. She was frustrated that she had to screen the story from a laptop with poor speakers and, under pressure, screened a version that was not her final. The fact that the story is an audio-visual digital document clearly makes it harder to transcribe and quote. Despite this, Bronwen illuminates the story's impact on an unanticipated counter-public or intimate public composed of 'friends with kids':

> I think it's been valuable and supportive for friends with kids – both straight and queer – to look at, and talk about families, and different kinds of families – I know my sister in law did that with her daughter when we posted it.
> (Bronwen, email correspondence, 2012)

Bronwen's response reflects the difficulties of measuring impact of a story on any audience, let alone corresponding social change. However, shifts that occurred closer to home, changes that were not originally among her stated objectives, are more tangible:

> It gave me some ideas for different ways of talking about and presenting who we are – together. I [also] think it gave R's non-bio grandparents a stronger sense of being part of our family, sort of an acceptance of their importance/place in R's – and our – life.
> (Bronwen, email correspondence, 2012)

These small familial changes signal social change on a *micro* scale. People that have maintained silence in the face of homophobia previously, are more inclined to speak up as advocates when they know and love somebody who is affected by bigotry.

Kate, creator of *Kate's story* and *That's so Gay!*, offers a tangible measure of the influence of her story:

> **Kate's update:** I have recently had more success with my digi-doc – an ex-teacher of mine has agreed to show the documentary at a staff meeting to encourage teachers to be aware of alternative family structures. Study of alternative family structures will also be added to curriculum for the subject Health Studies for year twelves at my old high school. All inspired by my story!

This feedback has clearly had an impact on Kate, enabling greater advocacy. She has publicly affirmed her pride in her family and this ownership has helped her put aside some of the guilt she felt about the years that she hid them from her friends.

Greg, creator of *Me, Mum and Dad* and *Greg's Sermon*, speaks about the mixture of face-to-face and online environments in which his story has been screened:

> I [wrote] an article for Talkabout about the process (which is the NSW HIV magazine). I put the links [to my story] on [the online publication]... I have put it on two different Private Facebook HIV positive groups to high praise. At the launch... of *Positive Stories* I was overwhelmed with the response from everyone... so were Mum and Dad who came over for the event. I have shared my story with nieces and nephews who are teens and I felt a strong urge to educate them... I have two nephews under twenty who are gay and have expressed a lot of pride in their 'old' uncle for telling his story about being positive... and it also has radically changed how they have treated my parents!
>
> (Greg, email correspondence, 2011)

Greg's approach to distribution might be described as ad hoc in that he followed up on a variety of unanticipated opportunities to share his story. However, the activist zeal with which he applies himself pulls him into closer alignment with the 'targeted' category. He believes his story deserves a variety of audiences, while ad hoc distributors are often surprised by the places their stories unexpectedly travel.

Ad hoc sharing

Some storytellers think very little about where their stories might be seen. They grant permission for them to be uploaded with a degree of blind faith and return to their daily lives. When they receive feedback, particularly from unforeseen audiences, they are surprised.

> [on Facebook]... a comment from a Korean friend [who I haven't seen for many years] who lives in the US – she reposted to all of her newsfeed too. [Also] someone from playgroup... talked about watching it over and over with her daughter – a way of connecting [her] with a family that is in some ways (though not all!) similar to her own...
>
> (Bronwen, email correspondence, 2012)

Many storytellers do not necessarily think of their digital story as a form of cultural participation or as part of a wider social discourse. Mahdi, a gay Muslim immigrant and storyteller of *Islam and Me* reveals a casual and unexpected moment of civic engagement:

> Ian Hunter [gay Labour MP in South Australia] came up to me one day and said 'omigod your story is beautiful!' I said thankyou! I'd kind of forgotten all about it after showing a few friends... so it was really... out of the blue... I was proud!
> (Mahdi, interview, 2011)

While Mahdi has gone on to use digital storytelling in his own work as a community health worker and certainly sees it as a vehicle for expression of marginalised voices, he is reluctant to actively share his own story.

> I don't want to seem too egoistic... self-indulgent... yes it feels like blowing your own trumpet... maybe agencies can do that but it's difficult to do that myself... my story is quite a personal one...
> (Mahdi, interview, 2011)

Interestingly, Mahdi's ambivalence about distributing his work is reflected in his approach to the text itself – apparently pseudonymous. Mahdi uses only publicly available, non-personal images in his story of reconciling sexuality with spirituality. His narration speaks of gay people being persecuted and killed in many countries and initially it seemed that his choice to use generic images in his story was a means of protecting his identity and that of his friends and family, still in Malaysia. This seemed at odds with the use of his real name and photograph on his *Rainbow Family Tree* profile, which is directly linked to his story. In an interview, Mahdi reveals that his choice was not so much political as pragmatic. He didn't have many photos of his childhood in Malaysia and certainly none that captured the desperate and lonely mood he was aiming for. More importantly, perhaps, he also spoke of being a bit 'shy' about making his story, not especially wanting it to be 'about me' but nevertheless needing to draw on personal experience in order to speak to others who may be struggling with similar conflicts. Other storytellers report similar reticence:

> I do hang back a little bit [from distributing my film]. I don't know, I think it's more about this weird thing that I do... I feel compelled to put myself out there and do what I do... but on the other

hand I'm still quite shy... yeah it's an oxymoron, two parts of me battling... It's silly...

(Ad'm, interview, 2011)

The shyness many storytellers spoke of when discussing their ad hoc distribution strategies is actually one of the largest obstacles to the use of digital stories as a tool for everyday activism. While this 'tall-poppy syndrome' – or, in this case, a reluctance to be seen as remarkable – emerges in many interviews, some storytellers report being reassured by the collective context in which their individual story travels, for example on a DVD compilation or on the *Rainbow Family Tree* website.

Proxy sharing

Auspicing agencies, advocates or web spaces – proxies – may distribute pseudonymous stories widely as long as their origins are not traceable. Both Frank, and Molly and Brendan, have active profiles on *Rainbow Family Tree* (one under a pseudonym) but the profiles are not linked to their stories. In both cases the storytellers track their story's progress in the world (through reading comments and/or following viewer statistics) but do not promote them personally to audiences using their real names. They are able to engage in activism by pseudonymously sharing their stories with interest groups (especially web-based lobby groups, many of which can be located on Facebook) and encouraging viral circulation by community members. All of the stories made during *What's Your Story?* and *Positive Stories* have been included on a DVD compilation and widely circulated in an educational context. Both ACSA and SHine SA promote the compilations at conferences and in a variety of social service and health sector publications. Both initiatives also celebrated completion with a theatrical screening of the stories.

For storytellers who elect to use both pseudonymity and proxy distribution, attending a physical screening of their own stories (especially in a small community in a small city) is fraught with personal risk. Frank, the pseudonymous author of *My Secret Story* attended the launch of the *Positive Stories* compilation during the Feast Festival. His workshop peers sat on stage for a post-screening community forum and Frank sat among the audience. During the celebratory drinks and nibbles that followed he was witness to both praise and critiques of his story without ever knowing whether anyone recognised him. While this caused some awkwardness, Frank's approach allowed his carefully crafted story to 'stand in' as a sort of proxy for him in face-to-face discussions with audiences.

In a contrasting example of pseudonymity and proxy sharing, Molly and Brendan attended the launch of *What's Your Story?* hoping to identify themselves to select audience members. Sean and Molly had been inspired by one another's stories during the workshops and Sean was particularly keen that his parents have an opportunity to meet some other parents of a trans child. This meeting was a highlight of the launch for all involved.

Agency and ownership

Digital storytellers frequently describe the experience of creating their own story as 'empowering'. This is a term that has become ubiquitous in modern Western societies, particularly in social service sectors, and here I reflect upon what it actually means for participants. In popular usage empowerment is an amorphous concept ranging from feelings of confidence through to the acquisition of tangible skills that enable an individual to have greater control over their life. The following quote describes several intersecting aspects of empowerment: gaining concrete expertise; gaining a sense of independent responsibility; and challenging how one is perceived:

> It's one of the few things I've done in connection to 20 plus years of being positive where the end result was NOT... there you go dear, you poor little AIDS victim, we will do this and do this and do this for you... it's the one thing that I've walked away from and actually felt empowered by because I've learnt skills and it sort of forced me to stand up.
> (Greg, ACSA group evaluation, 2011)

Other participants report feeling empowered as a result of discussions with friends and family members about their stories-in-progress. For some people, this process catalyses conversations that have been avoided for years, often about behaviour or issues that have been steadfastly ignored. Receiving positive feedback from viewers both face-to-face and online is also frequently cited as an empowering occurrence. Sometimes empowerment is experienced as a sense of accomplishment at undertaking and succeeding in a challenging task; sometimes it's a sense of 'doing one's bit' and contributing to social change in a small way. In sum, storytellers speak of several key elements as indicators of empowerment. First, they develop technical skills and social capital. Second, they feel entitled to speak as a representative (of self, or 'people like me'). Third, they fulfil a sense of duty ('I hope that sharing my story helps others'). Fourth, they negotiate confidently with publics (familiar, intimate, counter and unknown).

Empowerment in this context might also be defined as a combination of agency (to define and create a congruent self) and ownership (the right to curate identity on own terms). Through networked identity work, storytellers build bridges across personal and social differences and this activity confers agency. The resulting stories are the outcomes of negotiations among divergent publics and represent an identity that the storyteller can 'own'. This is not to say that they control their self-representation in all contexts (something that is arguably unattainable among digitally mediated networks), rather that they exercise conscious self and social awareness in constructing and sharing a preferred identity narrative. Unlike coherence or authenticity, which are largely conferred by an audience, a storyteller retains agency in the creation of congruent self-representation. Similarly, ownership of this self-representation is manifest in the choice to share with select publics – networks of friends and family as well as imagined unknown allies and antagonists.

While agency and ownership over self-representation in digital stories amplifies empowered cultural participation, it is mostly accessible to a cohort with a pre-existing degree of social capital (well-educated people with a proclivity towards group participation and public sharing) and those nominated by public policy as 'in need'. Further, as a tool for queer everyday activism, digital storytelling can be displaced by many easier options. Spontaneous face-to-face enactments of queerness are arguably less labour-intensive and social participation mediated by digital platforms like blogs, Flickr, Facebook and Twitter require minimal effort and technical aptitude compared to that required of a digital storyteller.

In terms of emotional investment, sharing an anecdote with a sales person in a hardware store is notably less risky than sharing a digitised version of the story with unknown online publics. However, the ramifications for sharing in either space depend on individual perceptions of 'publicness' and 'privacy'. Moreover, these perceptions are a synthesis of personal understandings in combination with diverse understandings among networked publics. 'Oversharing' is not in itself a source of conflict so much as the clash of values regarding privacy and publicness. Sean's dad and Max's grandfather are proud of their progeny. However, they are also of the opinion that 'these things are private and not to be aired in public'. The process of digital storytelling provokes awareness of these socially contingent judgements of preferred identity, publicness and privacy. As a result, many participants start challenging perceptions among their networked publics more actively. This networked identity work constitutes a form of cultural citizenship that, in turn, generates erosive social change.

This chapter has distinguished 'audiences' from 'publics' and detailed a variety of definitions of publics from both theoretical and storyteller perspectives. I canvassed a similar range of understandings of 'privacy' and 'publicness' and offered examples of how storytellers curate their digitally amplified and curated exhibitions of selfhood. Finally, I provided a typology of outness and otherness that catalogues examples of visible, bounded and pseudonymous approaches to textual representation and targeted, ad hoc and proxy modes of sharing content. In sum, I argue that the agency demonstrated by storytellers in constructing their stories and the ownership, apparent in careful distribution, is evidence of a new manifestation of digitally mediated civic engagement. In the following two chapters, I discuss how some of the obstacles to digital storytelling as a tool for everyday activism might be countered as Intimate Citizenship 3.0.

6
Provocations: Digital Storytelling ≠ Social Change

Everyday activists frequently refer to their storytelling as a 'drop in the ocean' or a 'ripple in a pond'. While I have heard these expressions used almost interchangeably, brief consideration reveals that they represent almost opposite ends of a spectrum of hope. 'A drop in the ocean' is typically used as an analogy for the slight significance of one contribution compared with what is needed to affect change. On the other hand a 'ripple in a pond' refers to the continuing and expanding results of an action. If a drop of water represents a story or storyteller then the energy and motion relayed to the proximal drops might be called networked identity work. However, this analogy is not as appropriate as it first appears. Networked identity work relays energy simultaneously across time and space, between people who are both real and imagined, past, present and future. It is hard to think of a natural or visual metaphor that illustrates the kind of social change that is catalysed. While the first five forms I describe in the introduction are to some degree tangible, erosive change takes longer to observe. It is nevertheless observable and perhaps, over time, the impact of networked identity work is also measurable. This chapter reviews, in brief, both the obstacles and opportunities for digital storytelling as a catalyst for social change.

As I noted in the introduction, an underpinning presumption of everyday activism is that sharing divergent personal stories has a persuasive capacity to reshape prevailing conservative attitudes. While this may be a contested presumption, it is nevertheless a common one and not one that I take issue with. Some of the difficulties I detail in the following are characteristic of many modes of rhetorical communication while others arise from postmodern and queer representations of identity. Additional obstacles emerge from current forms of workshop practice while some concerns are pertinent primarily to digital stories as a genre. Thus far, intersecting themes have been examined in discrete chapters (categorised as identity, voice and networked publics), However, in the following, these threads coalesce, with analysis unfolding loosely from the personal (*micro*) to the social (*meso*) and cultural (*macro*). I argue that some of the apparent obstacles to digital storytelling as everyday activism can be re-framed as opportunities. For example, while it seems that coherence in digital storytelling may be an unachievable social imperative, congruence affords self-representation that has a ripple effect upon networked publics catalysing many kinds of social and cultural change.

Micro

Some of the most significant barriers to the use of digital stories as tools for everyday activism occur as digital storytellers negotiate congruence, preferred nominalisations and shared meanings of identity. While some analyses of digital storytelling consider class, race, gender and sexuality, few consider the ramifications in detail and many, many people lack the requisite social capital, confidence or agency to commence involvement in a workshop. Fundamental issues of self-representation, while arguably common to all people, are profoundly exacerbated by social marginalisation. Despite this, digital stories are an example of 'mass self-communication' (Castells, 2007, p. 238) and therefore wield a degree of power in public space.

> The emergence of mass self-communication offers an extraordinary medium for social movements and rebellious individuals to build their autonomy and confront the institutions of society in their own terms and around their own projects.
> (Castells, 2007, p. 249)

While Castells is optimistic about the potential of mass self-communication (like digital stories) to catalyse social movements, he points out that technology, both as a tool and a medium, is nevertheless a social construction and therefore reflects cultural values that privilege autonomy and agency. I take this point up again further as a *macro* issue in discussion of the implications of self-broadcast for social change. In the following, I revisit the most significant issues confronted by storytellers – coherence, nominalisation and negotiating meaning.

'Authenticity', coherence and congruence

A normative social code of conduct challenges us to live logically and rationally from one performance or incarnation of identity to the next; in other words, to be 'authentic' or coherent. Postmodern and queer understandings of identity as fluid and contextual nevertheless conflict with prevailing social discourses like 'inner truth'. Even breakfast cereal packets espouse aspirational philosophy like 'Be happy, be real, be relaxed and be yourself!' ('Be Natural' cereal, Australia, 2012). What exactly does 'real' and 'yourself' look like? How is it performed? Butler (2005) points out that individuals are fundamentally incapable of having anything other than a partial awareness of the multitudinous complexities of their own existence. They are invariably hampered by faulty memory, inadequate language, fears of being misunderstood, social influence and so on. Also, stories have a constitutive influence on culture and a tendency to reinforce existing knowledge and limitations.

> ...the explanations individuals offer of their lives are inevitably shaped by the prevailing norms of discourse within which they operate... social influence shapes not only public action but also private self-understanding. To the degree that this is true, social control takes on a more ominous aspect. For now it appears that the alternatives one recognises as possible or moral are constrained in the marrow of individual self-representation. Those strictures in turn limit personal and political emancipation.
> (Rosenwald & Ochberg, 1992, pp. 4–5)

If telling stories only serves to limit personal potential and perpetuate social norms, then certainly there would be no great utility in sharing personal narratives in pursuit of social change. Butler and other queer theorists offer some optimism by postulating that analysis of the performative nature of identity, and consideration of what function particular gendered and sexualised identity categories serve in a wider social context, may deconstruct this self-perpetuating cycle. Further, I argue that the process of digital storytelling helps many people to see their lives as 'story' and therefore something that can be scripted and replete with imagined possibilities.

Stories make meaning out of mess. Crafted representations of self, while always incomplete and therefore, in a technical sense, incoherent, are nevertheless meaningful to numerous publics, in numerous ways. They build bridges across what are sometimes previously unacknowledged differences. Further, whereas limitations to self-awareness exist on a metaphysical plane, limitations to self-expression are frequently enacted by constantly shifting relationships between self and imagined publics. Networked identity work, as a crucial component of digital storytelling, involves active renegotiations of these limitations, thereby acknowledging social influence while simultaneously describing new worlds.

The notion of coherent identity is quite a conservative construct, at odds with even the most obvious example of evolving identity – 'growing up' from child to teenager to adult. Digital stories, however, are frequently beholden to genre conventions that privilege coherent narrative; further, they are fixed in time and located in space. This rigidity is true both of the world of the story (i.e. 'I was this; then I became that... now I am...') and its screening context (theatre, training room, office, bedroom, etc.). Staking identity in a digital story – alongside any impassioned public announcement made in persistent and searchable form – may later generate accusations of inconsistency and personal incoherence, causing embarrassment or loss of social capital. As many politicians and celebrities can testify, ill-considered public disclosure of stories that conflict with newer iterations of identity may cause discomfort and renewed guilt many years later. However, having choice or agency over the construction of their stories and awareness of them in perpetuity also enables storytellers to own them. Rather than striving for the unachievable goal of authenticity, storytellers can reconcile different versions of themselves on their own terms. Rather than coherence, they attain congruence.

Congruence results from a conscious reconciliation of private and public presentations of self and from considering and understanding one's position, situated among multiple publics. It is reflected in capacity to articulate who, when and how I am; thumbing nose at risk; claiming 'I don't care' status. Where coherence pivots on logical consistency as understood through the eyes of an imagined audience, congruence reflects harmony between disparate representations of self. It considers the ramifications of staking a nominalised self, both positive and negative – this is who I am now, but I may not be this way forever. I reserve the right to 'change my mind' (Valerio, 2003).

In *Sisterhood* Karen pays homage to the sister who supported her through the early years of gender transition. When this journey unexpectedly changes course, veering back towards masculinity, Karen is hopeful that this relationship will endure. In an interview, Karen describes congruence as having some alignment between internal understandings of self and external representations, or being 'true to yourself'. When her inner feelings shift, so does her external alignment, thereby maintaining congruence. Karen is nevertheless aware that transgendered friends (by comparison with their own journey) might regard her as inconsistent, uncommitted or 'incoherent'. She accepts she will lose many of them. However, as Karen points out, regardless of where you are on your personal journey: 'you've got to build networks of like minded people who you relate to and can eventually build some connection with...' (Karen, interview, 2011). A poignant digital story, despite its somewhat arbitrary rendition of an isolated moment within an ongoing life drama, can facilitate social connection.

However, while all people manage their public identities by putting forth their best selves (Goffman, 1959) this is problematic for people who understand themselves to be 'spoiled identities', stigmatised by the reactions of others (Goffman, 1963). Regrettable formative decisions, and behaviours and personality traits that are socially unacceptable, or a source of personal shame, tend not to be first choice as subjects for exploration in digital stories. Digital storytelling however, affords spoiled identities a process for selective public disclosure; a mechanism for partially opening the closet door. These storytellers can choose to share 'shameful' material that is carefully constructed and distributed in order to preserve a degree of privacy. For example, in *My Secret Story* Frank makes details of his seroconversion public. Frank is cognisant that friends who see the story (including those who were actually on the fated houseboat trip that he speaks of) will find out, for the first time, the fact that 'I let him fuck me not once, but twice without a condom' (Frank, story excerpt, 2010). Frank's disclosure is a risk laden one. He is aware that it is likely to impact upon some of his friendships (intimate publics) and very much hopes his mum will never see the story. He simultaneously considers the consequences should a neighbour in his small country community stumble upon it:

> ...part of me thinks they would be ok with it but then, instead of them thinking 'oh that's the gay guy on the corner...' they'd be thinking 'oh that's the HIV pos guy...'. So you go to the pub and have a sip from your schooner and you wonder whether they'll be looking at your schooner going 'how do they wash that schooner?'...Everything becomes much more slow motion...
>
> (Frank, interview, 2011)

While Frank is pragmatic in pointing out that it is unlikely that anyone in town will see the story (unless they are actively seeking out queer

HIV positive material online), he simultaneously describes an encounter in which this possibility seems quite likely. He'd been having problems with his laptop and took it to a local computer service where the repair person regaled him with stories of the 'interesting' and 'entertaining' material he regularly comes across on people's hard drives. Frank describes the anxiety he felt as he realised his story was on his laptop and that he didn't absolutely trust the repair person. Nevertheless, Frank maintains a very generous rationale for understanding and forgiving people who violate his confidentiality:

> I s'pose I work on the basis that people need to talk and share things and when you share something with them that's really powerful... then they need to understand it better so they need to talk to someone else... and ultimately things get around... which is both a good and a bad thing... so it's just easier to keep it to myself...
> (Frank, interview, 2011)

Frank acknowledges that his compassionate understanding of information sharing is also, in effect, a barrier to forming close friendships.

The problem of speaking across differences among networked publics plays out even in the intimate context of face-to-face workshops. In *Greg's Sermon* he rails against young gay men who should know about HIV (like Frank) but nevertheless act irresponsibly and he accuses them of being 'fucking idiots' (Greg, story excerpt, 2010). As a facilitator I was concerned that both Frank and Greg had opportunity to realise their stories without feeling judged or chastised by their peers or one another. As it happened, the two men benefited from discussing and comparing the themes of their apparently discordant stories. They modelled mutual acceptance, agreeing that they each had an equally valid though different contribution to make and the initiative's target audiences (young gay men) would benefit from hearing both stories. Out of these discussions there also emerges awareness that storytellers cannot control what an audience might make of a story.

While storytellers who share 'spoiled identities' (Goffman, 1963) risk affirming rather than deconstructing negative social stereotypes this is countered by the positive affirmations that emerge from their networked identity work.

> I feel more confident and at peace for having made the short film. It has allowed me to air a secret and in a way has liberated that part of my brain... I don't feel apologetic for being gay and the depth of the religious hang up seems diminished, so I think it has helped me

settle... Having worked out where I stand on keeping my HIV status to myself and why was also useful.

(Frank, email correspondence, 2012)

Despite obstacles to self-understanding, the requisite networked identity work undertaken throughout the digital storytelling production and distribution process offers opportunities to develop increased self-awareness and to evaluate fears, eventually arriving at personal congruence rather than socially determined authenticity or coherence.

Nominalisation, framing devices and bracketing

Naming and describing an identity can enact new normative codes and perpetuate a cycle of entrapment in social stereotypes. Regardless of ameliorations offered by queer theory (i.e. that awareness and critique counters entrapment), the possibility of unintentionally reinforcing norms is something to guard against. As Waidzunas points out, the creation of a 'gay youth' identity category over the last 10 years in the United States is frequently linked in popular discourse with suicidal ideation (Waidzunas, 2011). The popular 'Born This Way' blog (and unrelated 'Born This Way Foundation') perpetuate and reinforce understandings of identity as being innate and biologically determined. Meanwhile campaigns like 'It Gets Better' affirm normative values around emotional wellbeing, espousing happiness as an idealised state. Greater resilience might emerge from acknowledging that 'it gets better, then worse again, and then better for another little while, before something else brings you down'. Meanwhile 'I choose my cultural identity and I require acceptance of it' might be more enabling than social difference being inscribed in biology and therefore something uncontrollable.

Nominalising *any* identity without being limited by its boundaries is a paradigmatic problem – a problem that is nevertheless amplified by the fact that some identities are more socially acceptable than others. Choosing to identify as gender queer (i.e. presenting as neither male nor female), might seem a sensible way of casting off prescribed gender norms but, the fact is, social life is constructed around gender binaries. Unisex toilets are relatively rare and many schools maintain rigid and discrete school uniforms for boys and girls. For children who explore the boundaries of gender norms there is a clear choice to be made. Any ambivalence or hesitation at the boundaries is likely to induce anxiety in a host of adults, concerned about whether they are supporting the child on the 'right' journey. Adults making digital stories that implicate their children, regardless of whether the nominalised identity category is perceived as chosen, biologically or spiritually endowed, exhibit similar anxiety about how they represent their children. The parents who made *Blue for Boys? Pink for Girls?* alleviate this concern somewhat by concealing the child's identity. It is interesting to note that the child herself was not only aware of the story and quite proud of it, but saw no need to blur her image. The story ascribes no shame to her journey and therefore she saw no need to be ashamed. Despite this, in other circumstances, she remains concerned about 'who knows'. This vacillation and ambivalence aligns with the anxiety many queer storytellers feel – seemingly trapped between making public statements of self-acceptance and the fear of prejudice and social ramifications. I contend however, that having agency and ownership over a preferred nominalisation, despite associated risks, is affirming.

I use 'framing devices' in this sub-heading to refer to the ways storytellers frame stories within social contexts, in some cases with explicit nominalisations of preferred identities. Many digital stories start with 'I am a proud (insert identity descriptor here)' or 'I was born into a typical (descriptor) family in (insert place) during (insert era)'. Framing devices offer points of similarity and difference with which audiences can connect. For example, an explicit frame like 'same-sex attracted parents make a loving family unit' rests upon an implicit frame of assumed common values like 'good parents love their children and want the best for them'. Like nominalisation, framing devices are also conscious gestures on the part of the storyteller as they proclaim their position apart from or a part of stated publics. Whether overt or implicit, these framing devices allow storytellers to map the terrain and define the boundaries across which they hope to speak.

I use 'bracketing', in deference to Habermas, to signify the putting aside of prejudicial personal influences in order to engage in public debate. In this evocation of the public sphere such actions also constitute an attempt to speak and listen across difference. Digital storytellers bracket their values by diminishing narrative alternatives. They may be guided by personal moral motivations, for example 'I put aside the hurt and resentment I have felt as a result of social and/or personal exclusion and/or rejection...and I forgive you for your complicity'. They may also be guided by political goals to put aside personal disquiet that conflicts with the discourses of a social movement. For example, 'Marriage is a patriarchal capitalist construct, one that elides the diversity offered by queer familial alternatives' is sublimated in favour of 'same-sex marriage signifies social acceptance that will have positive repercussions for our children'. Other manifestations of bracketing traverse the personal and political, as in 'this is who I am and where I sit in relation to you. However, I'm going to try and see past our differences... will you?'. Bracketing and framing devices are related aspects of speaking and listening across difference, nevertheless the extent to which deeply ingrained social values can be comprehensively put aside is a contentious subject (Benhabib, Butler, Fraser & Cornell, 1995; Fraser, 1990; Young, 2011).

Nominalisation, framing devices and bracketing are narrative gestures that are significant for several reasons. Storytellers model the kind of active engaged listening (to the publics they perceive themselves apart from) and critical self-awareness (of the publics they are a part of) that they hope for in their audiences. Nominalisations that articulate an already enacted construct – for example 'this is what family means to us' in *Rowan's Family Tree, Where did we come from?* and *Our Conception Story* – inscribe this variation from social norms in a cultural space. Conscious decisions to represent self in relation to other are a measure of agency and ownership.

Negotiating meaning

Like social convergence, context collapse refers to the fact that digital (especially online) distribution allows a multitude of audiences to access and bring different interpretations to a story. As discussed above, when storytellers understand and frame an apparently incoherent identity and share this on their own terms, new possibilities of agency and ownership emerge.

Storytellers may sculpt a congruent identity by coding and layering their stories for divergent audiences. Molly (*Where did we come from?*) and Greg (*Me, Mum and Dad*) handle the social convergence of disparate audiences by anticipating what meaning might be made of their stories. Molly chooses a beguiling kid-friendly tone in the hope that adult audiences be alerted to the irreproachability of children caught in the midst of moral disputes over family structure. Greg chooses homegrown flowers, recognisable to family members, in order to represent their love without identifying them and exposing them to potential homophobia. Agency is apparent in networked identity work – the negotiated meaning-making implicit in self-representation as a part of/apart from divergent publics.

Claire made a story called *Kitchen Table Wisdom* about how families share profound insight in mundane domestic places. She reflects

Provocations: Digital Storytelling ≠ Social Change   183

upon change, both personal and social, being more spiralled than circular, and shares the belief that 'at kitchen tables everywhere we're slowly and steadily making progress...' (excerpt from *Kitchen Table Wisdom*). Here she describes what she conceives of as the slow ripples of change:

> I am glad the digital story is out there as part of my journey. I have asked my partner to marry me, and move in one day (when we have the room and when the laws change here!) that's the next step... Interestingly I have not yet formally shown [the story] to my mum and she has never commented on it, even though there have been links to it sent to her in the past via Facebook. Neither has my brother/step-siblings commented on it. [Nevertheless] I think [the story has] been part of a process of helping bring my partner and I closer in being able to share feelings about coming out more openly between ourselves, the kids and our extended families; it helped her come out to her own family and for us to go visit them overseas recently, for them to come see her Feast Hub art exhibition (also a public coming out statement for her) and to join in queer community events, to be herself more openly because she felt supported by her partner. I feel the same too because her helping me make the story and sharing her art in it etc. has strengthened our relationship and resolve to be ourselves, and together, no matter what. It also helped us feel supported by friends who saw it.
>
> (Claire, email correspondence, 2012)

Claire describes both the story-making process and the product itself having multiple effects. She affirms her relationship with her girlfriend (and also their coupled identity), among numerous intimate publics made up of her children, her partner's extended family, their friends, etc. Affirming an identity is 'taking control', declaring responsibility for one's actions and performances of self. In making herself visible before her networked publics, Claire challenges less-than-accepting attitudes and, in doing so, she transforms herself. She has become an active advocate for marriage equality, writes songs on the subject ('Civil Unity' posted on *Rainbow Family Tree*) and regularly posts calls to action on Facebook.

Stories that function principally as tributes also consolidate social (and personal) change among networked publics. In *Back to Happiness* (Figure 5.1), Sean declares his version of growing up, a history he shares with his family and, in publicly acknowledging a transgendered identity, also positions himself in reference to future identities. While he is happy to acknowledge that he is selective in how he represents himself to different publics – 'as Male, but also Queer/Gay and Pan/Bi' (Sean, forum excerpt, 2009) – the visible declaration of a transgendered history, distributed across networked publics online, allows that this information may always be discovered, foreclosing his capacity to 'go stealth' or pass consistently and coherently as a biological male. This is a declaration that he considered deeply and is happy to own. It positions his embodied identity in congruence with his political beliefs in which taking a stand against personal shame, mental illness and fear is central.

Provocative declarations that document a particular version of history (*Dear Sister, La La Land*) enable differences, at least potentially, to be acknowledged and overcome. My sister, after watching *Marriage Is So Gay!* phoned to offer her sympathies to our family and my daughter in particular. She was horrified that 'so-called Christians' would express their views (views she had previously expressed herself) in such a public and vociferous fashion. While we have not had explicit conversations about how her views have changed, she now encourages her children to spend time in the company of my unconventional family, thereby demonstrating acceptance.

The labour undertaken in making digital stories – networked identity work that underpins Intimate Citizenship 3.0 – is a vehicle for agency, congruence, ownership and bridging difference.

> Doing that work on building relationships indirectly through making digital stories is proving to be something of a theme for me. It is much safer to weave around the edges, and say what I want to say in a Digital Story, than to raise matters face-to-face and deal with the ensuing discomfort of conflict. This is not new for me. I have always used writing as a tool for getting my voice out. My voice in person is very different from my voice in production.
>
> (Melina, email correspondence, 2012)

As a tool for making provocative statements in public, digital storytelling is dependent upon evaluating the relationship between risk and reward. Melina's reference to writing as 'a tool for getting my voice out' refers to her digital self-representations in blogs, mailing lists, Facebook and so on, all spaces where she has previously reconciled the risks of disclosure versus the potential of personal and social change action. Owning a particular interpretation of an anecdote in digital story form, declaring it and sharing it in public, is also taking responsibility for unforeseen future consequences.

Meso

A *meso* account of digital storytelling canvasses the mediation of voice from institutional (facilitation) and storyteller (orchestration) perspectives. I briefly revisit obstacles to grassroots independent storytelling practice. Following this, I consider perennial difficulties for mediating voice in an institutional environment. I suggest, however, that these are not paralysing problems and can be managed with careful consideration of collective engagement and mindful listening.

Grassroots sustainability

Digital storytelling practice is traditionally beholden, for the most part, to workshops, funding and institutional agendas. This is problematic for minorities that do not in some way align with policy priorities. For example, it is only in the past two or three years that organisations like 'GetUp!' and platforms like change.org have undertaken GLBTQIS equality as a cause ('All about this campaign selection business | GetUp Campaign Blog', 2012). While it has been unacceptable to overlook racist behaviour or attitudes for some decades now, 'that's so gay!' is widely used and rarely challenged in playgrounds, workplaces and so on. In the last two years, gay and lesbian issues are taking up more space in the public sphere, however trans, intersex and gender queer issues are still poorly understood and polyamory or non-monogamy remain in widespread social disrepute.

For digital storytelling to evolve and grow as a creative practice, let alone a vehicle for activist communication, it has been suggested that the practice needs to be liberated from its institutional origins (Hartley & McWilliam, 2009; Lundby, 2008). How then might individual storytellers use digital stories as activist tools without the endorsement of institutions? Theoretically, anyone with broadband access, technical skills and basic digital tools like iMovie or Movie Maker can make and upload a story. However, in practice, and as I've already expanded upon at length, obstacles are more complex and numerous than mere technical access and aptitude. Melina, the most prolific storyteller on *Rainbow Family Tree*, describes some of these obstacles as 'logistical factors':

> There are certain logistical factors that have changed in my life, and these affect my willingness to make more digital stories. Firstly, there's the fact that I don't have a computer anymore. I use [my partner's] computer that she bought for herself before coming to Adelaide. It's not mine, I don't store anything on it, and I don't feel

that sense of power that I did when I had a laptop from school. That laptop was well-maintained and serviced through school, so it was a great privilege to have all that technology at my disposal! I have [my daughter's] old desktop computer which I use for storing photos. It is hopeless in other respects – possibly because it's out in the Big Room I haven't successfully accessed the net with it, but I can use it for Word. I can't however, make any pdf and then jpg files from Word with that computer, because it only has very basic programs. It means I'd have to take the photos off, put them somewhere else with the necessary programs, and work – where? You see?

(Melina, email correspondence, 2012)

In addition to these logistic factors, marginalised individuals in the community are less likely to develop the social capital or agency with which to undertake unsupervised digital storytelling compared with a cohort who are supported through a workshop process. Further, depending on the level of hands-on technical engagement, many workshop participants finish the process without the basic skills necessary to undertake storytelling independently. Broadly speaking, those non-professional media makers who have sufficient interest and motivation to seek out and acquire skills with which to create and share personal stories online appear more inclined to self-publish blogs and vlogs using platforms like YouTube and numerous blog hosting sites. While some of these media practices are audio-visual, few include the rich media tropes of digital stories, principally, first person narration combined with personal photographs. Digital stories require a greater investment of technical skills, time and emotional energy (by virtue of the networked identity work involved) than many other modes of online personal storytelling and are therefore harder to undertake as an individual. And so, it would seem that, despite the possibility of more sustainable and independent practice, the majority of traditional digital storytelling production currently occurs and is likely to remain within the context of auspiced workshops, regardless of whether they take place online or face-to-face.

Online curation

Both online and face-to-face workshops still need to be designed and facilitated which is an obstacle for unfettered organic communal self-expression. Interactive web platforms and/or archives like *Rainbow Family Tree* and *Stories for Change* are actively curated and thereby exert a framing influence upon content. Even when this frame has been determined by consensus, ongoing facilitation of engagement is a phenomenal task. Unless the site is funded or supported by a commercial agenda this is a task that must be undertaken by unpaid volunteers. Should key individuals move on or step back, this central role must be passed on and, as is the case in any volunteer-based communal activity, this turnover absorbs energy (in re-training, re-establishing trust, passing on 'corporate memory') and can destabilise critical momentum.

In the case of *Rainbow Family Tree* it is difficult to evaluate the project in terms of success or failure. It remains small, with only sporadic bursts of activity. Despite this, most members report that they appreciate the site, and value it as an archive of stories that they can direct people to when they are looking for audio-visual material or GLBTQIS resources. After being invited to offer feedback on the future of *Rainbow Family Tree*, the majority of storytellers responded with 'not sure', 'don't use it that much but like having it as a resource', 'it's fine and valuable just as it is' and 'I'd like to be more involved but I don't have enough time'. The fact that the space was initially established as a facilitated workshop space inevitably established a hierarchical status quo that has been difficult to reconfigure.

While it is not the focus of this book, a large body of scholarship in marketing, business and community development disciplines focuses upon critical aspects of engaging and growing communities online. However, much of this work describes hierarchical constructs that echo the 'for' or 'to' of Leadbeater's 'For, To, By, With' (2009). Social movement scholars offer analyses of mediated communication from a different theoretical perspective and yet in many cases they also describe hierarchical contexts in which power is located in charismatic leadership or institutions (Benford & Snow, 2000). It seems that, regardless of context, it is necessary to acknowledge the discursive influence of production, distribution and curation upon digital storytelling practice. Rather than abandon the practice entirely it seems appropriate to simply recognise these mediating influences, making them visible rather than regarding them as definitively good or bad.

Institutional facilitation

If digital storytelling is a practice that prospers best in a mediated and collaborative workshop environment, how might institutions and facilitators think about their power to influence hegemonic discourses in both positive and negative ways? Would greater awareness and acknowledgment enable a stepping back from top-down agendas and imposed objectives and outcomes? Digital storytelling is consuming of emotional and intellectual energy. It requires substantial networked identity work in addition to time, financial resources and social capital. Risks associated with self-exposure often outweigh, at least from the perspective of participants, perceived rewards. Workshop practice, if poorly managed by institutions or agencies, can not only miss an opportunity to affirm agency and ownership but fail to respect or understand the fundamental risks that storytellers undertake.

In actuality there is substantial goodwill among the social service providers, community arts and community media organisations that actively mediate voice in digital storytelling initiatives. Additionally, many institutions are staffed by social workers, therapists and arts/media workers who have excellent and nuanced listening skills. Deferring to the storyteller as an authoritative voice, expert in their own story, is common practice in narrative therapy. However, it is not necessarily understood by filmmakers, editors and facilitators. Further, there are no codes of ethical practice to guide facilitators in the increasingly complex dimensions of digital production practice let alone negotiating licensing arrangements, online distribution or related educational or marketing materials.

As an illustrative case in point, it is interesting to reflect upon the *What's Your Story?* case study in which a team of SHine SA project workers collaborated on a facilitator's guide to accompany the digital story compilation. The DVD compilation was intended for use in disparate social contexts. However, by the time the stories were completed, the general consensus among SHine SA staff was that teachers would regard the content as being too provocative for primary schools. In any case, the steering committee were tasked with imagining divergent publics ranging from conference contexts to 'train the trainer' and specialised 'gender and sexuality awareness' workshops and hopefully high schools. Each steering committee member was asked to distil 'take home messages' for three or four stories and pair stories with appropriate group exercises that were already being used in SHine SA's education/training programme. Over a period of three or four meetings it became apparent that some stories were more difficult to interpret and distil into neat teaching points. As an intermediary who was much closer to the experiences of the storytellers, I found myself inviting the steering committee to consider how they would feel if they were to read similar analytical summaries of their own lives. Efforts were made to adopt a neutral tone that avoided well-meaning but somewhat condescending judgement. It was also agreed that the booklet that accompanied the DVD would include reflections directly from the storytellers, while the facilitator's guide would attempt a more educational and purportedly objective distance. In this way the stories themselves were contextualised within several layers of interpretation from different analytical perspectives and the hope was that this would offer both a richer learning experience and a more respectful understanding of the role the stories played in the storytellers' lives.

Outside of my case studies, I have met many people who have become disillusioned with digital storytelling either because they were unhappy with the collaboratively produced end product or because they were not well-informed of the scope and potential ramifications of widespread distribution. This kind of disillusionment, a product in most cases of naïve, ill-informed or insensitive facilitation, undermines the potential of digital storytelling. Additionally, any social change that may be catalysed by digital stories is severed from its original impetus, located in an individual's narrative. The ripple effect is generated by story, storyteller and production process, situated in the wider context of a storyteller's life. Full acknowledgement of the contribution made by each actor engaged in co-creative enterprise – the storyteller, by association their networked publics, the facilitator, the editor, the photographer, the musician and the institutional representative – amplifies communicative and catalytic power. The multitude of actors involved in production and distribution actually constitute an intimate public for the storyteller and each one of them has capacity to influence their own intimate publics. Like the ripple in a pond, the original action is amplified by advocates, and cumulatively this is a large populace.

In sum, institutions and facilitators must support participants to manage a balance between personal risks and rewards both at the time of storytelling and in the future, in overlapping face-to-face and online contexts. While this can be challenging for workers who may be more accustomed to resolving immediate and tangible conflict or focussing upon current wellbeing issues, the complex everyday realities of technologically mediated publicness and privacy can no longer be neglected in any social initiatives that engage with personal and public communications. Both institutions and facilitators have an ethical responsibility to acknowledge their shaping influence and actively engage with methods and methodologies of practice that attempt to 'shape well'.

Collective engagement and mindful listening

Digital storytelling is a discursive practice that mediates the interface of many to one. It also mediates private and public understandings of identity and everyday life. Like any group initiative, storytelling practice is shaped at multiple points of intervention – initially determining that this is the kind of initiative that a community needs and wants, setting objectives, allocating resources, determining timeframes and outcomes, recruitment – and all of these stages occur before active facilitation of a group has even begun.

Any production initiative that brings together a group of individuals positions them within a collective frame – a frame that consequently determines practical engagement and establishes the terms by which the group may be understood. The same can be said of most web spaces that frame engagement either implicitly or explicitly, by defining the space and outlining expectations of the user. Analogously, any story that speaks for many individuals positions them within a frame, casting them in a pre-determined role in the story so that the narrative as an entirety may be understood. In all of these examples the rendering of many individuals as one collective necessitates mindful listening on the part of the empowered actor who is tasked with distillation and representation.

One of the storytellers involved in *What's Your Story?*, Fanny, is also a filmmaker, social worker and group facilitator. As someone with 32 years' experience of facilitation and who is currently undertaking further postgraduate study in the field, she has spent many hours reflecting upon what constitutes best practice and considering how the collective energy of a community might be better harnessed for social change:

> There's a whole bunch of us who could be working more together, which would take up less time, and less energy, and accomplish more. But we're so stuck in doing our own little things, and our own little spaces, and saying we've got no time... [these] determinants are what makes that ripple out effect happen, fast or slower...
> (Fanny, interview, 2011)

Because personal social change projects are so prone to losing focus, Fanny sees a place for institutional involvement in facilitation. However, she is also extremely aware of the shaping influence of any kind of intervention.

> The one thing that I think really does need to happen, is that we're really sure that what we are proposing, is really wanted by the communities, which might mean that you've actually got to take four years to sit around and just listen to what the community are saying,

without ever asking anybody a question. And putting the responses that you hear, into categories, until you've got a longitudinal study of what people in the queer community want...

(Fanny, interview, 2011)

Fanny points out that this kind of process is problematic for institutions with limited time and resources. On the question of how a group, having formed, might be facilitated she again advocates for minimalist intervention. Fanny wonders whether regular meetings of a non-hierarchical storytelling group might unfold into a more distinct project over time. She describes the practice of a spiritual group she is involved in:

> We get in a circle, and we all smudge each other. And then we meditate for maybe 10, 15 minutes. And then the circle is opened, and people tell their stories. There's a time keeper. And somebody might do a reading to evoke a sense of emotional connectedness. Something that is personal and meaningful for them. And then it is just silence. And you sit in the circle, until somebody agrees to speak. So you then have about three to four minutes. And it can be anything. You know: 'I'm so fucked off with...', you know: '...my life...I just wanna be dead'. (makes noise) Ding. It's a process where people tell their stories into the middle of the circle. There's a candle. And then at the end of it, it's like, 'Is everybody clear? Is everybody done? Complete?' And then we all lean over to the middle and blow out the candle.

(Fanny, interview, 2011)

Fanny is inspired by this approach and wonders how effectively it might map onto other institutionally facilitated group practice. She imagines, having listened to community issues for years, inviting a group of people to meet regularly to tell stories. Over time these stories could be sorted into categories around 'common themes' or 'most frequently heard' or 'most popular', in fact whatever criterion is arrived at by group consensus. Then the process begins again, this time encouraging the group to develop stories that move into collective exploration: 'you use the circle process to rehearse the stories, to make them thicker...To tease out their underlying narratives' (Fanny, interview, 2011). Fanny acknowledges that even this imagined process effectively imposes a format and structure. Further, potential incompatibilities with institutional preferences for objectives, deadlines and outcomes remain. She also highlights the fact that non-hierarchical groups like this do not necessarily resolve problems of how to facilitate the expression of quiet, withdrawn voices. Similarly, the recruitment process can be problematic:

> ...do we go for people who are likely to take part? And then, you know, you're preaching to the converted. But that group of people might well be the people who will create ripples. So what it means, is that you're using resources for a privileged group of people already. But on the other hand, you know that they're the kind of people who are going to be interested in moving it along. You know, using it in their work, doing it, you know...
> (Fanny, interview, 2011)

Fanny admits that she often feels trapped by what may be regarded as the intrinsic complexities of mediating voices. As somebody who is naturally inclined to organise by sorting people into groups, getting them to write down their ideas, creating 'to do' lists and so on, she did not regard herself as a good facilitator: 'Give me a group and I turn into a Nazi!' (Fanny, interview, 2011). Eventually, despite all her concerns, Fanny hopes that it is enough to personally commit to good listening:

> Really good listening, is placing yourself in positions where you're likely to hear things... Also, well maybe one thing, is to be authentic in what your concern is. [Not] framing the situation [by tabling an agenda]... I'm thinking, more within [gestures to heart]...
> (Fanny, interview, 2011)

Alongside these aspirations, representative of profound goodwill, Fanny also wonders whether there is a fundamental fallacy in empowered institutions/facilitators attempting to mediate marginalised voices:

> ...is trying to be a non-invasive facilitator actually a hoax? Are we putting ourselves... you know, is it actually authentic to propose a non-structure or a... when clearly we need things to happen?
> (Fanny, interview, 2011)

While it appears there are some dimensions to listening, speaking and mediating voices that are eternal conundrums of communication and power, Fanny's sensitivity to these issues and willingness to confront them in practice may in itself be a measure of best practice. It is also important to acknowledge that all spaces and interactions are mediated regardless of whether they take place face-to-face or online and that mediation in itself is not inherently negative. While non-influential mediation might remain an unattainable goal, in the face of dire social problems and a culture of inequity that marginalises many divergent individuals, 'best efforts' at reflective community engagement strategies is infinitely better than no efforts at all.

Macro

On a *macro* or cultural level, I discuss concerns with the digital storytelling genre as a communicative medium, and problems reaching audiences, particularly those who are inclined to be unreceptive. I consider difficulties in measuring the value of digital storytelling as a change catalyst and suggest re-framing our understandings of this value.

Appeal of genre

How appealing is the digital story genre to conventional audiences and unknown publics? Digital stories are often not very entertaining or fun. However, as a rich media first person narrative form, they broaden and diversify stereotypical representations that prevail in broadcast media. Digital platforms have expanded the spaces in which audiences might consume autobiographical content (previously monopolised by books, theatrical documentaries and occasional television broadcast). As brief amateur insights, digital stories align more closely with content shared via YouTube and Facebook than that broadcast in traditional arenas. In parallel there has been an arguable expansion in audience acceptance of user-generated content or the aesthetics of amateur production. Memes like 'Charlie bit my finger!'[1] have accustomed audiences to mundane everyday insights, and widely read blogs have increased the social value of personal stories and opinions, expressed in colloquial language by ordinary people. A wider understanding of how/when/where traditional audiences consume narrative content, increasingly spread across mobile and online platforms also shifts the boundaries of what is regarded, socially and critically, as quality narrative content. On this question of what constitutes a good story, it is worth revisiting Gubrium and Holstein, cited earlier:

> To expect a definitive answer to the question of what a good story is, is to expect the impossible in practice. Standards, generalized criteria, or codes are not the issue, even while they are perennially present in everyday life. Rather, the issue centers on the question, What is narratively adequate in the circumstances? Put in these terms, the

answer requires a view to application, to something that is reflexively discerned. It requires an aesthetics of narrativity that draws inspiration from the relevancies and contingencies of everyday life, from operating purposes, from the functions of accounts, and from the consequences for those concerned. To say 'that's a beautiful story' is as much a reflexive measure of its situated utility as it is a judgment of the story's narrative quality.

(Gubrium & Holstein, 2009, p. 210)

Rather than striving to replicate genres and narrative forms that are palatable for broadcast TV, digital storytellers participate in a cultural landscape by appealing to the situated aesthetics of everyday life. Further, carefully constructed 'ordinary' digital stories offer the flavour of lived experience in such irrevocable and evocative detail, that they may be more difficult for audiences to summarily dismiss or forget than some other personal story-sharing vehicles like Facebook updates, photographs or blog posts. For example, consider the hypothetical situation of Molly's Facebook 'friends': capable of scorning innocuous photographs of her daughter, would they have been capable of same if they had they viewed *Blue for Boys? Pink for Girls?*. Regardless of whether they were inclined to approve or disapprove of transsexualism, it seems likely that the situated story might have provoked a more nuanced discussion and a degree of empathy. In sum, rather than measuring against the aesthetics and significance of broadcast media, researchers need to examine user-generated rich media content alongside the situated significance of the networked identity work that underpins it.

Marketing

Regardless of the nature of their content or the proficiency with which their message is communicated, digital stories can only be effective catalysts of social change if they are actually watched by audiences. Many of the initiatives I have become aware of during this research and in the years prior do not undertake any active distribution of the stories beyond a collective screening for friends and family members of the storytellers. Distribution difficulties often result from lack of digital literacy on the part of both facilitators and storytellers – for example storytellers may receive a DVD version of their story but not the digital file that would enable them to upload the story to the internet. Even if they are in possession of a digital file, many storytellers lack skills to upload or have residual fears about sharing their stories online.

Where digital education ceases at the end of production, an opportunity to actively engage with a wider public is missed. Digital sharing of self has become increasingly ubiquitous (especially in the context where Facebook routinely encourages expansion of social networks and self-marketing through 'friending') and storytellers can be better supported in exploring these distribution possibilities by institutions, facilitators and web curators. Of course some storytellers have limited desire to undertake distribution and many speak of not wanting to appear to be self-indulgent and overly self-interested. This is normative social behaviour, partially overcome by better awareness of the benefits of networked identity work. The different distribution strategies undertaken by storytellers lobbying for same-sex marriage and same-sex parenting recognition offer rich material for analysis.

Following the IDAHO 2011 rally in Adelaide, *Gay Rights Rally, Adelaide, 2011*, was widely circulated via Facebook, links on interest based e-lists and direct emails. I embedded it on the *Rainbow Family Tree* where it received 172 views. The current YouTube statistics reveal 3,504 views. Public access to statistics have been disabled, hence it is difficult to know where this traffic or view referrals originated. *Marriage Is So Gay!* was not uploaded until 2 weeks after the rally and therefore missed an initial peak in audience interest. After embedding the video on *Rainbow Family Tree* I did a blog post in which I described my anxiety about engaging my daughter in public activism. I also sent a message to all members of the site alerting them to the new content and inviting them to share it. I sent the link to various friends and e-lists of which I am a member. I tweeted the link and posted it on my personal Facebook page and the *Rainbow Family Tree* Facebook page. Following that I spent 3 or 4 hours posting the link to numerous other interest-based (marriage equality, GLBTQIS parenting, etc.) Facebook pages both nationally and internationally. This strategy resulted in 1,600 views in the 2 weeks following upload and 2,058 views to date. I published a further blog about the various distribution strategies I engaged with including a visit to and screening for my local federal liberal member of parliament.

Apart from the unmeasurable influence the video had in its circulation among unknown publics there were some interesting ripples created among intimate publics. Numerous friends got in touch and were cross that my girlfriend and I had gotten 'married' without fanfare or invitations. Several *Rainbow Family Tree* site members, previously unknown to me, shared their own anxieties about exposing their children to social conflict (including Jacqui Tomlins whom I later interviewed on this subject). I've already mentioned that my sister was also forthcoming in her support, signalling a significant shift from her previous silence. I met with the principal and vice principal at my daughter's school and invited them to share the story among staff. I gave them a copy of the *What's Your Story?* DVD and facilitator's guide and asked them to consider using it for staff awareness raising and potentially in classroom contexts. The last images in the video include a call for action in which supporters are encouraged to make their acceptance visible by voting in online polls, adding their names to petitions and contacting their member of parliament. While it is impossible to know what effect either the story or the call to action had, various national polls have indicated a slow and steady increase in community support over the last two years for same-sex marriage. It seems likely that the cumulative influence of personal storytelling and everyday activism may have contributed to this social change. Digital storytellers can be guided and encouraged to undertake a range of strategies (targeted, ad hoc and proxy) for distributing their stories, just as they can be supported through the production process. Active and considered distribution and marketing offers potential to amplify both the personal and social benefits of digital storytelling.

Speaking across difference

Many storytellers share concerns that their stories only preach to the converted, begging the question of how to communicate with people who are not interested or antipathetic. As I have noted previously, as far as I am aware, no storytellers actively targeted their stories at unknown religious fundamentalist groups. However, in several instances (*Dear Sister, Notice One, La La Land*) stories were made as provocations and were shared directly with the people they were made about and for, in every instance catalysing some degree of change. *Notice One* opened up a conversation about Kirsten's unhappy childhood with her mother; *La La Land* contributed to Bronwen's grandparents flying to Adelaide to welcome both Melina and their new baby, Rowan, into the family. Perhaps the true power of a digital story is in bridging many small differences rather than gulfs of difference. Perhaps witnessing to ambivalent familiar publics, and eventually recruiting them as advocates does, in itself, represent social change, recalling the movement of a ripple, expanding across the surface of a pond.

Bridge building is reflected in the capacity to negotiate one's position as a part of or apart from networked publics – including familiar, intimate, counter and unknown. Digital storytelling creates opportunities to 'bring things up', to broach difficult discussions 'out in the open'. Ownership of one's position in society (as represented in a digital story) is reflected in the capacity to receive and give affirmation. Further, public expression of marginalised voices opens space for others to speak as they also negotiate how and where they fit in the world. As a medium that facilitates speaking across difference and bridge building, digital storytelling evokes the profound significance of participatory media as a widespread global phenomenon. The capacity for ordinary individuals, formerly barred from access to media production, to make and distribute self-representations, represents a shift in a cultural ecosystem towards dialogic engagement.

Measuring social significance

My study intentionally avoided any attempt to quantify social impact. Not only is it very difficult to track and enumerate how many people have viewed stories, it is also difficult to measure the effect of shifts in attitude. Audiences may be moved by stories and yet not undertake direct quantifiable action (like calling their local politician, voting in online polls etc.). Further, audiences may note alternate representations with interest but nevertheless give more credence to professionally produced and authoritative content that perpetuates stereotypes. Couldry argues that, regardless of the alternate representations of identity disseminated by mass self-communication, it remains less influential than mass media.

> ...self-communications do not stop mass media circulating, nor do they influence the degree to which mass media are even-handed in their representation of the social world: nor, given the difficulty of becoming visible online... do they necessarily have any wider effect beyond the momentary satisfaction of expression.
> (Couldry, 2012, p. 203)

Gray, in online discussion with Couldry, argues that participatory media has not replaced the traditional one-to-many model of broadcast but has grown alongside it.

Rather than see mass media as large-scale, hegemonic spaces of representation (thinking of the power of documentary here) and social or digital media as small-scale platforms that provide individual voices (thinking of the 'It Gets Better' campaign here), what might come of seeing media as interlocking articulations/echoes of hegemonic discourses of who we 'really are' or 'what's' really going on'? With this formulation in mind, how might we build a media praxis that invites deeply contextual representations that can't stand in for what's universally true or authentic – or at the very least ask us to see what's presented as a partial, possible truth?

(Couldry & Gray, 2012)

Gray's call for acknowledgment of user-generated content, like digital stories, as valid and useful representations alongside the equally 'partial, possible truth' countered in any other media environments (including broadcast and theatrical) is pertinent to digital storytelling.

For some storytellers, being liberated from the pressures of a genre that is packaged primarily for audience entertainment may be construed as an opportunity rather than an obstacle. Where words are inadequate, storytellers like Kirsten can describe their experience in artistic form, through visual rather than verbal communication. In *Notice One* Kirsten presents a rapid montage of famous art works alongside her own art works to represent her reconstructed, fragmented memories of childhood mental illness. In Kirsten's case it seems that the microcosmic social changes (including challenging and cathartic conversations with her mother, also an artist) that have taken place individually and among her networked publics may outweigh concerns of whether her story (and in fact her identity) is palatable to a wider public: '[Now] I have much more of a sense of my identity and instead of disliking myself I can see the progress that I have made since then.' (Kristen, email correspondence, 2012) Kirsten's testimony suggests that she is more capable of engaging in social discussions about wellbeing which, in itself, affords opportunities for others to listen and contribute their own stories. Among her family, Kirsten's digital story has raised to the surface an issue that was previously difficult to discuss.

Meanwhile unconscious choices made by storytellers offer grist for further analysis. They reflect interesting social and personal resonances that are often hard to access and are therefore invaluable for cultural research. For example, many storytellers in these case studies sought out emblematic representations of homophobia and acceptance online. In several stories (notably *My Secret Story* and *O.M.G....Is she really?*), iconographic and widely distributed images of Westboro Church banners are used despite the fact that these are American points of reference. Australian equivalents may be less numerous and harder to find but they nevertheless exist. Similarly, Frank uses an image of buffed and suntanned 'jocks', leaning against a wall and one another, as they stare off into an imagined happy future, blue sky in background. These are clean middle-class white American men and for Frank, they represent romantic happiness. The image is so notably not-Australian that it provoked a question at the public screening. As Frank, in an effort to maintain pseudonymity, was among the audience rather than on stage with his peers he was unable to directly address the question. After the screening he admitted he hadn't thought about the choice that much and pointed out he had limited time and broadband access with which to find appropriate images. This anecdote reflects the unpredictable and paradoxical ways in which culture is shaped and re-shaped. While the prevalence of American images online make them easier to find, this cultural hegemony is also internalised by storytellers who, perhaps unconsciously, default to American representations of happiness, innocence, pride and homophobia. Just as many Australians have grown up with Sesame Street as a dominant representation of urban community (despite its dissimilarity to Australian or in fact most American realities) many young gay people are profoundly influenced by American cultural frames of reference. The profound and mundane everyday absorption and re-production of culture is evident in many digital story texts analysed in this research.

The storytellers in my case studies report that their sense of belonging as respectable citizens of the world is not necessarily correlated to whether or not they are heard by, or visible to, powerful people. Rather than exclusively targeting power brokers, they negotiate new understandings with intimate circles of friends and family. In workshops and interviews they frequently speak about uncovering the support of friends and family members (and in some cases strangers) as an unexpected benefit of the digital storytelling process. They identify this as an underestimated *micro* element of *macro* social change. In imagining future worlds, storytellers make these worlds possible, a prospect they seed in the imaginations of their audiences.

> So what's the point of this short film? I hope you learn from my mistakes? I hope you are empowered to protect yourself... I hope society changes and adopts positive messages about gay people. I passionately hope that gay marriage is legalised and that dedicated, caring, loving gay relationships are acknowledged, celebrated and supported. I also hope that the young religious gay person loves themselves and understand that god loves them too...
>
> (*My Secret Story*, excerpt)

In the closing words of his story, Frank explicitly articulates his dreams of a more equitable and accepting society. It is the first time he has done so in this public fashion, demonstrating a form of actively engaged cultural citizenship that is, in itself, a measure of social change. Rather than attempting to quantify the social impact of digital storytelling, it seems more useful to gauge the way it increases capacity for social and cultural engagement. This research was originally framed around 'everyday activism' to distinguish the specific intentions of participant storytellers from the infinitely varying motivations of generalised digital storytelling practices. Everyday activist storytellers are motivated to effect change in their social environments, regardless of whether or not that change actually happens. Nevertheless, changes perceived by the storytellers among their networked publics are significant. They reflect a more subtle form of change, as illustrated in Figure 1.1 that erodes stereotypes and conventional heteronormative attitudes to gender and sexuality.

Digital storytellers engage with inventing, enacting and publicly celebrating selves of their own making. Through networked identity work they arrive at new understandings of both individual and collective constructions of identity and in doing so they consolidate their connections with the world, something they frequently refer to as becoming 'empowered' or feeling 'affirmed'. While there are many obstacles to the use of digital storytelling as a personal grassroots tool for activist communication, it nevertheless serves a useful social purpose. Further, these obstacles are characteristic of numerous forms of digitally mediated self-representation and better awareness of them is of use to designers of social policy and cultural development programmes. In the concluding chapter I argue that employing a conceptual framework of Intimate Citizenship 3.0 does just this.

7
What Lessons to Bear Forth?

This book has offered unique insight into specific textual approaches and modes of sharing used by marginalised (and in some cases stigmatised) people. I have highlighted the labour involved in negotiating and managing privacy and publicness across networked online and face-to-face environments. While Intimate Citizenship 3.0 is fraught with risk, the rewards include greater cultural and civic engagement and erosive social change. These new understandings can be usefully mapped onto other contexts in which digital tools and platforms are being used to facilitate engagement and empowerment, for example among young people who strive to overcome bullying, or older people who seek a way out of social isolation. In the following I present **four summative points** as they emerge during my representative chapters on voice, identity and networked publics.

Retracing the journey ... and takeaway insights

In *Chapter 1* I established definitions for key terms including *digital storytelling, everyday activism, erosive social change* and, briefly, *Intimate Citizenship 3.0.* To summarise: I see everyday activism as a permutation of more conventional and strategic activism; it takes place spontaneously in everyday life and is both provocative and frank, echoing the public speech of Foucault's parrhesiastes. I clarified my specific use of 'networked publics' – a convergence of social networks across face-to-face and online spaces, both familiar and unknown, whom we imagine as we perform our preferred identities. Later, I considered what role digital tools and platforms may have in amplifying the impact of everyday activism and whether this constitutes a kind of 'digitally enabled citizenship' (Papacharissi, 2010). I outlined six kinds of *social change* that may result from everyday activism among networked publics, and suggested *erosive change* as a slow and hard-to-discern result of *networked identity work*. Out of this emerges the conceptual framework of Intimate Citizenship 3.0. I argued that my work with queer storytellers and research participants, while specific of circumstance and in some ways extreme, was nevertheless illustrative of the obstacles and opportunities experienced by less marginalised people and a wider population.

In *Chapter 2* I canvassed some of the social and historical uses of personal storytelling as a tool for speaking across difference. I evaluated different genres of personal storytelling, from embodied and performed witnessing, to autobiographical prose and self-reflexive documentaries. I described the emergence of digital storytelling situated as community media, and briefly surveyed other critical problems canvassed in a burgeoning scholarship. I considered what impact increasingly accessible digital tools, web platforms and associated social convergence has on the production and distribution of personal stories in a variety of forms, including individual and communal blogs (like 'Same Plus' and 'Born This Way'), vlogs (like 'It Gets Better') and as facilitated by organisations (like 'Creative Narrations' and 'BAVC'). Finally I pondered new potentials for digital storytelling in online spaces, situated aside life-streaming social network platforms like Facebook, Twitter, Instagram and Tumblr.

This review illuminates the **first** finding of this research. Clearly, *widespread online distribution represents new possibilities for conventional digital storytelling practice*. Because media content doesn't need to be professionally produced to find an audience online, 'ordinary people' can contribute to platforms like YouTube and feel like they are having a say in shaping the kind of world they would like to live in. Further, greater acceptance of amateur aesthetics in user-generated and user-distributed content affords new opportunities for rich media activism, particularly by disenfranchised people.

In *Chapter 3: Identity: Nominalisation, Authenticity and Incoherence* I considered a *micro* 'up close' unit of analysis – stories as representations of identity. I began with a review of philosophical understandings of identity and considered how and when vernacular understandings, as articulated by my participants, align and diverge. I examined difficulties with nominalising queer identities, and described the everyday disruption of categories undertaken by participants in their digital stories. The second section of this chapter analysed the more generalised problems posed by narrative coherence, partial self-awareness and/or 'opacity' (Butler, 2005) and the limitations of language. These obstacles thwart purportedly 'authentic' self-representation and they are difficulties experienced by both disenfranchised minorities and a more privileged 'mainstream'. I argued that efforts to conceptualise 'authenticity' should move away from *social expectations of coherence* towards *self-ascribed congruence*. I foreshadowed ideas of 'empowerment' through agency and ownership that I then developed further in Chapters 4 and 5. The analysis presented in these chapters highlights a **second** significant finding of this research. *Agency over storytelling + ownership of contextually located stories = greater control* over privacy and publicness and > *reconfigures how people think about what is private and public*. In other words, conscious reflection about how to represent oneself to many different people in different times and places, affords empowered self-representation.

I tackled *Chapter 4: Case Studies in Voice* by dividing it into two sections, both analysing a *meso* level of digital storytelling practice. First, I described in detail the ways in which voice was *facilitated* in each of the three case studies, primarily from a facilitator/institutional point of view. Second, I considered how storytellers *orchestrate* voices in their efforts to speak across difference, including particular *rhetorical strategies* and the *use of emotives* in shaping social movements. Finally I argued that expression of voice has a *constitutive effect* in enacting identity and articulating normative values. *Mediation is inevitable,* either via facilitation and orchestration of voice online, and/or face-to-face environments. I concluded however, that this mediation is *not implicitly positive or negative,* rather a serious factor that must be considered by institutions, facilitators, web curators and storytellers themselves. In *Chapter 5: The Private in Networked Publics* I considered the ways storytellers define audience and think of themselves as *a part of* or *apart from* divergent imagined publics, both familiar and unknown. I detailed the networked identity work storytellers undertake as they create stories that *build bridges between multiple co-existent understandings of self, family and community*. I reflected upon the ramifications of social convergence, particularly for privacy and publicness. I offered examples of storytellers as they managed textual approaches to self-production and distribution as they continue to curate intimate exhibitions of self, simultaneously on and offline. I categorised these processes in a typology of otherness and outness and argued that they provide substantial evidence of digitally mediated *agency* and *ownership*. Chapter 5 provided evidence for a **third** proposition. *Networked identity work facilitates social connection among divergent publics, bridging differences and creating new space for other disenfranchised voices*. For participants, active reflection upon all the people who are in some way involved in their stories often led to discussions about these relationships. These affirm meaning, and a safe social context. Networked identity work also extends the capacity for participants and their networked publics to listen to other people's points of view. Many participants reported a ripple effect in which other people, inspired by their stories, found impetus to speak out and share their own perspectives.

In *Chapter 6: Provocations: Digital Storytelling ≠ Social Change*, I analysed key issues in digital storytelling practice and considered how they may be re-framed in order to arrive at better understanding of this specific tool for everyday activism. I proposed that heightened awareness of the obstacles and opportunities implicit in negotiating modern, fluid and persistent digitally mediated identity, is the networked identity work that constitutes Intimate Citizenship 3.0. This chapter synthesises material from throughout the book that can be summarised as a **fourth** significant finding. *Articulating congruent non-normative identity to imagined and networked publics reconstitutes culture.* Boundaries around gender and sexuality (or, arguably, any rigidly constructed and normative identity) particularly as depicted in media and culture, blur and start to take new shape. On an individual level of personal identity construction, Melina provides an apt summary:

> The digital stories do change the way I feel about myself, and they also change the perceptions I have about myself. The technical and creative satisfaction I get from producing them has been beneficial. On a personal level, there is potential there for change action, but also for recognition and acknowledgment.
> (Melina, interview by email, 2011)

Melina highlights the benefits of creative and digitally literate self-expression (increased self-esteem and opportunity for personal growth) as well as the amplified opportunity provided by digital distribution for engagement with networked publics (potential for political/policy change and social recognition of cultural participation and queer identity). On the subject of conscious and unconscious enactment of identity for divergent publics she is also eloquent:

> Sometimes I have positioned myself in a particular way in order to elicit a particular reaction from my perceived audience, but most of the time that positioning has not been deliberate, and it's the making and showing of the digital stories that finally reveals to me where I was coming from, and why.
> (Melina, interview by email, 2011)

The cultural consequences of sharing personal narratives are greater than the sum of their parts – these digitally mediated narratives of identity in flux inscribe culture with new patterns for being, and potentially, new patterns for communication. It seems that, for all their difficulties, digital storytelling processes offer potential as tools for catalysing social change. Further, extrapolating core communication strategies – processes of listening, interpreting and consciously representing – into other cultural engagement initiatives, offers potential for greater 'digitally enabled citizenship' (Papacharissi, 2010) and widespread Intimate Citizenship 3.0.

My research questions sought understanding of the particular practices of an activist oriented queer cohort of digital storytellers as they were presented with particular digital tools and platforms. In sum the four aforementioned core findings offer evidence that grounds some guidelines for best practice and ideas for further research.

New horizons

Social service providers and community development workers, filmmakers, journalists, individual storytellers and researchers have great capacity to shape social discourses and enact new normative values in both profound and mundane ways. What constitutes best practice in situations where normative values need to be actively re-negotiated with communities? How can mediators of voice curate communities that are affirming across intersecting face-to-face and online networked publics? How might co-creative cultural renewal – an active and collaborative process of listening across difference, interpreting, and representing non-normative identities – networked identity work that catalyses erosive social change – be facilitated?

Here I have **four proposals** that are applicable to digital storytelling practice but also map, at least in theory, to *any* creative initiatives that entail the sharing of private stories with networked publics. In essence, they are a guide to the facilitation of Intimate Citizenship 3.0.

First, framing and nominalisation have profound influence upon the processes and products of creative community initiatives and, in turn, shape how we think about and describe ourselves as individuals and groups. Institutions and facilitators can be transparent in *actively acknowledging their discursive mediating influence upon the construction of individual and collective identities*. In my case studies, drawing attention to mediation allowed storytellers, facilitators and auspicing institutions to act with mutual respect and consideration, especially in the distribution and marketing stages of initiatives.

Second, *awareness of networked identity work* provides an opportunity to sculpt *congruent rather than coherent narratives* and this labour can have both *personal value* and *constitutive cultural value*. For example, representations on LinkedIn need not be consistent OR inconsistent with those on Facebook or 'real life', rather they can be affirmed as different aspects of a complex and fluid identity. For storytellers (like Karen in *Sisterhood*, Figure 3.6) whose identity is evolving, conscious curation of a personal identity 'exhibition' can model acceptance of personal and social complexity and fluidity.

Third, *active consideration of distribution* of private stories amplifies personal and social benefits, especially as a tool for everyday activism. Despite the obstacles, discomfort and/or risks implicit in actively sharing personal stories, rewards can include greater self-acceptance and understanding of and among networked publics. While the digital stories in my case studies did not always result in material policy or law reform (though on several occasions they contributed), storytellers frequently referred to changes accelerated by their networked identity work that in turn catalysed *erosive social change*.

Fourth, initiatives benefit from reflective analysis of *cross-disciplinary community engagement strategies*, social movement theory and strategic listening across difference.

I pose an additional **two queries** for further research. **First,** how can understandings of Intimate Citizenship 3.0 support mediators of voice to *actively engage in co-creative curation of communities of affirmation*? **Second,** *how can social change be reimagined* both qualitatively and quantitatively through complex description of Intimate Citizenship 3.0? How can we develop new ways of thinking about and describing ideas like 'cultural engagement' and new methodological approaches to studying digitally enabled citizenship?

Can the conceptual framework of Intimate Citizenship 3.0 be applied in other contexts – theoretical, methodological and pragmatic? For instance, could congruent and curated self-representation be used to support young queer people in schools, or more generally, in anti-bullying initiatives? The evolving use of digitally mediated tools and platforms for everyday activism demands ongoing, methodologically diverse, interdisciplinary research.

Even as I ponder the construction of these closing passages, I am surprised to observe the storytelling capacity encoded in my automated screensaver. The cover image of this book represents a small sample. The screensaver loads images from my iPhoto library and presumably uses facial recognition to identify frequently reoccurring people and frame analysis features to detect areas of light and dark. If you wait long enough, a single image slowly becomes smaller. As it zooms into the middle distance it is surrounded by more and more images, in concert telling a new story of intimate domestic lives. Eventually the original images become part of an abstract pointillist canvas. Out of this indistinct mass of frames a single shot slowly emerges again. It's quite mesmerising to watch as one's mind casts back to the events and people represented in the photos and ponders the apparently abstract life narrative that emerges from odd correspondences between images. One is reminded of the somewhat staid PowerPoint displays that are routinely screened at birthdays and funerals, with images painstakingly selected by loved ones in order to generate summative meaning. However the screensaver is random, drawing upon a library to generate an aesthetically pleasing non-linear summation. Watching it is both an invigorating and mildly disturbing experience, depending on your point of view. As automated technology and the predictive capacities of big-data becomes ubiquitous across multiple platforms and devices, what significance will there be for social and personal narratives of identity? As self-representation is increasingly mediated by a plethora of digital technologies, tools and platforms, how will people evolve in their management of Intimate Citizenship 3.0?

While this book has focussed upon self-representation through digital storytelling for activist purposes, further research might examine capacity to curate online exhibitions of self in divergent social contexts – for example what happens if we deliberately link incoherent representations in discrete spaces? Does agency and ownership over curation *necessarily* impute greater cultural engagement and empowerment? Will better social understanding of the complexities of coherence, congruence and postmodern understandings of identity make for a wider array of socially acceptable identities?

In the context of online communities there is more work to be done on actively facilitating affirmative communities and co-creative practice. Using the example of 'It Gets Better' it seems that unresolved discordances between online and offline spaces, between affirming and antagonistic publics, has potential to harm as well as increase personal resilience. This is the 'what doesn't kill you will make you stronger' school of personal development. Jamey Rodemeyer's digitally mediated everyday activism increased his exposure to bullying online and at school and did little to overcome his isolation. In contrast, the kind of nuanced Intimate Citizenship 3.0 that is central to digital storytelling practice (and apparent in the strategies of 'Make It Better') might actually help erode the value of bullying, changing a social landscape that privileges power. Some of the processes established by Myerhoff and utilised in narrative practice facilitate 'definitional ceremonies' and the use of 'outsider witnesses' as audience for storytellers. What might these processes, extended into simultaneously online/offline environments, look like and could they achieve similar communal affirmation?

Just as mediation strategies derived from narrative practice and anthropology may be usefully applied to the facilitation of storytelling in a variety of contexts, it seems likely that social movement theory might offer clues for nurturing communal activity. Social movement scholars recognise that growth is dependent on complex combinations of related factors, including charismatic leadership, existing social networks, cultural capital, financial resources, community consensus and community ownership. These are strikingly similar to the complex processes individual storytellers undertake as they construct their narratives via networked identity work. In particular there are analogous parallels between 'political opportunity structures, cultural opportunities and constraints, and targeted audiences' (Benford & Snow, 2000). Future research might consider these alignments and investigate their leverage as interdisciplinary models for best practice in the community development and civic participation sectors.

In concluding, it is useful to consider again the discrete objects that have been examined in this book – first, digital story *products*; texts that represent specific content (in this case, queer identity); second, digital storytelling *process* (in this case a mix of face-to-face and online production and distribution); and third, the significance of the aforementioned two objects in the *context* of simultaneously private/public lives and networked social spheres. While my case studies are located in queer communities, their concerns align with similarly marginalised communities. They evoke larger social questions of how individuals find voice and how collectives and institutions discover capacity to listen. Similarly, while my observations regarding Intimate Citizenship 3.0 are made in the context of specific digital tools and platforms, they map well onto other forms of publicly distributed self-representation. What are the possibilities for facilitated interventions that harness both the viral energy and the chaotic fragmented inclusivity of digital platforms? Can they promise greater agency over self-representation, ownership of personal congruence and sustainable change?

Intimate Citizenship 3.0

In the early moments of Occupy Wall Street, blogs, tweets, hash tags and sharing via memes, facilitated public personal storytelling as everyday activism. Intimate Citizenship 3.0, as manifest in Occupy Wall Street and the case studies in this book, demonstrates networked engagement that deconstructs false digital dualisms and puts the nail in the coffin of binary oppositions like public/private, online/face-to-face. When conventional megaphones were banned, participants in Occupy general assemblies utilised a 'human microphone' that allowed speech to be amplified across large crowds. The fractal and self-replicating nature of communication via the human microphone finds parallel, in some ways, with the 'story circle' at the heart of most digital storytelling workshops. Everybody takes a turn to answer questions like 'tell a story about your name ... a favourite object, person, memory'. Trust is established in an environment of mutual vulnerability, encouraging listening across difference. Depending on the storytelling cohort and the issues that draw them together (i.e. what makes them an intimate public) some of the listening and speaking skills acquired are replicated as participants negotiate the content of their story with the friends and family who are part of it.

While the human microphone circumnavigates laws on electronic amplification, Occupy Wall Street nevertheless employed a plethora of digital tools (e.g. smart phones, cameras, photocopiers), genres (e.g. memes, distributed personal storytelling) and platforms (e.g. blogs, e-lists, bespoke websites, community media) to disseminate their complex and disparate messages. Like digital storytelling, when discourse is mediated by technology it can be sustained over an extended time frame and reach multiple publics, representing the slow creep of erosive cultural change. Mapping these networked strategies has the function, like much narrative practice, of bringing awareness and insight into communal and personal meanings that have previously been obscure – for example 'what do we mean by privacy now, anyway?'.

As a conceptual frame, Intimate Citizenship 3.0 makes apparent the emergent digital expertise and resilience of communities and people that transgress social norms. These people use technology to claim belonging and active citizenship for even the most taboo, intimate and formerly private aspects of selfhood. At an education, policy and advocacy level, this toolbox of networked strategies could be implemented for better listening, sharing and acceptance of 'the other'. Mapped even more broadly, this toolbox is of use to anybody navigating contemporary life beyond digital dualisms. Meanwhile the personal benefits of practicing Intimate Citizenship 3.0 include a consolidation of networked connections that support agency and ownership of curated congruence.

As a facilitated (by people or platforms or both) and creative everyday practice, Intimate Citizenship 3.0 constitutes an intervention – a strategic and targeted experiment in catalysing erosive change. Well-articulated strategies are likely to map broadly onto banal transitions (e.g. young person to adult) that are currently tangled in digitally mediated concerns about privacy and publicness. Thus, the selective curation undertaken by those at the most extreme at-risk borders of intimate transgression is equally useful to the confused teen and the overwhelmed caregiver, alongside social-service providers and policymakers. When understanding of the selective self-representation strategies of Intimate Citizenship 3.0 becomes widespread and routine, we may witness greater acceptance of the multitude of intimate differences among us.

To return to my friend, the lesbian mum, who is called upon to negotiate her family identity in the queue at the hardware store: rather than endlessly recount and perform her story in face-to-face encounters for time immemorial, a communication mode is at her disposal. If she can counter the obstacles (including time, energy, access and aptitude) Intimate Citizenship 3.0 offers opportunity to amplify her everyday activism, hopefully (though not necessarily) catalysing social change. In making her queer and congruent family structure visible, she makes their family a little more 'acceptable'. For her kids, life becomes a little easier. For participants like Bronwen, Melina and the two Mollys, this is demonstrably the case. It is also the case for my own family. Our children might grow up to regard all identity as queer – that is in flux and opaque, inconsistently performed – recognising that agency over storytelling and ownership of self-representation are fundamental tools in negotiating an empowered congruent identity. Meanwhile they live in a time when the convergence of networked publics is forcing increased social awareness of the impossibility of authentic coherent self-representation. Their capacity to curate a congruent digitally mediated identity is central to their active, networked, and culturally engaged Intimate Citizenship 3.0.

Notes

Preface and Acknowledgements

1. This acronym stands for Gay, Lesbian, Bisexual, Transgender, Queer, Intersex, Same-sex attracted people. It is commonly used albeit with many variations.

1 Introduction

1. SHine SA is a government-funded sexual health and education network in Adelaide, Australia.
2. ACSA is the government-funded South Australian AIDS Council.
3. While people use the term 'queer' in different contexts to mean different things, I use it as an expression that encapsulates GLBTQIS identities and in deference to queer theory. I follow transgender theorist Susan Stryker in its employment 'as a term that refers to all identities or practices that cross over, cut across, move between, or otherwise queer socially constructed sex/gender boundaries' (Stryker, 2006, p. 254). It is also the contraction that is most often used by the storytellers I worked with (which is not to say that all the people that I include under this umbrella would necessarily embrace the term themselves).
4. See Chapter 2 for a critical analysis of this summary and problematic phrase.
5. An independent community group of GLBTQIS parents and their kids and friends. We meet for play group weekly and irregular social activities as well as a camp twice a year. There is no formal leadership or political affiliation and events are co-ordinated either face-to-face or via Facebook.
6. 'Authenticity' is used widely in digital storytelling practice to refer to the apparent truthfulness and sincerity of many digital stories. It is a highly subjective and somewhat problematic term. I deconstruct it further in Chapter 4.

3 Identity: Nominalisation, Authenticity and Incoherence

1. Preliminary analysis of this story and the experiences described by Molly have been included in several publications (Vivienne, 2011a, 2011b; Vivienne & Burgess, 2012).
2. Preliminary analysis of *I am Sarah* (Figure 4.5), *Sisterhood* (Figure 4.6) and *Back to Happiness* (Figure 5.1) has been published in Vivienne (2011c).

4 Case Studies in Voice

1. Here I follow Berlet's definition of 'Christian right' as a social movement that 'uses a pious and traditionalist constituency as its mass base to pursue the

political goal of imposing a narrow theological agenda on secular society' (Berlet & Lyons, 2000).
2. Preliminary analysis of the *What's Your Story?* initiative has been published in several articles (Vivienne, 2011a; Vivienne & Burgess, 2012).
3. Preliminary analysis of this story was published in a book chapter in *Queering Paradigms II* (Vivienne, 2011b).

5 The Private in Networked Publics

1. The concept of 'networked identity work' was first developed and employed in a co-authored article published in the *Journal of Broadcast and Electronic Media* (Vivienne & Burgess, 2012).
2. A preliminary analysis of Max's experiences has been published as a chapter in *Queering Paradigms II* (Vivienne, 2011b).
3. Wikipedia currently describes the Westboro Baptist Church as 'an American, Independent Baptist church known for its extreme ideologies, especially those against homosexuality.' Their web home page has the URL www.godhatesfags.com.
4. Hogan's concept of 'curated exhibitions' is also canvassed in a co-authored article published in *Journal of Broadcast and Electronic Media* (Vivienne & Burgess, 2012).
5. This typology was developed and employed (though not nominalised as 'outness and otherness') in Vivienne and Burgess (2012).

6 Provocations: Digital Storytelling ≠ Social Change

1. 'Charlie bit my finger' a 56-second clip of two young English brothers engaged in sibling play is reputedly the most watched clip on YouTube. As of October, 2012 the video has nearly 500 million views ('Charlie Bit My Finger – Wikipedia, the free encyclopedia' 2012).

Bibliography

Ahmed, S. (2006). *Queer Phenomenology: Orientations, Objects, Others.* Durham & London: Duke University Press.

Ahmed, Sara (1998). *Differences that Matter: Feminist Theory and Postmodernism.* Cambridge: Cambridge University Press.

Alasuutari, P. (1995). *Researching Culture: Qualitative Method and Cultural Studies.* London: Sage Publications.

Alasuutari, P., Bickman, L., & Brannen, J. (2009). *The Sage Handbook of Social Research Methods.* London: Sage Publications.

Alexander, B., & Levine, A. (2008). Web 2.0 Storytelling: Emergence of a New Genre. *Educause Review*, 43(6).

All about this campaign selection business GetUp Campaign Blog. (2012). Retrieved October 7, 2012, from http://blog.getup.org.au/2010/11/16/261/.

Ausqueer: Yahoo! Group. (2012). Retrieved October 8, 2012, from http://groups.yahoo.com/group/ausqueer/.

Austin, J. L. (1978). *How to Do Things with Words.* (J. O. Urmson, Ed.). Cambridge: Harvard University Press.

Australian Civil Unions. (2012). Retrieved June 20, 2012, from http://www.australianmarriageequality.com/wp/australian-civil-unions/.

Bakhtin, M. (1982). *The Dialogic Imagination: Four Essays.* (K. Brostrom & V. Liapunov, Trans., M. Holquist & V. Liapunov, Eds.). Austin: University of Texas Press.

Bakhtin, M. (1986). *Speech Genres and Other Late Essays.* (M. Holquist & C. Emerson, Eds.). Austin: University of Texas Press.

Baym, N. K. (2010). *Personal Connections in the Digital Age.* Cambridge: Polity Press.

Benford, R. D., & Snow, D. A. (2000). Framing Processes and Social Movements: An Overview and Assessment. *Annual Review of Sociology*, 26, 611–639.

Benhabib, S., Butler, J., Fraser, N., & Cornell, D. (1995). *Feminist Contentions: A Philosophical Exchange.* London: Routledge.

Berlant, L. (1997). *The Queen of America Goes to Washington City: Essays on Sex and Citizenship.* Durham & London: Duke University Press.

Berlant, L. (2008). *The Female Complaint: The Unfinished Business of Sentimentality in American Culture.* Durham & London: Duke University Press.

Berlant, L., & Warner, M. (1995). What Does Queer Theory Teach Us about X? *PMLA*, 110(3), 343–349.

Berlet, C., & Lyons, M. N. (2000). *Right-Wing Populism in America: Too Close for Comfort.* New York: Guilford Press.

Berners-Lee, T., & Kagal, L. (2008). The Fractal Nature of the Semantic Web. *AI Magazine*, 29(3), 29.

Bernstein, M. (1997). Celebration and Supression: The Strategic Uses of Identity by the Lesbian and Gay Movement. *American Journal of Sociology*, 103(3), 531–565.

Bickford, S. (1996). *The Dissonance of Democracy: Listening, Conflict, and Citizenship*. New York: Cornell University Press.
Blumer, H. (1986). *Symbolic Interactionism: Perspective and Method*. Berkeley: University of California Press.
boyd, danah. (2008a, Fall). *Taken Out of Context: American Teen Sociality in Networked Publics* (PhD in Information Management and Systems). Berkeley: University of California.
boyd, danah. (2008b). Facebook's Privacy Trainwreck: Exposure, Invasion, and Social Convergence. *Convergence: The International Journal of Research into New Media Technologies*, 14(1), 13–20.
boyd, danah. (2011). Social Network Sites as Networked Publics: Affordances, Dynamics, and Implications. In Z. Papacharissi (Ed.), *Networked Self: Identity, Community, and Culture on Social Network Sites* (pp. 39–58). New York: Routledge.
boyd, danah. (2012). Four Difficult Questions Regarding Bullying and Youth Suicide Social Media Collective. Retrieved March 6, 2012, from http://socialmediacollective.org/2011/12/12/bullying-suicide-questions/.
Burgess, J. (2006). Hearing Ordinary Voices: Cultural Studies, Vernacular Creativity and Digital Storytelling. *Continuum: Journal of Media & Cultural Studies*, 20(2), 201–214.
Burgess, J., & Green, J. (2009). *YouTube: Online Video and Participatory Culture*. Cambridge: Polity Press.
Burgess, J., & Klaebe, H. (2009). Digital Storytelling as Participatory Public History in Australia. In J. Hartley & K. McWilliam (Eds.), *Story Circle: Digital Storytelling Around the World* (pp. 155–166). West Sussex, UK: Wiley-Blackwell.
Butler, J. (1990). *Gender Trouble: Feminism and the Subversion of Identity*. New York: Routledge.
Butler, J. (1993). *Bodies that Matter: On the Discursive Limits of 'Sex'*. London: Routledge.
Butler, J. (2001). Giving an Account of Oneself. *Diacritics*, 31(4), 22–40. doi:10.1353/dia.2004.0002.
Butler, J. (2005). *Giving an Account of Oneself*. New York: Fordham University Press.
Butler, J. (2006). Doing Justice to Someone: Sex Reassignment and Allegories of Transsexuality. In Susan Stryker & Stephen Whittle (Eds.), *The Transgender Studies Reader* (pp. 183–193). New York: Routledge.
Campbell, J. (1949). *The Hero with a Thousand Faces*. Michigan: Pantheon Books.
Castells, M. (2007). Communication, Power and Counter-Power in the Network Society. *International Journal of Communication*, 1, 238–266.
Charlie Bit My Finger – Wikipedia, the free encyclopedia. (2012). Retrieved October 7, 2012, from http://en.wikipedia.org/wiki/Charlie_Bit_My_Finger.
Charmaz, K. (2006). *Constructing Grounded Theory: A Practical Guide through Qualitative Analysis*. London: Sage Publications.
Chatterton, P., & Pickerill, J. (2010). Everyday Activism and Transitions towards Post-Capitalist Worlds. *Transactions of the Institute of British Geographers*, 35(4), 475–490. doi:10.1111/j.1475-5661.2010.00396.x.
Citron, M. (1999). *Home Movies and Other Necessary Fictions* (Vol. 4). Minneapolis: University of Minnesota Press.
Clarke, A. E. (2003). Situational Analyses: Grounded Theory Mapping after the Postmodern Turn. *Symbolic Interaction*, 26(4), 553–576.

Cole, C. E., Quinlan, M. M., & Hayward, C. C. (2009). Aesthetic Projects Engaging Inequities: Documentary Film for Social Change. In L. M. Harter, M. J. Dutta & C. E. Cole (Eds.), *Communicating for Social Impact: Engaging Theory, Research and Pedagogy* (pp. 21–32). New Jersey: Hampton Press.

Corboz, J., Dowsett, G., Mitchell, A., Couch, M., Agius, P., & Pitts, M. (2008). *Feeling Queer and Blue: A Review of the Literature on Depression and Related Issues among Gay, Lesbian, Bisexual and Other Homosexually Active People*. Melbourne: Australian Research Centre in Sex, Health and Society, La Trobe University, Beyond Blue.

Couldry, N. (2012). *Media, Society, World: Social Theory and Digital Media Practice*. Hoboken: Wiley & Sons.

Couldry, N., & Gray, M. (2012, September 17). Digital In/Justice/Culture Digitally. Culture Digitally: Examining Contemporary Cultural Production. Collective Scholarly Blog. Retrieved September 18, 2012, from http://culturedigitally.org/2012/09/digital-injustice/?utm_source=feedburner&utm_medium=feed&utm_campaign=Feed%3A+nsfworkshop+%28Culture+Digitally+Feed%29.

Dolan, J. (2001). *Geographies of Learning: Theory and Practice, Activism and Performance*. Middletown: Wesleyan University Press.

Dreher, T. (2009). Listening across Difference: Media and Multiculturalism beyond the Politics of Voice. *Continuum: Journal of Media & Cultural Studies*, 23(4), 445–458.

Edmond, M., & Spurgeon, C. (2013). Introduction – Community Uses of Co-creative Media: User-Created Citizenship. *Cultural Science*, 6(1), 1–3. Retrieved from http://cultural-science.org/journal/index.php/culturalscience/issue/view/13.

Erhart, J. (2009). 'Pink Parent' Pictures: In the Digital Domain. *Gay and Lesbian Issues and Psychology*, 5(1), 45.

Ess, C., & AoIR Ethics Working Committee. (2002). Ethical Decision-Making and Internet Research: Recommendations from the AoIR Ethics Working Committee. Retrieved from www.aoir.org/reports/ethics.pdf.

Fosl, C. (2008). Anne Braden, Fannie Lou Hamer, and Rigoberta Menchu: Using Personal Narrative to Build Activist Movements. In Rickie Solinger, Madeline Fox, Kayhan Irani (Eds.), *Telling Stories to Change the World: Global Voices on the Power of Narrative to Build Community and Make Social Justice Claims* (pp. 217–226). New York: Routledge.

Foucault, M. (1979). *Discipline and Punish: The Birth of the Prison*. London: Vintage Books.

Foucault, M. (2001). *Fearless Speech*. (J. Pearson, Ed.). Los Angeles: Semiotext(e).

Fraser, N. (1990). Rethinking the Public Sphere: A Contribution to the Critique of Actually Existing Democracy. *Social Text*, (25/26), 56–80.

Fraser, N. (1995). False Antithesis: A Response to Seyla Benhabib and Judith Butler. In *Feminist Contentions: A Philosophical Exchange* (pp. 59–74). London: Routledge,.

Freeman, M. (2010). 'Even Amidst': Rethinking Narrative Coherence. In M. Hyvärinen, L.-C. Hyden, M. Saarenheimo & M. Tamboukou (Eds.), *Beyond Narrative Coherence* (pp. 167–186). Amsterdam: John Benjamins Publishing.

Gamson, J. (1995). Must Identity Movements Self-Destruct? A Queer Dilemma. *Social Problems*, 42(3), 390–407.

Gamson, W. (1992). *Talking Politics*. Cambridge: Cambridge University Press.

Gibson, P. (1989). *Gay Male and Lesbian Youth Suicide* (Report of the Secretary's Task Force on Youth Suicide No. Volume 3) (pp. 110–142). Washington, DC: U.S Department of Health and Human Services.

Giddens, A. (1991). *Modernity and Self-Identity: Self and Society in the Late Modern Age*. Cambridge: Polity.

Goffman, E. (1963). *Stigma: Notes on the Management of Spoiled Identity*. New York: Simon & Schuster.

Goffman, Erving. (1959). *The Presentation of Self in Everyday Life*. New York: Anchor Books.

Goffman, Erving. (1974). *Frame Analysis: An Essay on the Organization of Experience*. Cambridge: Harvard University Press.

Goldman, S., Booker, A., & McDermott, M. (2008). Mixing the Digital, Social, and Cultural: Learning, Identity, and Agency in Youth Participation. *Youth, Identity, and Digital Media*, Edited by David Buckingham. The John D. and Catherine T. MacArthur Foundation Series on Digital Media and Learning (pp. 185–206). Cambridge, MA: The MIT Press.

Goodwin, J., & Jasper, J. M. (2003). *The Social Movements Reader: Cases and Concepts*. Hoboken: Wiley & Sons.

Gould, D. (2001). Rock the Boat, Don't Rock the Boat, Baby: Ambivalence and the Emergence of Militant AIDS Activism. In J. Goodwin, J. M. Jasper & F. Polletta (Eds.), *Passionate Politics: Emotions and Social Movements* (pp. 135–157). Chicago: University of Chicago Press.

Gould, D. B. (2009). *Moving Politics: Emotion and ACT UP's Fight against AIDS*. Chicago: University of Chicago Press.

Gray, M. (2009). Negotiating Identities/Queering Desires: Coming Out Online and the Remediation of the Coming-Out Story. *Journal of Computer-Mediated Communication*, 14(4), 1162–1189. doi:10.1111/j.1083-6101.2009.01485.x.

Gray, M. (2012). A Message to the 'First Responders' in Gay Kids' Lives: Why We Need to Ditch the Politics of Blame, Stop Talking about 'Cyberbullying,' and Move toward Sharing Responsibility for the Loss of Tyler Clementi Social Media Collective. Retrieved March 6, 2012, from http://socialmedia collective.org/2012/03/ 02/a-message- to-the-first-responders-in-gay-kids-lives-why-we-need-to-ditch-the-politics-of- blame-stop-talking-about-cyberbullying-and-move- toward-sharing/.

Green, J. (2006). Look! No, Don't! The Visibility Dilemma for Transsexual Men. In Susan Stryker and Stephen Whittle (Eds.), *The Transgender Studies Reader* (pp. 499–508). New York: Routledge.

Gross, L. (2005). The Past and the Future of Gay, Lesbian, Bisexual, and Transgender Studies. *Journal of Communication*, 55(3), 508–528. doi:10.1111/j.1460-2466.2005.tb02683.x.

Gross, L. (2007). Foreword. In K. O'Riordan & D. J. Phillips (Eds.), *Queer Online: Media, Technology and Sexuality* (pp. vii–x). New York: Peter Lang.

Gubrium, J. F., & Holstein, J. A. (2009). *Analyzing Narrative Reality*. Los Angeles: Sage Publications.

Hacking, I. (2004). *Historical Ontology*. Cambridge: Harvard University Press.

Halberstam, J. (2005). *In a Queer Time and Place: Transgender Bodies, Subcultural Lives*. New York: NYU Press.

Hall, S. (1980). Encoding/Decoding. In *Centre for Contemporary Cultural Studies: Culture, Media, Language*. London: Hutchison.

Hall, S. (1996). Who Needs Identity? In P. Du Gay & S. Hall (Eds.), *Questions of Cultural Identity* (pp. 15–30). London: Sage Publications Limited.

Haraway, D. (1988). Situated Knowledges: The Science Question in Feminism and the Privilege of Partial Perspective. *Feminist Studies*, 14(3), 575–599.

Haraway, D. (1991). *Simians, Cyborgs and Women: The Reinvention of Nature*. London: Free Association.

Hartley, J., & McWilliam, K. (2009). *Story Circle: Digital Storytelling around the World*. West Sussex, UK: Wiley-Blackwell.

Haythornthwaite, C. (2009). *Crowds and Communities: Light and Heavyweight Models of Peer Production* (pp. 1–10). Presented at the System Sciences, 2009. HICSS '09. 42nd Hawaii International Conference on.

Hertzberg Kaare, B., & Lundby, K. (2008). Mediatized Lives: Autobiography and Assumed Authenticity in Digital Storytelling. In Knut Lundby (Ed.), *Digital Storytelling, Mediatized Stories: Self-Representations in New Media* (Vol. 52, pp. 105–122). New York: Peter Lang.

Hillier, L., Dempsey, D., Harrison, L., Beale, L., Matthews, L., & Rosenthal, D. (1998). *Writing Themselves in: A National Report on the Sexuality, Health and Wellbeing of Same-Sex Attracted Young People*. Carlton, Australia: National Centre in HIV Social Research, La Trobe University.

Hogan, B. (2010). The Presentation of Self in the Age of Social Media: Distinguishing Performances and Exhibitions Online. *Bulletin of Science, Technology & Society*, 30(6), 377–386. doi:10.1177/0270467610385893.

Holmlund, C., & Fuchs, C. (1997). *Between the Sheets, in the Streets: Queer, Lesbian, Gay Documentary* (Vol. 1). Minneapolis: University of Minnesota Press.

Hull, G. A., & Katz, M.-L. (2006). Crafting an Agentive Self: Case Studies of Digital Storytelling. *Research in the Teaching of English*, 41(1), 43–81.

Hyvärinen, M., Hyden, L.-C., Saarenheimo, M., & Tamboukou, M. (Eds.) (2010). *Beyond Narrative Coherence*. Amsterdam/Philadelphia: John Benjamins Publishing Company.

It Gets Better Project. (2012). Retrieved December 18, 2012, from http://www.itgetsbetter.org/.

Jenkins, H. (2006). *Fans, Bloggers, and Gamers: Exploring Participatory Culture*. New York: New York University Press.

Jenkins, H., Clinton, K., Purushotma, R., Robinson, A. J., & Weigel, M. (2006). *Confronting the Challenges of Participatory Culture: Media Education for the 21st Century*. Chicago: MacArthur Foundation.

Jurgenson, N. (2011, February 24). Digital Dualism versus Augmented Reality Cyborgology. Retrieved November 20, 2013, from http://thesocietypages.org/cyborgology/2011/02/24/digital-dualism-versus-augmented-reality/.

Jurgenson, N. (2012, June 28). The IRL Fetish – The New Inquiry. Retrieved November 20, 2013, from http://thenewinquiry.com/essays/the-irl-fetish/.

Kaminsky, M. (1992). Myerhoff's 'Third Voice': Ideology and Genre in Ethnographic Narrative. *Social Text*, (33), 124–144.

Karlsson, L. (2004). We're Still Connected in a One-Sided Sort of Way: Acts of Reading Personal Journal-Type Weblogs. In Mia Consalvo and Kate O'Riordan (Eds.), *Internet Research Annual: Volume 3* (pp. 75–91). New York: Peter Lang.

Kaveney, R. (1999). Talking Transgender Politics. In Kate More & Stephen Whittle (Eds.), *Reclaiming Genders: Transsexual Grammars at the Fin De Siècle* (pp. 146–158). London: Cassell.

Keller, J. R. (2002). *Queer (Un)Friendly Film and Television*. Jefferson: McFarland.
Klaebe, H. G. (2006). *Sharing Stories: Problems and Potentials of Oral History and Digital Storytelling and the Writer/Producer's Role in Constructing a Public Place*. Brisbane: Queensland University of Technology.
Lambert, J. (2002). *Digital Storytelling: Capturing Lives, Creating Community*. Berkeley, CA: Digital Diner Press.
Lambert, J. (2009). Where It All Started: The Centre for Digital Storytelling in California. In J. Hartley & K. McWilliam (Eds.), *Story Circle: Digital Storytelling around the World* (pp. 79–90). West Sussex, UK: Wiley-Blackwell.
Lane, J. (2002). *The Autobiographical Documentary in America*. Madison: University of Wisconsin Press.
Lange, P. (2008). Publicly Private and Privately Public: Social Networking on YouTube. *Journal of Computer-Mediated Communication*, 13, 361–380. doi:10.1111/j.1083-6101.2007.00400.x.
Law, J. (2004). *After Method: Mess in Social Science Research*. Oxon: Routledge.
Leadbeater, C. (2009, March). *The Art of With*. Cornerhouse. Retrieved from http://www.charlesleadbeater.net/home.aspx.
Lejeune, P. (1989). The Autobiographical Pact. In P. J. Eakin (Ed.), K. Leary (Trans.), *On Autobiography*. Minneapolis: University of Minnesota Press.
Linde, C. (1993). *Life Stories: The Creation of Coherence*. Oxford: Oxford University Press.
Livingstone, S. M. (2005). *Audiences and Publics: When Cultural Engagement Matters for the Public Sphere*. Bristol, United Kingdom: Intellect.
Love, H. (2004). 'The Right to Change My Mind': New Work in Trans Studies. *Feminist Theory*, 5(1), 91–100.
Lukasiewicz, T., & Straccia, U. (2008). Managing Uncertainty and Vagueness in Description Logics for the Semantic Web. *Web Semantics: Science, Services and Agents on the World Wide Web*, (6), 291–308.
Lundby, K. (2008). *Digital Storytelling, Mediatized Stories: Self-Representations in New Media* (Vol. 52). New York: Peter Lang.
Make It Better Project (2012). Retrieved December 18, 2012, from http://www.makeitbetterproject.org/.
Mansbridge, J., & Flaster, K. (2007). The Cultural Politics of Everyday Discourse: The Case of 'Male Chauvinist'. *Critical Sociology*, 33, 627–660.
McLaughlin, T. (1996). *Street Smarts and Critical Theory: Listening to the Vernacular*. Madison: University of Wisconsin Press.
Meadows, D., & Kidd, J. (2009). 'Capture Wales': The BBC Digital Storytelling Project. In J. Hartley & K. McWilliam (Eds.), *Story Circle: Digital Storytelling around the World* (pp. 91–117). West Sussex, UK: Wiley-Blackwell.
Meyrowitz, J. (1985). *No Sense of Place: The Impact of Electronic Media on Social Behavior*. Oxford: Oxford University Press.
Milliken, M., Gibson, K., & O'Donnell, S. (2008). User-Generated Video and the Online Public Sphere: Will YouTube Facilitate Digital Freedom of Expression in Atlantic Canada? *American Communication Journal*, 10(3), 1–14.
Myerhoff, B. (1982). Life History among the Elderly: Performance, Visibility and Re-membering. In J. Ruby (Ed.), *A Crack in the Mirror: Reflexive Perspectives in Anthropology* (pp. 99–117). Philadelphia: University of Pennsylvania Press.

Myerhoff, B. (1986). 'Life Not Death in Venice': Its Second Life. In Victor Witter Turner & Edward M Brumer (Eds.), *The Anthropology of Experience* (pp. 261–287). Illinois: University of Illinois Press.

Neilsen, P. (2009). Digital Storytelling as Life-Writing: Self-Construction, Therapeutic Effect, Textual Analysis Leading to an Enabling 'Aesthetic' for the Community Voice. In *Speculation and Innovation: Applying Practice Led Research in the Creative Industries*. Kelvin Grove, Brisbane: Queensland University of Technology.

Nelson, M. E., & Hull, G. A. (2008). Self-Presentation through Multimedia: A Bakhtinian Perspective on Digital Storytelling. In Knut Lundby (Ed.) *Digital Storytelling, Mediatized Stories: Self-Representations in New Media* (Vol. 52, pp. 123–144). New York: Peter Lang.

Nicholson, L. (1995). Introduction. In *Feminist Contentions: A Philosophical Exchange*. Oxon: Routledge.

O'Donnella, P., Lloyd, J., & Dreher, T. (2009). Listening, Pathbuilding and Continuations: A Research Agenda for the Analysis of Listening. *Continuum: Journal of Media & Cultural Studies*, 23(4), 423–439.

Olson, M. (1965). *The Logic of Collective Action: Public Goods and the Theory of Groups*. Cambridge: Harvard University Press.

Ostrom, E. (2000). Collective Action and the Evolution of Social Norms. *The Journal of Economic Perspectives*, 14(3), 137–158.

Papacharissi, Z. A. (2010). *A Private Sphere: Democracy in a Digital Age*. Cambridge: Polity.

Penn, P., & Sheinberg, M. (1991). Stories and Conversations. *Journal of Strategic & Systemic Therapies*, 10(3–4), 30–37.

Peppard, J. (2008). Culture Wars in South Australia: The Sex Education Debates. *Australian Journal of Social Issues*, 43(3), 499–516.

Pisano, G., & Verganti, R. (2008). Which Kind of Collaboration Is Right for You? *Harvard Business Review*, 86(12), 78–86.

Plummer, K. (2002). *Telling Sexual Stories: Power, Change and Social Worlds*. London, New York: Taylor & Francis.

Plummer, K. (2003). *Intimate Citizenship: Private Decisions and Public Dialogues*. Washington, DC: University of Washington Press.

Poletta, F. (2006). *It Was Like a Fever: Storytelling in Protest and Politics*. Chicago, Illinois: University of Chicago Press.

Preece, J., & Shneiderman, B. (2009). The Reader-to-Leader Framework: Motivating Technology-Mediated Social Participation. *AIS Transactions on Human-Computer Interaction*, 1(1), 13–32.

Prestage, G., Bradley, J., Down, I., Brown, G., Hurley, M., & McCann, P. D. (2010). *PASH: Pleasure and Sexual Health*. National Centre in HIV Epidemiology and Clinical Research. Retrieved from http://notes.med.unsw.edu.au/NCHECRweb.nsf/resources/TOMS/$file/PASH2009-final.pdf.

Prestage, G., Bradley, J., Down, I., Ellard, J., Brown, G., Grulich, A., & Jin, F. (2009). *HIV Seroconversion Study Newly Diagnosed Men in Australia 2007–9* (p. 48). Australian Research Centre in Sex, Health and Society. Retrieved from http://www.nchecrsurveys.unsw.edu.au/hivss/Reports/SeroconReportOct09.pdf.

Rainbow Family Tree. (2012). Retrieved from http://www.rainbowfamilytree.com.

Raun, T. (2010a). *DIY Therapy: Exploring Affective Aspects of Trans Video Blogs on YouTube*. Presented at the Affective Fabrics of Digital Cultures: Feelings, Technologies, Politics, Manchester: Research Institute for Cosmopolitan Cultures.

Raun, T. (2010b). Screen Births: Exploring the Transformative Potential in Trans Video Blogs on YouTube. *Graduate Journal of Social Science*, 7(2). Retrieved from http://www.gjss.org/images/stories/volumes/7/2/8.%20Raun.pdf.

Reddy, W. M. (1997). Against Constructionism: The Historical Ethnography of Emotions. *Current Anthropology*, 38(3), 327–351.

Riggs, D. W., & Willing, I. (2013). 'They're All Just Little Bits, Aren't They': South Australian Lesbian Mothers' Experiences of Marginalisation in Primary Schools. *Journal of Australian Studies*, 37(3), 364–377.

Rosenwald, G. C., & Ochberg, R. L. (1992). *Storied Lives: The Cultural Politics of Self-Understanding*. London: Yale University Press.

Ruby, J. (1991). Speaking for, Speaking about, Speaking with, or Speaking Alongside – an Anthropological and Documentary Dilemma. *Visual Anthropology Review*, 7(2), 50–67.

Sartwell, C. (2000). *End of Story: Toward an Annihilation of Language and History*. New York: State University of New York Press.

Savin-Williams, R. C. (2005). *The New Gay Teenager*. Cambridge: Harvard University Press.

Scheff, T. (1994). Emotions and Identity: A Theory of Ethnic Nationalism. In C. Calhoun (Ed.), *Social Theory and the Politics of Identity* (pp. 277–304). Cambridge, Massachusetts: Blackwell.

Scheff, T. (2000). *Bloody Revenge: Emotions, Nationalism and War*. Bloomington: iUniverse.

Schradie, J. A. (2009). *The Digital Production Gap: The Digital Divide and Web 2.0 Collide*. In *American Sociological Association Conference*. San Francisco, CA.

Seidman, S. (1994). Queer-Ing Sociology, Sociologizing Queer Theory: An Introduction. *Sociological Theory*, 12(2), 166–177.

SHine SA, Incite Stories. (2010). *What's Your Story: Facilitator's Guide*. Adelaide, Australia: SHine SA.

Shirky, C. (2009). *Here Comes Everybody: The Power of Organizing without Organizations*. London: Penguin Books.

Soep, E. (2006). Beyond literacy and Voice in Youth Media Production. *McGill Journal of Education*, 41(3), 197–214.

Soep, L., & Chavez, V. (2010). *Drop that Knowledge: Youth Radio Stories*. Los Angeles: University of California Press.

Stryker, S. (2006). My Words to Victor Frankenstein above the Village of Chamounix: Performing Transgender Rage. In Susan Stryker and Stephen Whittle (Eds.), *The Transgender Studies Reader* (pp. 244–256). New York: Routledge.

Tacchi, J. A. (2006). Information, Communication, Poverty and Voice. In *Mapping the New Field of Communication for Development and Social Change*. Brisbane, Queensland, Australia.

Tacchi, J. A. (2009). Finding a Voice: Participatory Development in Southeast Asia. In John Hartley & Kelly McWilliam (Eds.), *Story Circle: Digital Storytelling Around the World* (pp. 167–175). West Sussex, UK: Wiley-Blackwell.

Tacchi, J. A. (2010). Open Content Creation: The Issues of Voice and the Challenges of Listening. *Continuum: Journal of Media and Cultural Studies*, 14: 652–668.
Tannen, D. (1989). *Talking Voices: Repetition, Dialogue and Imagery in Conversational Discourse*. Cambridge: Cambridge University Press.
Taub-Pervizpour, L. (2009). Digital Storytelling with Youth: Whose Agenda Is It? In *Story Circle: Digital Storytelling Around the World* (pp. 245–251). West Sussex, UK: Wiley-Blackwell.
Thompson, J. (2000). *Political Scandal: Power and Visibility in the Media Age*. New Jersey: Polity Press.
Thorson, K., Ekdale, B., Borah, P., Namkoong, K., & Shah, C. (2010). YouTube and Proposition 8: A Case Study in Video Activism. *Information, Communication & Society*, 13(3), 325–349.
Thumim, N. (2008). 'It's Good for Them to Know My Story': Cultural Mediation as Tension. In Knut Lundby (Ed.) *Digital Storytelling, Mediatized Stories: Self-Representations in New Media* (Vol. 52, pp. 85–104). New York: Peter Lang.
Thumim, N. (2009). Exploring Self-Representations in Wales and London: Tension in the Text. In John Hartley & Kelly McWilliam (Eds.), *Story Circle: Digital Storytelling around the World*. West Sussex, UK: Wiley-Blackwell.
Tomlins, J. (2012). SAME Plus. Retrieved June 20, 2012, from http://jacquitomlins.com/.
Tregoning, W. (2006). Authentic Self, Paranoid Critique and Getting a Good Night's Rest. *Continuum: Journal of Media and Cultural Studies*, 20(2), 175–188.
Tremayne, M. (2007). *Blogging, Citizenship, and the Future of Media*. New York: Routledge.
V, P. (2012). Born This Way Blog. Retrieved December 18, 2012, from http://borngaybornthisway.blogspot.com.au/.
Valerio, M. W. (2003). The Joker Is Wild. Retrieved July 16, 2003, from http://www.anythingthatmoves.co/ish17/jokers-wild.html.
Van den Berg, B. (2008). Self, Script, and Situation: Identity in a World of ICTs. In S. Fischer-Hübner, P. Duquenoy, A. Zuccato & L. Martucci (Eds.), *The Future of Identity in the Information Society* (Vol. 262, pp. 63–76). Boston: Springer.
Vivienne, S. (2011a). Shouting from the Rooftops: Queer Digital Storytelling for Social Change. In B. Scherer & M. Ball (Eds.), *Queering Paradigms II: Interrogating Agendas* (pp. 171–190). New York: Peter Lang Pub Inc.
Vivienne, S. (2011b). Trans Digital Storytelling: Everyday Activism, Mutable Identity and the Problem of Visibility. *Gay and Lesbian Issues and Psychology Review*, 7(1), 43–54.
Vivienne, S. (2011c). Mediating Identity Narratives: A Case Study in Queer Digital Storytelling as Everyday Activism. *AOIR Selected Papers of Internet Research, IR12.0*. Retrieved from http://spir.aoir.org/ir12.html.
Vivienne, S. (2012). Standing Up and Finding My Voice through Positive Digital Storytelling. *HIV Australia*, 10(1), 3234.
Vivienne, S., & Burgess, J. (2012). The Digital Storyteller's Stage: Queer Everyday Activists Negotiating Privacy and Publicness. *Journal of Broadcasting & Electronic Media*, 56(3), 362–377. doi:10.1080/08838151.2012.705194
Vivienne, S., & Burgess, J. (2013). The Remediation of the Personal Image in Queer Digital Storytelling. *Journal of Material Culture*, 18(3), 279–298.

Waidzunas, T. (2011). Young, Gay, and Suicidal: Dynamic Nominalism and the Process of Defining a Social Problem with Statistics. *Science, Technology & Human Values*, 1–27. doi:10.1177/0162243911402363.

Walker, J. (2004). Distributed Narratives: Telling Stories across Networks. In Mia Consalvo & Kate O'Riordan (Eds.), *Internet Research Annual: Volume 3* (pp. 91–104). New York: Peter Lang.

Warner, M. (2005). *Publics and Counterpublics*. New York: Zone Books.

Weintraub, J. (1997). The Theory and Politics of the Public/Private Distinction. In J. A. Weintraub & K. Kumar (Eds.), *Public and Private in Thought and Practice: Perspectives on a Grand Dichotomy* (pp. 1–42). Chicago: University of Chicago Press.

Wertz, F. J., Charmaz, K., McMullen, L. M., Josselson, R., Anderson, R., & McSpadden, E. (2011). *Five Ways of Doing Qualitative Analysis: Phenomenological Psychology, Grounded Theory, Discourse Analysis, Narrative Research, and Intuitive Inquiry*. New York: Guilford Publications.

White, M., & Epston, D. (1990). *Narrative Means to Therapeutic Ends*. New York: Norton.

Wolfe, A. (1997). Public and Private in Theory and Practice: Some Implications of an Uncertain Boundary. In J. A. Weintraub & K. Kumar (Eds.), *Public and Private in Thought and Practice: Perspectives on a Grand Dichotomy* (pp. 182–203). Chicago: University of Chicago Press.

Young, I. M. (1997). *Intersecting Voices: Dilemmas of Gender, Political Philosophy, and Policy*. Princeton: Princeton University Press.

Young, I. M. (2011). *Justice and the Politics of Difference*. Princeton: Princeton University Press.

Zimmermann, P. R. (1995). *Reel Families: A Social History of Amateur Film*. Bloomington: Indiana University Press.

Index

aboriginal, 69
activism, *see* everyday activism
agency, 3, 5, 15, 18, 45–8, 63–4, 85–7, 98, 131, 152, 171–3, 175, 182, 203, 210
Ahmed, Sara, 48, 65
AIDS Council of SA (ACSA), 2, 97–8, 170, 211
analysis
    textual, 44, 219
    see also macro; meso; micro
anonymity, 154
    see also pseudonymity
a part of and/or apart from, 2, 8, 17, 50, 117, 131–5, 139, 181–2, 203
audience, 7, 9–10, 14, 17–26, 33–5, 41–6, 63–6, 73–6, 109–11, 133–4, 182, 193–9
    see also publics
authenticity, 16, 19, 33–4, 44, 46, 63, 65, 75, 85, 172, 176, 211, 217
authorship, 47–8
autobiography, 19, 21–3, 47, 217

Berlant, Lauren, 17, 36, 132, 135, 137, 147
boyd, danah, 7, 13, 17, 43, 135–6, 150
Burgess, Jean, 11–12, 28–35, 211–12
Butler, Judith, 16, 34, 47–8, 56–7, 71–2, 77, 176

childhood, 15, 32, 74, 139, 169, 196, 198
children, 5–6, 14, 35–8, 56, 83, 86, 112, 114, 116–17, 127, 135, 144–7, 156, 160–3, 180–4, 210
Christian, Christianity, 15, 91, 120, 125–7, 141, 184, 212
Citizenship, *see* Intimate Citizenship
coherence, 63–4, 67, 71, 75, 172, 175–7, 203, 207
    narrative, 16, 44, 65, 68, 73, 85
collaboration, 24, 29, 89, 101, 161

community engagement, 91, 92, 107, 193, 206
community ownership, *see* ownership, community
congruence, 16, 44, 63, 71, 175–8, 184, 203
context
    collapse, 132, 182
    commercial, 31, 106, 187
    familial, 111, 119, 122, 159, 167
    institutional, 1, 16, 27, 49, 138, 185, 187–91
    social or cultural, 4, 7–8, 13, 18, 47, 50, 64, 71, 122, 137
convergence, *see* social convergence
Couldry, Nick, 30, 197–8
Creative Commons, 39, 106
creativity, co-creative, 14–15, 25, 27–9, 60, 68, 87, 98, 101, 189, 204–6
crip, 50, 52–3
    see also Stealth
curator, curation, 17, 38, 86, 90, 106–8, 150–2, 172–3, 186–7, 203, 206–7, 210

difference, 6, 14, 43, 49, 53, 56, 114
    speaking and/or listening across, 2, 10, 16, 74, 86, 88, 108–10, 116, 119–20, 127, 139, 159, 162, 172, 179–84, 196, 209–10
digital literacy, 25, 29, 106, 194
digital storytelling
    genre of, 14, 32, 44, 65, 175, 177, 193, 198
    history of, 24–7, 43
    seven elements of, 26, 67, 110
    tradition of, 3, 24, 26, 29, 44, 66, 89, 98, 185–6
    distribution, 2–3, 41, 86–90, 173, 189, 194–6, 206
    online, 7, 9–11, 90, 97, 101, 106, 132, 147, 150, 182, 188, 202, 204

223

distribution – *continued*
three modes of, 166, 168, 170
see also sharing
documentary, 22, 35, 88, 156, 197

engagement, civic, 1–2, 6, 11, 41, 169, 173, 201
everyday activism, 1, 3–7, 9, 14, 21, 23, 36, 43, 53, 86, 118, 127, 130–1, 155, 170, 172–5, 196, 200–1, 210
exhibition, 150–2, 173, 206–7

Facebook and risk, 12, 82, 106, 144, 149–51
facilitation, 32, 40, 86–90, 95, 104, 131, 185, 187, 189–90, 208
faith, *see* Christianity, Judaism, Islam
family, *see* context, familial
Feast Festival, 71, 101, 170
fluidity, 74, 76, 206
Foucault, Michel, 5, 46–7, 201

gay marriage, 4, 93, 111, 119–24, 143, 199
Goffman, Erving, 13–14, 16, 64–5, 89, 137, 148
Gray, Mary, 15, 38, 197–8

Hartley, John, 28–9, 185
Hogan, Bernie, 150–8
homophobia, 37–8, 68, 73, 111, 113, 120, 122–7, 156, 164, 182, 198

identity, 44–9
performance of, 7, 15–16, 20, 34–5, 56–7 63–8, 75, 147, 150–1
see also networked identity work
indigenous, 15, 92
see also aboriginal
Intimate Citizenship, 3, 9–10, 14, 42–3, 131, 134–9, 150, 173, 184, 200–1, 205–10
invisible, invisibility, 11, 79, 104, 112–13, 122, 136, 144, 147, 156, 160–2
see also visible, visibility
Islam, Muslim, 15, 169

Jewish, Judaism, 15, 66, 120

listening, *see* difference, listening across
Livingstone, Sonia, 133–4

macro, analysis, 2, 8, 16–17, 132, 135, 175, 193, 199
marketing, 31, 187–8, 194–6
membership, 104, 107, 129, 133
memory, 19, 72–3, 88, 176, 209
meso, analysis, 2, 8–9, 15, 17, 86, 175, 185, 199
micro, analysis, 2, 8, 15, 17, 44, 167, 175, 199
moral panic, 84, 91
Myerhoff, Barbara, 23, 66, 88–9

narrative
theory, 26, 70
therapy, 26, 70, 188
see also coherence, narrative
networked identity work, 9–10, 12–13, 132, 136–9, 172–4, 202–8
networks, *see* social networks
nominalisation, 44, 54, 59–60, 84, 129, 175, 180–2, 205

ownership
agency and, 101, 107–8, 208
community, 107, 208
see also agency

Papacharissi, Zizi, 12, 17, 134–5, 201
parenting, 113–16, 195
parrhesia, parrhesiastes, 5–6, 201
participatory culture, 3, 10–11, 134
performance, *see* identity, performance of
performativity, 14, 16, 34, 44
Plummer, Ken, 34–5, 42–3
political campaign
Love Makes a Family, 36, 114
Same Sex Marriage, 37, 55, 125–6, 195
Same Sex Parenting Recognition, 113–16
see also gay marriage
Positive Stories, 2, 16, 85, 101–2, 170

privacy, 2, 6, 13–15, 59, 61, 79–80, 143, 145–7, 161, 164–5, 209
and publicness, 2, 7, 12–13, 35, 132, 143, 150, 172, 189, 203
settings, 105–6
production
  bounded, 17, 106, 132, 153, 158–9
  pseudonymous, 17, 106, 132, 153, 163, 169–70
  textual approaches, 2, 12–13, 15, 17, 43, 129, 132, 143, 172, 202–3
  visible, 17, 132, 153
pseudonymity, 7, 149, 163–70, 199
publics
  antagonistic, 207
  counter, 36, 135–9, 167
  familiar, 135–6, 154, 196
  imagined, 13, 17, 131–6, 177
  intimate, 8, 17, 36, 71, 125, 132–9, 167, 178, 183, 189, 209
  networked, 1–3, 9, 12, 16–17, 43, 101, 135–6, 172–3, 175, 183–4, 196, 200–6

queer, 2, 14–16, 22, 36–8, 53

Rainbow Family Tree, 2, 16, 60, 62, 84, 94–7, 101–3, 106–8, 124–7, 150, 154–5, 164–6, 169–70, 187, 195
recruitment, 92, 97–8, 156, 190, 192
religion, 15, 82
  see also separate entries for Christian, Islamic, Jewish
re-member, 66, 88
rhetoric, 10, 18, 30, 66, 109–10, 127, 203

secrecy, 53, 77, 145–6, 155
self, partial opacity of, 16, 71–2, 202
self-representation, 1, 63, 151–2, 207–8, 210
sharing
  rhetoric of, 8, 11, 13, 17, 21, 34, 89, 108–9, 127, 153, 172, 174
  selective, 106

three modes of, 150; ad hoc, 166, 168; proxy, 166, 170; targeted, 166
sharing, consequences of
  embarrassment, 64, 177
  employment related, 6, 152
  relationship related, 82, 99, 117, 133–5, 144, 160, 177, 183–4, 203
social capital, 7, 154, 171–7, 186, 188
social change
  form of, 1, 4, 8–14, 18, 155, 173–4, 201, 206
  measurement of, conditions for, 8, 27, 32, 35, 38, 109, 167, 189, 196, 200
social convergence, 7, 12–13, 85, 135
  see also context, collapse
social movement, 16, 20, 22, 55, 86, 108, 118–19, 124, 129–30, 175, 181, 203, 208
social networks, 43, 148, 195, 201, 208
social or cultural norms, 1, 3, 6, 24, 46, 49, 71, 86, 127, 139, 176, 182, 209
software, 27–8, 93–5
speaking, *see* difference, speaking across
stealth, 53, 61, 184
  see also crip
sustainability, 185

transgender, 6, 54–6, 60, 76, 139, 178, 183–4, 211

Vimeo, 106, 108
visible, visibility, 8, 14, 17, 32, 35–6, 50, 126, 129, 145, 153, 155–6, 162, 183–4, 196–7, 210
  see also invisible, invisibility
voice
  emotive, 75–6, 118, 127–8, 161, 203
  mediating, 2, 8, 10, 16, 87, 122, 192
  orchestration of, 87, 130, 185, 203

voice – *continued*
  tone of, 7, 10, 99, 112, 114, 116–17, 122, 125, 128, 182
  see also rhetoric

Warner, Michael, 17, 36, 135, 144–7
What's Your Story?, 2, 16, 56, 62, 72, 91, 97, 107, 111, 120, 138, 150, 156, 161, 170–1, 188, 190, 196

website, design, architecture, 102–8
workshop
  design, 17, 90, 93, 98, 101–3, 186
  facilitation, 93, 98

Young, Iris Marion, 10, 22, 109–10
You Tube, 10–11, 30, 39, 106, 123–5, 195, 212

PGMO 06/08/2018